Policy Evaluation for Community Development

Shimon Awerbuch
William A. Wallace

The Praeger Special Studies program—utilizing the most modern and efficient book production techniques and a selective worldwide distribution network—makes available to the academic, government, and business communities significant, timely research in U.S. and international economic, social, and political development.

Policy Evaluation for Community Development
Decision Tools for Local Government

PRAEGER SPECIAL STUDIES IN U.S. ECONOMIC, SOCIAL, AND POLITICAL ISSUES

309.262
A966p

163698

Praeger Publishers New York Washington London

Library of Congress Cataloging in Publication Data

Awerbuch, Shimon.
 Policy evaluation for community development.

 (Praeger special studies in U.S. economic, social, and political issues)
 Bibliography: p.
 Includes index.
 1. Cities and towns—Planning—United States. 2. Municipal government—United States. 3. Decision-making in public administration. I. Wallace, William A., 1935- joint author. II. Title.
HT167.A87   309.2'62'0973   75-23953
ISBN 0-275-55940-8

AUG 7 '78

PRAEGER PUBLISHERS
111 Fourth Avenue, New York, N.Y. 10003, U.S.A.

Published in the United States of America in 1976
by Praeger Publishers, Inc.

All rights reserved

© 1976 by Praeger Publishers, Inc.

Printed in the United States of America

ACKNOWLEDGMENTS

Many individuals and organizations have helped in the development of this work. Of particular importance is the cooperation provided by the citizens and officials of Cohoes, New York, especially staff of the Cohoes Planning and Development Agency. Assistance in undertaking a second case study was provided by The Institute on Man and Science, Rensselaerville, New York, through its field personnel in Dunbar, Pennsylvania.

We also extend our appreciation to Professors Albert Paulson and Charles E. Lawrence, Rensselaer Polytechnic Institute, for their technical review of the material in chapters 7 through 9.

Special thanks are due to Dean W. W. Cooper, School of Urban and Public Affairs, Carnegie-Mellon University, for his interest in the work and confidence in the applicability of quantitative techniques to enhance community participation and the municipal planning process, and to Dr. Harry Smith, Jr., Chairman, Department of Biostatistics, Mount Sinai Hospital (formerly Dean, School of Management, Rensselaer Polytechnic Institute), for his encouragement and financial support during the early part of the research.

The Sloan Foundation assisted by providing financial support through a grant to the Program in Engineering and Public Affairs, Carnegie-Mellon University.

CONTENTS

	Page
ACKNOWLEDGMENTS	v
LIST OF TABLES	xii
LIST OF FIGURES AND EXHIBITS	xv

Chapter

1 INTRODUCTION   1

    Scope of the Problem   2
    Overview of the Text   2

2 THE AMERICAN CITY AND CITY PLANNING, COLONIAL PERIOD-1850   7

    Early Planning Examples   8
        Colonial Williamsburg   8
        William Penn's "Large City or Town"   9
    Legal Foundations of American City Planning   10
        Zoning and Its Foundations in English Nuisance Law   11
        Extension of Police Power in Land-Use Planning   12
    The "Boom" Years   14
        Early Development of the Eastern Cities: New York and Philadelphia   15
        Washington, D.C.   16
        A Midwest Example: Jeffersonville, Indiana   17
        Other Economic Pressures on Municipal Government   17
        Speculation in the West   18
    Summary   19
    Notes   20

3 THE FOUNDATIONS OF MODERN CITY PLANNING   22

    "City Pestilential": The Industrial City 1850-1900   23
        Perceptions of the Period   23
        Bases of Modern Planning in the "City Pestilential"   25

Chapter		Page
	"City Beautiful" and the Emergence of Modern Planning	26
	Zoning vs. Planning	27
	Development of the Planning Profession	28
	New Directions in the 1930s	31
	Conclusion	33
	Notes	34
4	THE NEW PLANNING	36
	Pluralism and Citizen Participation in Planning	38
	Citizen Participation	38
	Advocacy in Planning	39
	The Planning Process: Observations, Definitions, and Prescriptions	40
	Goal Setting	44
	Review of Existing Planning Models	47
	The Pittsburgh Urban Renewal Simulation	47
	The San Francisco Urban Renewal Model	49
	A Land-Use Plan Design Model	49
	A Plan-Evaluation Methodology for the Small City	50
	Notes	51
5	A METHOD FOR ASSESSING THE IMPACTS OF COMMUNITY DEVELOPMENT PROPOSALS	56
	Cost-Revenue as a Basis for Plan Evaluation	58
	Generalizing the Cost-Revenue Approach	58
	Expansion of the Cost-Revenue Approach	59
	Cost-Revenue Applied to the Planning Process	60
	The Community Development Impacts Model: An Overview	62
	Industrial Development Submodel	65
	Gross Acreage and Land Coverage	66
	Full Value of Industrial Real Estate	67
	Employment Densities	68
	Type of Employment	70
	Capture Rate	70
	Housing Demand by Type of Dwelling	74
	Summary of the INDUST Submodel	75
	Housing Submodel	77
	Characteristics of Residential Development	77
	Computation of Physical Development Characteristics	78
	Summary and Sample Output	81

Chapter	Page
Demographic Submodel	82
Total Population and Age Distribution	82
Population Per Unit	85
Age Distribution of the Household Head	87
Computations	88
Summary and Sample Output	90
Number of School Children	91
Household Income Submodel	93
Stability of Current Residents' Income Distribution over Time	93
1970 Income Distribution of Residents	95
Income Distribution of New Residents	95
Output of the INC Routine	99
Assessing the Impacts of Development on Retail Sales	100
Public Sector Submodel	101
Municipal Tax Base	101
Sources of Revenue: State Revenue Sharing and Sales Taxes	104
Computation of Nonproperty Tax Revenues	105
Municipal Expenditures	106
A Method for Estimating Municipal Expenditure Increases Resulting from Development	109
Expenditures and Revenues for Education	114
State Aid for Education	115
Property Tax and School Tax Rates	116
Output of the PUBSEC Routine	116
Summary	117
Notes	118
6 AN APPLICATION OF THE MODEL	122
Geographic and Economic Overview	122
Historic Overview	124
Demographic Characteristics	124
Population	124
Households	125
Housing Stock	128
Age and Structural Characteristics	128
Vacancy Rates	128
Household Income	128
Potential for Residential Development	131
Economic Base	131

Chapter		Page
	Cost-Revenue Analysis of Three Projects	133
	Description of the Projects	133
	Municipal Cost-Revenue Summary	135
	School District Summary	138
	A Comparison with Results of CODIM	140
	Discussion of Results and Recommendations	148
	Conclusions	150
	Notes	150
7	COMMUNITY DEVELOPMENT PLANNING: NORMATIVE APPROACHES	152
	Utility Theory and the Attainment-Possibility Frontier	154
	Utility Theory	154
	The Concept of an Attainment-Possibility Frontier	155
	Efficiency: A Mathematical Approach	157
	Multiple Objectives	158
	Geometric Representation of Efficiency	159
	Efficient Points: Computational Assets	160
	Anomalies in Vector-Maximization Problems	161
	Concluding Remarks	163
	Linear Programming and Goal Programming: Prescriptive Tools for Community Development Planning	164
	Optimization Versus Simulation	164
	Linear Programming, Goal Programming, and Multiple-Objective Programming	166
	Externalities	168
	Preemptive Goal Programming	170
	Notes	172
8	A LINEAR GOAL FORMULATION AND SOME INHERENT DIFFICULTIES	176
	The Hidden Nonlinearity in Goal Programming	177
	Results of the Linear Goal-Programming Model	180
	Interpretation of the Dual	182
	Conclusion	184
	Notes	185
9	GOAL PROGRAMMING AND MULTIPLE-OBJECTIVE OPTIMIZATION: NONLINEAR FORMULATIONS	187

Chapter		Page
	Methods of Nonlinear Programming	188
	A Nonlinear Goal-Programming Formulation	189
	Disadvantages of the Nonlinear Goal Program	193
	A Nonlinear Multiple-Objective Optimization	194
	The Model	194
	A Note on Parameter Weights	197
	Setting Goal Levels and Scaling the Functional	198
	Advantages of the Quadratic Formulation	199
	Application I: Better Than Best?	200
	Application II: Making Trade-offs Along the Attainment-Possibility Frontier	205
	Constructing the APF	205
	Interpretation	207
	Determining the Shadow Price	209
	Application III: A Set of Efficient Solutions to the Community Development Problem	211
	Results	212
	Sensitivity to Changing Goals	215
	Sensitivity to Changing Coefficients	216
	Conclusion	217
	Notes	218
10	SUMMARY, CONCLUSIONS, AND SUGGESTIONS FOR FURTHER STUDY	219
	Summary	219
	Extensions to Community Participation	221
	Description of the Citizen Task Forces	222
	Implementation and Results	223
	Suggestions for Further Study	224
	Conceptual and Technical Suggestions	224
	Usefulness of the Constructs as Decision Tools	226
	Municipal Costs and Revenues	228
	Efficient Solutions and Goal Priorities	228
	Notes	229

Appendix

A	NOTES ON CONSUMER BEHAVIOR AND SOCIAL WELFARE THEORY	231
	Consumer Behavior, Social Welfare, and the Impossibility Theorem	231

Appendix		Page
	Social Welfare	233
	Social Choice and the Impossibility Theorem	239
	Notes	241
B	NOTES ON THE FUNCTIONAL IN THE QUADRATIC FORMULATION	242
	Form of the Functional	242
	Application	244
	Discussion	244
	An Analytic Description of the Solution Space	246
	Defining the Convex Hull	246
	Discussion of the Analytic Approach	248
	Conclusion	249
	Notes	249
C	A SAMPLE OF EFFICIENT SOLUTIONS FOR THE COMMUNITY DEVELOPMENT PROBLEM	251
BIBLIOGRAPHY		260
INDEX		282
ABOUT THE AUTHORS		287

LIST OF TABLES

Table		Page
5.1	Illustrative Floor Space and Acreage Standards Used to Determine Industrial Space Requirements by Zone, Philadelphia, 1960	69
5.2	Production Workers and Total Workers by Industry, Albany-Schenectady-Troy SMSA, 1967	71
5.3	Motivating Factors in an Employee's Decision to Move His Residence Closer to His Place of Work	72
5.4	Industrial Employment and Total Population	73
5.5	Occupational Distribution by Dwelling Type	74
5.6	Dwelling Distribution by Occupational Type	75
5.7	Lot Sizes and Dwelling Densities	79
5.8	Lot Areas and Dwelling Densities	80
5.9	Sample Work Table Illustrating Forecast Procedure by Cohort Survival Method Using Five-Year Intervals, for Females	84
5.10	Household Size by Housing Type	85
5.11	Distribution of Household Size by Housing Type and Number of Bedrooms	86
5.12	Age Distribution by Housing Type	88
5.13	Public School Pupils, by Dwelling Type and Number of Bedrooms, as Reported by Six Surveys	92
5.14	1970 Income: Families and Unrelated Individuals	96
5.15	Annual Costs of Living for a Four-Person Family, Buffalo, N.Y., Spring 1967	97
5.16	Household Income Distribution by Housing Type	98

Table		Page
5.17	Tax Base Trends, Cohoes, N.Y., 1967-71	102
5.18	Volume of Trade in Retail Activity and Selected Services in Albany County, 1954-67	105
5.19	Unit Costs of Municipal Services and Their Allocation to the Residential Sector	107
5.20	Annual and Amortized Capital Costs for a Hypothetical Subdivision, Assuming Varying Minimum Lot Sizes	108
5.21	Residential Development Potential	110
5.22	Estimated Municipal Expenditures Under Two Development Scenarios	112
6.1	Some Economic Indicators, Cohoes Versus Region, 1958-67	124
6.2	Population Trends, Cohoes and Capital District, 1900-70	126
6.3	Number of Households, by Age of Head: Cohoes, Capital District, and United States	127
6.4	Distribution of Family Income, Cohoes and the Capital District Region, 1959 and 1969	129
6.5	Employment by Occupation, Cohoes and the Capital District Region, 1970	130
6.6	Summary of Projected Residential Characteristics	136
6.7	Increase in Municipal Property Tax Revenue	136
6.8	Total Additional Municipal Revenue	137
6.9	Additional Municipal Service Costs by Function	137
6.10	Additional Pupil Loading, by Project	138
6.11	Additional Educational Costs, by Project	139

Table		Page
6.12	School District Additional Revenue Summary	139
6.13	Summary of CODIM Output and Staff Report	146
C.1	Sample Results from Cases 1-138, Using Original Objectives	252
C.2	Sample Results from Cases 201-338, Using Modified Objectives	254
C.3	Sample Results from Cases 501-638, Assuming a Decrease in External Funding	256
C.4	Sample Results from Cases 701-838, Assuming an Increase in External Funding	258

LIST OF FIGURES AND EXHIBITS

Figure		Page
5.1	Interactive Planning System	61
5.2	CODIM Summary Flow Chart	63
5.3	Lorenz Curve: Stability of Income Distribution, 1950-70	94
6.1	Regional Location, Cohoes, New York	123
6.2	Sales Volume, Cohoes, New York	132
7.1	Attainment-Possibility Frontier	157
7.2	Illustration of Efficient Points	160
9.1	Optimal Tax Rate Versus Population	206
9.2	Taxation-Population APF	208
9.3	Taxation-Industrial Acreage APF	210
A.1	The Consumer's Problem	232
A.2	Production-Possibility Frontier	234
A.3	Utility-Possibility Frontier	236
A.4	Welfare Criteria	237

Exhibit		
5.1	Sample Input and Output of the INDUST Model	76
5.2	Sample Input and Output of the HOUS Submodel	81
5.3	Sample Output of the DEMOG Submodel	90
5.4	Sample Output of the INC Submodel	99
5.5	PUBSEC Output Pertaining to Tax Base	103

Exhibit		Page
5.6	Output of the PUBSEC Routine	117
6.1	Base Run	141
6.2	Project A	142
6.3	Project B	143
6.4	Project C	144
6.5	All Projects	145
9.1	Output of the Goal-Programming Formulation	192
9.2	Sample Output of the Interactive Model	202
9.3	Sample Output of the Nonlinear Formulation	204

CHAPTER 1

INTRODUCTION

During the past few years, municipal government has been called upon to perform an ever increasing and diversifying variety of services. It can be expected that this expanding role of local government will continue into new areas. In view of the increasing demand that is being placed on the small municipality as an administrator of programs for the enhancement of the populace, the environment, and urban functioning in general, it is incumbent upon the small and medium-size local governments to seek new efficiencies and new methods of ascertaining the impacts and interrelationships of proposed policies and programs. This function becomes especially important when a city is called upon to allocate and administer community development revenue sharing under the Housing and Urban Development Act of 1974.

Large-scale planning and renewal efforts have repeatedly demonstrated that the municipal system is complex and that it does not always respond in the anticipated manner. Thus, local programs that are designed to alleviate specific problems often have a counter-economic effect on other parts of municipal activity.

In order to help municipal management move away from haphazard decision-making, techniques must be developed that will help local governments to implement and allocate projects under the special revenue-sharing system. This will enable them to plan on a sound basis in order to meet desired objectives.

What has generally inhibited the use of various analytic and decision-making methods in many municipalities is the dearth of technical talent usually available to the chief executive. It is important, therefore, to stress that the research herein is aimed at the administrator of the smaller municipality and requires only his basic knowledge of its economic and fiscal functions for successful implementation.

The need for improved planning is greatest at the moment in view of the recent community development revenue-sharing legislation. In contrast with its role under the categorical grants procedure, the municipality will now have to do a far more extensive job of setting priorities, allocating resources to projects, and ascertaining the impacts and interrelationships of these projects in order to make the concepts embodied in the community development block grants system a success.

SCOPE OF THE PROBLEM

During the early history of urban development in the United States, the city was principally a provider of such basic services as police, water and sewers, and possibly schools and fire protection. By contrast, the municipality of today has expanded into service areas that have traditionally been the domain of private, volunteer, and philanthropic organizations. Yet the comprehensive plans of the past two decades generally have tended to concentrate on physical planning, while disregarding the important fiscal and socioeconomic implications of the comprehensive plan.

More recently, the planning community has been exposed to several intricate computerized algorithms for planning and evaluating municipal growth. These models, however, have proved too complex and are of little practical benefit to policy-makers in the small municipality. Thus the need for simple and effective plan-evaluation tools becomes apparent.

OVERVIEW OF THE TEXT

The objectives of the research are to develop decision-making tools that will improve the planning process in local government by providing a means through which the municipal official can better choose among alternative community development policies. In order to propose useful methodologies, the current nature of city planning, its foundations, and—most importantly—the mechanisms that directly influence urban development must be examined.

If improvements of the planning process are to be suggested, the weaknesses of the process as it exists must be identified; and an understanding must be gained of how and why the process has evolved

INTRODUCTION 3

to its present form. Since the solutions proposed in this research are analytical in nature, an understanding of the roots of planning and the axioms of the profession must be shown. Otherwise, we may pose solutions in a vacuum.

The second area that must be explored deals with the factors that have influenced the shape and form of today's city, and how the present planning process deals with them. Toward this end the heritage of the American city is a critical element that must be given consideration in any scheme that purports to improve planning and policy evaluation.

The issues raised above are addressed by examining the history of urban development and city planning in chapters 2 and 3. We find that the strong tradition of planning that existed prior to the Revolution quickly dissipated as the result of economic and commercial pressures in a developing nation, and the perennial concerns of the weak federal, state, and local governments regarding financial viability. Thus, fiscal processes have traditionally played a strong role in urban development but have, to a large extent, been neglected in present-day planning.

Formal planning was not accepted as a legitimate enterprise of government until the twentieth century. In the vacuum that existed between the Revolution and the 1900s, land-use practices developed that led to "pestilential" forms of the industrial city in the late 1800s. It was during this period that modern planning was spawned, primarily as an urban reform and beautification movement.

While there was some early recognition of the fact that economics and fiscal dynamics were fundamental to providing proper solutions to urban forms, the planning process tended to disregard these considerations. In addition, isolated pleas for flexibility and incrementalism in planning were largely ignored, and the profession instead concentrated on development of basic planning principles. These principles, largely an outgrowth of concerns for urban reform, are still followed today, with the resultant neglect of many of the factors that actually drive and influence urban development. These factors include the economic and fiscal considerations that every municipality must ultimately deal with, particularly in evaluating community development policies.

Chapters 2 and 3 lay the foundations for the argument that the first step in planning is not the drawing board, but the development of overall policy choices in the community. In order to make this argument, one must extract the policy-making or "end-stating" that is implicit in the planning process, and deal with it explicitly. Such end-stating in the planning process has, as a rule, been left to the planner, who implicitly formulates policy on the basis of the planning axioms. The analytical techniques proposed in this research are designed to deal with policy formulation explicitly. If the end-stating process, as presently used, is successful, further decision aids are unnecessary.

Chapter 3 describes the urban environment that gave rise to modern planning axioms. Development of planning both as a profession and as an enterprise of government is traced to show that these mechanisms, as they exist today, are outdated and that management decision tools can help in the first stages of planning—that is, policy formulation.

Chapter 4 discusses the literature pertaining to policy formulation and goal setting in the community development process. It shows that while some authors have been calling for the application of Simon's rational decision-making process to planning, methodologies that can assist in the implementation of that process do not exist. A survey is given of current large-scale urban simulations, some of which have been developed for plan evaluation of urban renewal. These models are cumbersome, require a great deal of data, and are not easily implemented.

The objectives of the research can now be defined more precisely as

- Developing a tool that will enable municipal policy-makers to rapidly evaluate the impact of alternative development strategies
- Transforming the descriptive constructs used in such a model to a normative approach that will assist in optimizing the attainment of multiple objectives.

An evaluation methodology based on cost-revenue impacts analysis is proposed. An impacts-analysis package, which draws from a number of previous applications, is presented in chapter 5. This chapter is devoted to

- Classifying the state of the art in impacts analysis and presenting the techniques in a systematic manner
- Evaluating the advantages and disadvantages of various approaches
- Developing a generalized computer-based methodology that is easily implemented and hence eliminates the burden of manual computation
- Providing a construct for optimization.

The impacts-analysis package presented shows what is currently being done, proposes improvements where appropriate, automates the process, and augments the results by including socioeconomic and demographic considerations in addition to the usual fiscal indicators. Another departure from the usual cost-revenue study is the method of developing a balance sheet for comparing alternatives. This to to be differentiated from the method of performing cost-revenue analysis

INTRODUCTION

for a given project only. An important argument, made in the chapter, is that once the impacts-analysis process is automated, it becomes useful for rapid examination of hypothetical development alternatives and therefore can assist in policy selection. Analogies substantiate this point.

Numerous processes pertaining to financial analysis have been automated, such as cash flow and lease-leverage analyses, and computerized income tax preparation. Although the original intent is to remove the burden of manual computation, the usual result is that having the rapid tool available will encourage users to explore alternatives for one that is suitable (scenario analysis). Such automated accounting tools perform straightforward computations rapidly. For example, given various data regarding money rates and income tax status, a lease-leverage analysis provides pertinent data on the leveraging obtainable from a corporate leasing policy. Likewise, a cash-flow model will yield the annual (or monthly) cash situation, given data on sales, expenditures, and costs of capital. The output is correct for the given input data.

The Community Development Impacts Model (CODIM) presented in chapter 5 is analogous to the above examples. That is, given input data on type of development, per-unit populations, and so forth, the model computes the impact on the municipality. However, the model presented has more general applicability than previous cost-revenue analyses that were locale-specific. An application of CODIM using a specific example is given in chapter 6.

While the interactive impacts model assists in policy formulation, it cannot deal with goals explicitly. In the community development planning process, goals are desired end-states, such as population, level of taxation, and economic opportunity. Policies are land-use strategies that will attain the goals. A normative approach that handles goals explicitly is introduced in chapter 7, which also discusses satisficing and optimizing models, and gives a rigorous treatment of efficiency in the vector-maximization problem. In addition, a brief discussion of welfare maximization and social utility is presented. This forms the basis for an argument that tools for maximizing welfare do not exist, and that the role of analysis is therefore one of providing the efficient points along the possibility frontier. It is then up to the decision-maker, using whatever notions he or she has regarding the utility of competing objectives, to select those points along the frontier at which he or she wishes to operate.

The goal-programming form of the multiple-objective problem is explored in chapter 8. It is shown that this model leads only to satisficing, although techniques for developing efficient goals are available in the linear case. For the community development problem the linear goal formulation proves to be correct only under conditions where all goals are met. Otherwise, hidden nonlinearities occur. Techniques for linearizing the constraints are reviewed but discarded in favor of a complete nonlinear formulation of the problem.

The nonlinear formulations are treated in chapter 9. The first is an extension of the goal program presented for the linear case. This model is discarded in favor of a quadratic form in which all policy constraints are eliminated and optimization is accomplished directly in the functional. It is shown that the quadratic form of the functional is uniquely suited to solving the vector-optimization problem where objectives containing ratios exist.

The quadratic form is first applied to see if it can improve on a solution found through use of the interactive model. In a second application an analogue to the production-possibility frontier is evaluated as an aid for making trade-offs among competing objectives. Finally, a set of efficient solutions is presented and discussed.

The purpose of this research is not to prescribe the best community development plan for a municipality but, rather, to describe techniques that can help the local policy-maker evaluate the fiscal and socioeconomic impact of community development alternatives on the municipality.

CHAPTER

2

THE AMERICAN CITY AND CITY PLANNING, COLONIAL PERIOD—1850

The beginnings of modern planning in the United States are usually traced to the Columbian Exposition, held in Chicago in 1893. The exposition was only a temporary fair, yet it inspired visitors to emulate its magnificent "white city" forms in municipalities throughout the nation. While it is said that Daniel H. Burnham, master architect of the Exposition, could hardly have imagined the widespread and lasting influence of his designs, an examination of his planning philosophy clearly indicates the grandeur and foresight of his approach. Indeed, Burnham's often-quoted words were to become the motto of American planning for nearly half a century:

> Make no little plans; they have no magic to stir men's blood and probably themselves will not be realized. Make big plans; aim high in hope and work, remembering that a noble, logical diagram once recorded will never die, but long after we are gone will be a living thing, asserting itself with ever growing insistency. Remember that our sons and grandsons are going to do things that would stagger us. Let your watchword be order and your beacon beauty.[1]

The grandeur of the Columbian Exposition spawned a widespread "city beautiful" movement. Important businessmen and civic leaders in major cities sought to beautify the urban environment, using as models the tree-lined boulevards of such romantic European cities as Paris and Vienna. "City beautiful" was urban planning and redevelopment in its renaissance.

Burnham and his disciples had the benefit of numerous examples of American planning that dated back to the pre-Revolutionary period.

Among them is Williamsburg, Virginia, to which John Reps refers as "the most successful essay in community layout in Colonial America."[2] Such early plans were for cities and towns that often were no larger than some of today's suburban subdivisions, and the commonly employed gridiron plan eventually led to high urban densities and the lack of light and air. The early gridirons did make ample provision for public space (commons) and parks. However, statutory and economic circumstances, brought about in part by the American Revolution and the preemption of municipal powers by states, led to intense speculation in land, violation of the original colonial land-use plans, and the transferring of public commons to private holders.

The "city beautiful" practitioner of the early twentieth century sought to alleviate the drabness of the urban environment primarily by creating parks and open spaces, widening streets, erecting classical edifices and constructed thoroughfares to unify the focal points of the plan—concepts not unlike those employed in the colonial period. Without detracting from the significant contributions made by Burnham, Frederick Law Olmstead, and other "city beautiful" planners, it does appear in retrospect that their planning was no more than the urban renewal of the early twentieth century.

This chapter describes early planning examples and traces their eventual downfall. Particular consideration is given to the legal and economic aspects of land development and how they influenced the evolution of planning processes that have resulted in the modern American urban forms.

EARLY PLANNING EXAMPLES

Colonial Williamsburg

In 1698 Francis Nicholson began planning the second of his Tidewater capitals, Williamsburg, Virginia. The legislation of 1699 which established the new town of Williamsburg was "beyond a doubt the most detailed town planning law yet adopted in the English colonies. It specified the exact amount of land to be set aside for the town proper, the capitol building site, the public landing areas on the two rivers, and the roads leading from the town proper to these outlying river port areas."[3]

On the main street, all houses were to be set back by an equal distance and to have similar facades. In addition, the town directors were given authority to adopt rules regarding dwelling size and setbacks on the remaining streets. The legislature further provided that

THE AMERICAN CITY AND CITY PLANNING

Williamsburg was to be divided into half-acre lots and that purchasers had to begin construction within two years. The larger houses along the main thoroughfare, the Duke of Gloucester Street, had to be enclosed with "a wall, or post and rails" within six months after completion. "Indeed, there was little omitted from this unique statute."[4]

Such painstaking attention to planning detail in legislation was not seen again after the Revolution and is, perhaps, only reappearing now (albeit through the mechanism of deed covenants) in planned unit developments and new towns.

William Penn's "Large City or Town"

Nearly two decades before Nicholson embarked on his Williamsburg plan, William Penn received a charter from King Charles II and was made governor of Pennsylvania. Shortly thereafter he published a general scheme for the colony and the conditions of settlement, including the statement that a "large city or town" would be developed and that every person buying 500 acres of land in the colony would be granted a ten-acre plot in the city.[5]

In September 1681, Penn gave specific instructions to the commissioners he had selected to find a suitable site on high ground along the Delaware River where a city of 10,000 acres could be laid out. His instructions for the layout specified a gridiron plan.

While Penn had numerous models, both European and American, from which to draw, his "Philadelphia plan" was nevertheless a unique contribution that was later widely emulated, some principal examples being Savannah, Lexington, Cincinnati, Pittsburgh, and Zanesville, Ohio.[6] The "Philadelphia plan" was important for several reasons. First, it was for a city much larger than previous colonial towns. Second, and more important, by designating four smaller squares as recreational areas, Penn in essence established America's first public parks. "Thus," concludes Reps, "in its scale, its open squares, and its consistent use of wide streets intersecting at right angles, Philadelphia represented something of an innovation in colonial town design."[7]

Many of the colonial settlements had sound planning and design. However, new forces soon emerged that caused the green country towns to become shabby and dingy, without light and without air. Penn, for example, published his final Philadelphia plan in 1683; yet as early as 1698 the recordings of one Gabriel Thomas describe the initiation of practices that led to later problems.

The generous blocks were cut up with additional streets, and the four park squares were encroached upon, one being used as a brickyard and another as a graveyard.[8] Front streets, which, according to the plan, were to have no development, soon turned into commercial and warehouse areas. Thus the Delaware and Schuylkill rivers, which initially were an important factor in the siting of the city, soon became inaccessible to its residents.

The factors that led to deviations from original plans in Philadelphia and other cities were, for the most part, economic and statutory. However, post-Revolutionary social forces also played in important role in destroying the achievements of the early American planners.

LEGAL FOUNDATIONS OF AMERICAN CITY PLANNING

Zoning law, as it is known today, is one of the most recent additions to the American jurisprudence.[9] Although many examples of "antinuisance" legislation date from the early and mid-nineteenth century, it was not until 1916, when New York City passed the first comprehensive zoning ordinance in the country, that the concept of "districting," as it was first called, began to be used as a tool for planning and land-use control.[10] And zoning itself did not receive wide acceptance until a decade later, when the Supreme Court upheld its validity as a proper extension of police power. In 1926, the Court, ruling on the case of Village of Euclid v. Ambler Realty Company ruled that "[A] municipal ordinance which divides the whole territory of the municipality into districts and imposes land-use restrictions on the basis of district classifications is within the police power of the municipal corporation."[11]

In discussing the proper criteria for determining whether an exercise of police power is valid, the Court referred to the common law of nuisance:

> In solving doubts, the maxim sic utere tuo ut alienum non laedas [Use your property in such a manner as not to injure that of another], which lies at the foundation of so much of the common law of nuisances, ordinarily will furnish a fairly helpful clew. And the law of nuisances, likewise, may be consulted, not for the purpose of controlling, but for the helpful aid of its analogies in the process of ascertaining the scope of, the power.[12]

It took nearly 150 years of deliberate hesitation before the police powers of American state and local government were finally extended to the point where courts were willing to accept their use as a means of balancing the community's living environment (general welfare) with individual rights to property and the freedom from deprivation of that property without due process.

Extension of police powers has always been approached cautiously, and rightly so. But the legal vacuum that existed in municipal planning and land-use control during the 150 years between the adoption of the U.S. Constitution (1788; the constitutions of the thirteen original states, except Rhode Island, were adopted between 1776 and 1780) and <u>Euclid</u> v. <u>Ambler Realty</u> fostered an evolution of land development processes that invariably led to the blighted conditions of American cities in the late nineteenth and early twentieth centuries. Many of the land-use practices that arose in the absence of definitive statutory pronouncement have become part of the American culture and heritage. Before discussing the origins and development of post-Revolution land-use forms, it is worthwhile to examine the process that led to the acceptance of the comprehensive zoning ordinance in the early part of the twentieth century.

Zoning and Its Foundations in English Nuisance Law

Originally the common law of nuisance attempted to provide a remedy for petty disputes between English peasants living on adjoining land—those regarding overhanging trees, obnoxious pigs, and the like.[13] Inherent in the common law is the precept that the right of a landowner to use his land is an important incident of his ownership, highly regarded by the community and vigorously upheld by the courts.[14] Robert M. Anderson notes, however, "The right to use land is not an unrestricted license to use it without regard to the impact of such use upon the land of others."[15] From the case-by-case decisions there evolved a body of law that restricted or limited the rights of landowners to use of their property.

Thus, long before the 1916 Comprehensive Zoning Ordinance in New York City and the state's enabling legislation that preceded it, specific nuisance conditions were being abated by the courts and municipalities were using the common-law precedents by establishing antinuisance ordinances. These ordinances did not intend general zoning or planning but, rather, as in the case of early examples that prohibited laundries from residential areas of San Francisco, were designed to alleviate a specific undesirable condition.[16]

While such early cases did not involve comprehensive zoning ordinances, they were nonetheless encouraging to planners, since they did establish official recognition of the fact that certain land uses are incompatible with others, and that the rights of all landowners are diminished unless they are subject to some reasonable restraints.[17] This is the basic premise of comprehensive zoning and planning.

Extension of Police Power in Land-Use Planning

Progress in planning and control of land use was achieved through increasingly broad interpretations of the extent to which the police powers were proper exercise of land-use controls by municipal corporations, towns, villages, and counties. The exact limits of police powers are still not defined precisely, although the courts of New York State have held that "The purposes and the scope of the police power is clearly defined and well established and the test is explicit."[18] While the proper extents of the police power may be under examination today, the concept itself did not even exist during the first half-century after the Revolution.

Chief Justice John Marshall is credited with originating the term in the case of Brown v. Maryland in 1827.[19] The term did not find wide usage until after the middle of the century.[20] Anderson defines police power as "the general power to regulate conduct for the protection of the public health, safety, morals, or welfare."[21]

Apparently the New York State Legislature felt it was a proper exercise of this authority when in 1807 it passed "An Act, Relative to Improvements, Touching and Laying out of Streets and Roads in the City of New York, and for Other Purposes."[22] This act, perhaps a landmark statute for the period, sets forth that for the "public good," and in order to "secure a free and abundant circulation of air," the state and the city have the authority to undertake the planning of thoroughfares and squares—an action that strongly and directly affects the individual and his property. Nonetheless, direct control and planning for private land, even in the form of antinuisance ordinances, was still several decades away. Anderson notes:

> Early ordinances which limited the use of land usually concerned matters which were clearly related to the health or safety of the community. . . . They were comfortably within reach of the police power and were upheld by the courts.[23]

THE AMERICAN CITY AND CITY PLANNING

With the passage of time, the interpretations of what constitutes a nuisance were progressively modified; and after the mid-nineteenth century it became relatively easy to seek abatement of operations that were in themselves not a nuisance, but that for all practical purposes became so because of their proximity to congested areas.[24]

The era of laissez-faire with regard to municipal planning and control of land use was drawing to a close. The premise that comprehensive planning controls were needed for the general welfare was becoming more widely accepted. After some brief excursions into the employment of eminent domain as a planning and land-use tool, the stage was set for the comprehensive zoning ordinances of the early twentieth century. Unfortunately, most of the eastern cities had already become relatively large and zoning was not to be retroactive.

The common law of nuisance may have been adequate for the needs of a rural society.[25] However, the rapid migration to urban areas that took place in the last half of the nineteenth century generated problems that could not be solved through such "modest restrictions."[26] Villages grew into cities; and as land became scarce and expensive, owners developed it intensively to maximum capacity. Thus, the essentially unrestricted use of land produced communities that were overcrowded, blighted, and a hazard to health. "The situation became so grave that the decisional law developed in nuisance litigation provided no satisfactory solution to the problem."[27]

Although the power of eminent domain did not encounter serious judicial difficulty as a planning and land-use tool, its application in this field was doomed to failure because it was cumbersome and expensive.

By the late nineteenth century it became clear to planners that extending the police power to include comprehensive planning and land-use controls was the only practical, long-term means for achieving the broad authority that was necessary in order for meaningful urban planning to be undertaken and enforced. The colonial plans, even those for the nation's capital, were repeatedly violated; and no general mechanism was available to enjoin such violations. Without a broadly based planning authority vested in the municipal government and the contingent power to enforce such planning, rectification of the blight and congestion that plagued most cities by the end of the nineteenth century would not be possible.

THE "BOOM" YEARS

The uncertainty with which the laws regarding municipal powers to plan and control land use evolved led to a vacuum in local authority. This vacuum was taken up by merchants and real-estate speculators who, in the absence of statutory and regulatory constraints, operationally defined and established land development processes that are still in effect. Governmental and political power was concentrated in the hands of landed individuals. Policies regarding land development and planning were made according to the convenient axiom that land was a commodity for enriching men and not a resource to be managed for the benefit of all.

Intense speculation in land took place not only in the older cities such as New York, but also in the West. As a result of favorable federal land-sale and land-grant policies (especially the Land Ordinance of 1785), "new city" promotion became a successful venture. In the East, merchants and businessmen were a strong element in fostering competition for growth among the various cities. Thus, municipal construction and planning efforts were directed at improving commerce and manufacture. Promotion by businessmen was a strong factor in what soon became a municipality's responsibilities with regard to planning and land-use controls.

Finally, the peculiar regard held for the federal government appears to have been no small element in the development of land-use regulatory authority. The Continental Congress was weak and no match for business and landed interests. Later governments, both federal and local, found themselves continually short of funds because of the absence of sufficient taxing authority. Governments at all levels, however, had one unique asset—large quantities of land. This asset, combined with what appear to have been strong growth pressures in the states and territories, soon resulted in a happy union between men interested in land development and promotion (which, from some of the literature, appears to have been almost a common pastime) and government.

Unfortunately, this union was beneficial only to the developers. Over the long term the American city, the American countryside, and the American populace were all detrimentally affected by the early economic "boom" of this nation.

Early Development of the Eastern Cities: New York and Philadelphia

In 1807 New York State passed legislation appointing three commissioners to formulate a street plan for New York City. This commissioners' plan was an early example of a state's use of its police power to plan and regulate land use. Much as this legislation marks an early case of government regulation in planning, it has been referred to by some authors as the "one event, [which] could be said to signal the death of the colonial [planning] tradition."[28]

Trade and manufacture were important in colonial New York, and by 1700 new streets and building sites were being laid out north of the old city boundary. Large developments were rare, and for the most part land sales were made one or two parcels at a time,[29] thus leading to growth without an underlying plan, motivated by economic considerations of individuals.

For the purpose of raising funds, New York City surveyed and platted the lands it owned in 1804. Two years later, the State Legislature was requested to appoint a commission to lay out new streets.[30] The appointment of the commissioners began a flurry of speculation. Owners quickly platted their property, hoping they could force the commission to confirm its plans.[31] Evidently the owners were successful, for the commission found it impossible to "adjust their plan to the irregular property boundaries and the random streets that already existed in the vast territory under their jurisdiction."[32]

The plan was simple, utilizing some dozen north-south avenues intersected by 155 cross streets every 200 feet. The total disregard for topography (which is only one of the features that differentiates the New York City grid from such colonial grids as Philadelphia) and the monotony of the many shallow blocks caused Frederick Law Olmstead to remark:

> Some 2000 blocks were provided, each theoretically two hundred feet wide, no more, no less; and ever since if a building site is wanted, whether with a view of a church or a blast furnace, an open house or a toy shop, there is, of intention, no better place in one of these blocks than another. Such distinctive advantage as Rome gives St. Peter's, London St. Paul's, New York under her system gives to nothing.[33]

The commission plan was also criticized for the scant amount of open space it left. In possible anticipation of such criticism, the commissioners explained:

> It may, to many, be matter of surprise, that so few
> vacant spaces have been left. . . . when, therefore
> . . . the price of land is so uncommonly great, it seemed
> proper to admit the principles of economy to greater
> influence . . .[34]

The commissioners' report thus made little effort to disguise the economic motivation of their plan, and they later defended it for its utility in the "buying, selling and improving of real estate."[35] On the grounds of economy and practicality, therefore, the plan ignored well-precedented principles of design that would have improved variety in street vistas and defined important focal-point sites. But then, the rectangular platting of land had received the de facto support of the federal government, primarily on those grounds, in the Land Ordinance of 1785.

The 1811 gridiron plan for New York was widely copied by other cities. The business and economic pressures that forced the acceptance of this plan also were not unique to New York City. Lewis Mumford writes:

> The beauty of this new mechanical pattern, from a commercial standpoint, should be plain. This plan offers the engineer none of those special problems that irregular parcels and curved boundary lines present. An office boy could figure out the number of square feet involved in a street opening or in a sale of land: even a lawyer's clerk could write a description of the necessary deed of sale, merely by filling in with the proper dimensions the standard document.[36]

Washington, D.C.

The planning of the nation's capital is another example of how efforts to establish planned cities conflicted with the pressures of a rapidly expanding capitalistic economy. While Washington was being built, real estate holders influenced decisions and continually attempted to alter the officially adopted L'Enfant plan for the city.[37] The government had obtained control of half the lots in the District of Columbia not reserved for public purposes. After the plan for the city had been completed in 1791, attention of the commissioners turned to its implementation. Pierre L'Enfant opposed the sale of lots at such an early date.[38]

THE AMERICAN CITY AND CITY PLANNING

However, the new government had already promised skeptical citizens that the city would be developed soon. The sale was held as planned, but L'Enfant's refusal to print copies of his plan made it impossible for potential buyers to determine the locations of their lots. A second auction, held in 1791, fared as poorly as the first.[39]

In order to secure funds to get construction of the Capitol and the executive mansion under way, the government felt compelled to accept the proposal of James Greenleaf, made on behalf of a syndicate controlled by himself and Robert Morris, to purchase 3,000 lots at a reduced price. The group later secured more land and eventually owned one-third of the available lots. The syndicate finally overextended itself, and went into bankruptcy in 1797, leaving behind unfinished construction and giving the District of Columbia the reputation as a bad place for investment.[40] Benjamin Latrobe, who supervised the construction of public buildings, made bitter comments about the "ruin left by the speculators."[41]

A Midwest Example: Jeffersonville, Indiana

In 1805, Thomas Jefferson commented on the yellow fever scourge and proposed that by building cities less densely, the epidemics would not spread as rapidly:

> Take, for instance, the chequer board for a plan. Let the black squares only be building squares, and the white ones be left open, in turf and trees.[42]

William Henry Harrison, governor of the Indiana Territory, wrote President Jefferson in 1802 that he had selected a site for a city; and, upon recommendation of a plan by Jefferson, the "Town has been laid out with each alternate square to remain vacant forever. . . . and I have taken the liberty to call it Jeffersonville. . . ."[43]

Jeffersonville quickly grew in importance as a trade center for the area. The open squares of the original plan were too much of a temptation, however, and within two decades the leading businessmen petitioned the legislature for a change. The legislature yielded, and Jeffersonville's open squares were promptly platted and sold.

Other Economic Pressures on Municipal Government

Pressures on land during the first half-century of urban development in this nation were intense, and short-term economic forces tended to outweigh overall planning considerations. "Planning had disappeared from the American civic lexicon. City lots were now a speculative business, not a matter of community policy."[44]

Municipal government (except in the old New England cities) was severely constrained by the states in the manner and amount of funds that could be raised through taxes. In 1780, for example, Lexington, Kentucky's levy could not exceed £100.[45] "Restrictions on other towns varied, but the rate never exceeded one per cent of real and personal property."[46] Thus municipal sale of land was an expedient that, in many cases, raised badly needed revenues.

In addition, the members of local governing bodies were influential and wealthy citizens who controlled large amounts of land and were not interested in regulatory restrictions on its future use. In 1819, for example, the members of Cincinnati's governing board held land within the municipal corporation valued at $225,000 and averaging $10,000 per member. This "placed most of them in a category with only 38 other well-to-do Cincinnatians."[47]

The records of St. Louis indicate that in 1811 the town's total assessment was $134,000, of which almost $83,000 was concentrated in the hands of six influential mercantile leaders.[48] Businessmen in many cities were successful in promoting municipal planning and land-use policies conducive to the conduct of trade and the disposition of land. The period in which business leaders realized their significant responsibility to press for urban improvement and elimination of blighted and congested conditions was still nearly 75 years away.

Speculation in the West

By the time the U.S. Constitution was adopted, most cities on the eastern seaboard were at least a century old. The move across the Alleghenies came swiftly; and after 1830, an increasing number of speculators saw an opportunity to make large gains through the purchase of cheap government land.[49]

The Land Ordinance of 1785 helped the promotion of western land tremendously. It provided for the sale of public lands to individuals in "townships" of 36 square miles or "sections" of one square mile.[50] In authorizing these subdivisions, the Ordinance established the use of the rectangular survey system. Although revenues realized under the Land Ordinance proved far less than anticipated, by the turn of the century there were numerous land companies and syndicates that each held millions of acres.

Robert Morris' North American Land Company held 6 million acres by 1795. The Ohio Company of Associates, a group of army veterans, negotiated the purchase of 1.5 million acres at one dollar per acre under the 1785 Ordinance. The Congress, badly in need of funds to operate the government, agreed to installment payments, with a portion of the purchase price payable within three months.

When Connecticut waived its claim to lands between extensions of its northern and southern boundaries west to the Mississippi, it reserved a 3.5 million-acre tract in Ohio.[51] In 1795 a sales agreement was concluded for $1.2 million under which the Connecticut Land Company received a deed by posting a bond and a deed of trust with the Ohio treasurer. Moses Cleaveland led a survey party that found a site for the "capital" of this reserve, the city eventually named after him.[52]

SUMMARY

Although there were some excellent examples of town planning in the colonial period, American city planning became almost nonexistent after the Revolution. Following the Revolution there was an absence of definitive regulatory authority that permitted municipal corporations, villages, and towns to undertake comprehensive planning and land-use control measures. Within this vacuum, speculators and businessmen initiated land-use practices that did not always result in well-planned urban forms. The rapid growth of cities and the resultant pressures on land created widespread interest in land promotion and development. The cultural value of rugged individualism, coupled with the laissez-faire posture of government, further spawned the land boom.

Federal, state, and local government owned vast tracts of land. While this provided one of the greatest opportunities for planning and controlling growth, government chose instead to divest itself of these holdings as a short-term economic expedient. The resultant land sales led to the concentration of political power and vast holdings in the hands of relatively few individuals.

Finally, a general attitude, developed early among intellectuals, that cities were "pestilential to the morals, the health and the liberties of man,"[53] caused widespread disillusion with urban form in general, and an apparent lack of motivation for the public sector to improve conditions. The myth of bucolic serenity pervaded the culture and remains to this day.[54]

NOTES

1. *Plan of Chicago* (Chicago: Commercial Club, 1909; repr. New York: Da Capo Press, 1970).
2. John Reps, *The Making of Urban America* (Princeton, N.J.: Princeton University Press, 1965).
3. John Reps, *Town Planning in Frontier America* (Princeton, N.J.: Princeton University Press, 1969).
4. Ibid.
5. Ibid.
6. Richard C. Wade, *The Urban Frontier* (Chicago: University of Chicago Press, 1964).
7. Reps, *Town Planning*, op. cit.
8. City ordinances passed in the early nineteenth century reestablished the squares and prohibited their use as dumps or burying grounds. (Smoking "segars" or pipes in the public squares also was outlawed.) Ibid.
9. Jacob Beuscher and Robert Wright, *Land Use, Cases and Materials* (St. Paul: West Publishing Co., 1969).
10. Norman Williams, Jr., *The Structure of Urban Zoning* (New York: Buttenheim, 1966).
11. 272 U.S. 365, 71 L. ed. 303, 47 S. Ct. 114.
12. Robert M. Anderson, *Zoning Law and Practice in New York State* (New York: Lawyer's Cooperative, 1963, p. 6.
13. Williams, op. cit., p. 11.
14. Anderson, op. cit., p. 5.
15. Ibid.
16. Robert Walker, *The Planning Function in Urban Government* (Chicago: University of Chicago Press, 1941).
17. Anderson, op. cit., p. 7.
18. Charles Rathkopf, *The Law of Zoning and Planning* (New York: Crosby Press, 1949).
19. Walker, op. cit., p. 51.
20. Ibid.
21. Anderson, op. cit., p. 9.
22. N.Y. Laws chapter 115; Beuscher and Wright, op. cit., p. 10.
23. Anderson, op. cit., p. 10.
24. Ibid.
25. Ibid., p. 8.
26. Ibid.
27. Ibid., p. 9.
28. James G. Coke, "Antecedents of Local Planning," in William Goodman, ed., *Principles and Practice of Urban Planning*

(Washington, D.C.: International City Managers' Association, 1971), p. 14.
    29. Ibid.
    30. Ibid.
    31. Coke, op. cit.
    32. Reps, Town Planning, op. cit., p. 198.
    33. "New Ideals in the Planning of Cities, Towns and Villages," in John Nolen, ed., City Planning (New York: D. Appleton & Co., 1916 and 1929).
    34. Reps, Town Planning, op. cit., p. 201.
    35. Ibid., p. 203.
    36. Lewis Mumford, The City in History (New York: Harcourt, Brace, 1961), p. 422.
    37. Charles Glaab and Theodore Brown, A History of Urban America (New York: Macmillan, 1967).
    38. Reps, Town Planning, op. cit., p. 326.
    39. Glaab and Brown, op. cit., p. 34.
    40. Ibid.
    41. Ibid.
    42. Letter to Devolney, in Glaab and Brown, op. cit., p. 54.
    43. Letter from Harrison to Jefferson in Reps, Town Planning, op. cit., p. 280.
    44. Coke, op. cit., p. 15.
    45. Wade, op. cit., p. 76.
    46. Ibid. As a comparison, note that the present statutory limit in New York State for operating budgets of cities is 2 percent of real property value. Additional levies are permitted for debt service, with certain capital spending being totally excluded from limitation.
    47. Ibid., p. 78.
    48. Ibid., p. 109.
    49. Ibid.
    50. Reps, Town Planning, op. cit., p. 282.
    51. Ibid., p. 355.
    52. Ibid.
    53. Thomas Jefferson in a letter to Benjamin Rush, in Glaab and Brown, op. cit., p. 52.
    54. Noel Gist and Sylvia Fava, Urban Society (New York: Thomas Crowell, 1964), p. 440.

CHAPTER 3

THE FOUNDATIONS OF MODERN CITY PLANNING

With few exceptions, American city and town planning prior to the twentieth century concentrated on the two-dimensional layout. Perhaps the primary reason for this is that while regulatory authority to control land use was developing by the end of the nineteenth century, its basis was in nuisance law; and hence it was used only to restrict entire categories of land use. Height and bulk regulations on buildings did not appear until the landmark New York City comprehensive zoning ordinance of 1916.

Nearly 25 years before that ordinance, however, Americans were introduced to the physical planning that considered height and facades of buildings at the Columbian Exposition of 1893. Visitors to the fair were dazzled by the white forms and open spaces. The architects of the exposition paid close attention to such factors as the homogeneity of cornice lines and fenestration. With its magnificent vistas, formal fountains, and courts, the exposition gave substance to the desires of many civic reformers.

The Columbian Exposition was held at a time when the housing and urban reform movement had already attracted widespread attention among such liberal reformers as Benjamin Flower in Boston and Jacob Riis in New York. The myth that large cities were "pestilential to the morals, the health and the liberties of man," in Jefferson's words, was pervading common thought. In 1857, Harper's Weekly referred to New York City as "a huge semi-barbarous metropolis" with "no practical or efficient security for either life or property."[1]

The anti-urban movement gained popularity in an era of general concern for social reform, and it received notable intellectual support. The British scholar Lord James Bryce had few compliments for urban America. In his book The American Commonwealth, he stated:

"The government of cities is one of the conspicuous failures of the United States." Other noted figures, such as the economist Henry George, argued against vast cities where the "general populations . . . are divorced from the genial influence of nature."[2]

More than reformers, these commentators on American city life, along with such early leaders in the profession as Frederick Law Olmstead, had a pervasive influence on the newly emerging city planning profession. Planning principles such as contact with nature, the importance of human scale, open spaces, and visual focal points, which first crystallized in the Gilded Age, went unchallenged until the late 1950s, when "non-planner" planners such as William Alonso, Melville Branch, and Jane Jacobs began to take issue with ther heritage of physical planning.

"CITY PESTILENTIAL": THE INDUSTRIAL CITY 1850-1900

Perceptions of the Period

In 1845, Dr. John Griscom filed a report with New York City that was one of the first systematic investigations of the relationship between city slums and health.[3] Indeed, health and sanitary conditions were extremely poor in the congested areas of the large cities. Drainage ditches carried urine and fecal matter into the streets. In 1857, there were only 158 miles of sewers for nearly 500 miles of New York streets. After the Civil War overcrowding became increasingly severe, and by 1893 over half of New York City's population lived in tenements.

In 1857, New York State appointed a commission to make a detailed, house-by-house survey of slum conditions in Brooklyn and Manhattan. Their report, a plea for housing improvement, discusses some of the familiar economic mechanisms that lead to housing blight:

> It was soon perceived, by astute owners or agents of property, that a greater percentage of profit would be realized by the conversion of houses and blocks into barracks and dividing their space into the smallest proportions capable of containing human life within four walls. . . . and rates of rent were established, . . . which . . . secured . . . an aggregate of profit from the whole barracks (risks and losses taken into account) of twice or thrice the amount which a legitimate lease of the building to one occupant would bring, if granted for business purposes at the usual rate of real-estate interest.[4]

Ten years after the commission published its report, New York passed its first tenement legislation and established the Health Department. The 1867 ordinance limited lot coverage to 90 percent, but in general it forced only slight improvements.[5] In 1879, following a competition for a model tenement, the dumbbell plan was adopted. So named because tenements constructed according to this ordinance have the appearance of squared-off dumbbells in the plan view, it necessitated the use of indoor light shafts along the lot lines to insure ventilation to all rooms.

None of these laws was well enforced. Writing in 1890, Jacob Riis deplored the conditions of the Fourth Ward in New York:

> Down below Chattam Square, in the old Fourth Ward, where the cradle of the tenement stood, we shall find the Other Half at home. . . . These [tenements] never had other design than to shelter, at as little outlay as possible, the greatest crowds out of which rent could be wrung.[6]

Benjamin Flower, in Civilization's Inferno, spoke in equally impassioned tones about the poverty and "soul-sickening" spectacle "below the social cellar."[7] Both Riis and Flower reported extreme overcrowding, with over 100 people in a two-story dwelling sharing one privy not uncommon.

Stirred by the efforts of these crusaders, a growing protest against the railroad flats and the dumbbell tenements emerged. In 1899, the Charity Organization Society conducted a contest for a new tenement house design that had such requirements as 70 percent maximum lot coverage, inside courts, and a specific volume of air per dwelling occupant. The competition led to passage of the Tenement House Act of 1901, which prohibited the dumbbell plan of 1879 and fairly well established 50-foot lots, as opposed to the old 25-foot railroad flats.[8]

Through the efforts of reformers, housing became accepted as a legitimate interest of city planning, along with landscaping and boulevard construction, both of which fell into the domain of planning almost automatically after the Columbian Exposition. The first national conference on planning, held in Washington, D.C., in 1909, gained its initiative from groups interested in housing.[9]

The "city pestilential" was the breeding ground for the romantic "city beautiful" movement. By and large the industrial city of the late nineteenth century, both in the United States and abroad, was drab, congested, and noisy. These characteristics are portrayed in pictures and captions in such periodicals of the day as Harper's Weekly. In an 1878 print, a thick layer of air pollution over Pittsburgh is plainly visible.

FOUNDATIONS OF MODERN CITY PLANNING

It was in this urban milieu, during a period known for its reform and romantic interests, that men directed their attention to city renewal and beautification. The "city beautiful" movement, which called for civic adornment through the construction of new public edifices and boulevards, was a perfect, if compromising, solution to the problems of the day. For the reformer, "city beautiful" was an inspiration for more significant improvements. For the civic leader and politician, it was a convenient bromide. In short, what more proper channel could exist for the investment of public funds than the improvement of civic appearance?

"City beautiful" did not rely on zoning, on private concessions, or on restrictions of private land-use activity. Its hallmark was the creation of grand civic monuments.[10] In short, it possessed all the qualities needed for political compromise and the consolidation of divergent interest groups, from liberal reformers to conservative civic leaders.

Bases of Modern Planning in the "City Pestilential"

Before proceeding with a full discussion of the "city beautiful" movement, it may be well to summarize the evils of the "city pestilential" as perceived by its contemporaries. These perceptions formed the basis for the axioms of orthodox planning theory and have become an integral part of American folklore.[11]

The contemporary notions regarding the "city pestilential" are perhaps best summarized in Lord James Bryce's address to the Second National Conference on Housing:

> First: From the point of view of health. In the city, and most of the great cities are crowded, there must be less oxygen and more microbes. . . .
>
> Second: It is a great evil in the city that people are cut off from nature and communion with nature. . . .
>
> Third: It is an evil in that it separates the greater part of the community into classes and disturbs the sentiment of neighborliness between the richer and the poorer, which existed formerly in smaller communities and which ought to exist. . . .
>
> Fourth: Life in the great city tends to stimulate and increase beyond measure that which is the menace of the American city—intensification of nervous strain and nervous excitability. Cities are the home . . . of every kind of noise.

> Fifth: . . . these conditions are not favorable for . . . the boys and girls. The boy living in the country has any amount of opportunity for the development of his vitality. . . . But if he is cooped up in the city he takes to rambling at night . . . and . . . is apt to get into all sorts of trouble. . . .
>
> Lastly: In the great cities there is a deplorable amount of economic waste. . . . The people want to live in the outer parts of the city. . . . If you will consider the amount of time that is taken from work to be given to mere transportation . . . you will see how great the loss is.[12]

These views of the "city pestilential," the spawning ground for the modern planning profession, have become the foundations of planning values, which in turn have been translated into planning axioms. Under the assumption, for example, that cities are, to some measure, crowded and cut off from nature—and, further, that such crowding and removal from nature are detrimental—city planners have developed schemes to ameliorate these conditions. Garden cities, broadacre cities, and greenbelts have all been design solutions that assume concrete is injurious to the health of people.[13] Jane Jacobs lists some additional axioms of orthodox planning, among them the notions that the "street is bad as an environment for humans; houses should be turned away from it and faced inward toward sheltered greens."[14]

The principles of city planning are, in reality, only a reflection of values that grew out of the reform age in the "city pestilential," yet they have been taken as articles of faith by practicing professionals and have served as principal goals to be achieved by any city plan. Only in the last decade have planners begun to question the validity of the fundamental planning axioms. The literature, with increasing frequency, has contained papers relating to pluralistic planning, multiple-plan evaluation, and community-directed goal setting. All these are indications of the increasing skepticism toward the traditional planning axioms. They are a tacit implication that considerations other than the traditional sets of planning values must be included in plan making, and that goal setting, which had always been implicit in planning, must be treated as an explicit first step.

"CITY BEAUTIFUL" AND THE EMERGENCE OF MODERN PLANNING

In 1916, after nearly a century of deliberate progress in the extension of police power to the control of land use, New York City

FOUNDATIONS OF MODERN CITY PLANNING

passed the Building Zone Ordinance. Zoning was originally intended as a means for restricting building height and bulk in the city; and although it was not clearly recognized at the time, "city beautiful" planning could not have been implemented without this legal foundation.

By 1893, the year of the Columbian Exposition, Americans had already been exposed to a resurgence of classic architectural styles. "The private palaces, the colossal monuments and the discovery of the American Baroque were milestones along the road to a new taste. Suddenly, a vision appeared on the shores of Lake Michigan. . . ."[15]

The passage of the Tarsney Act by Congress in 1893, the year of the Exposition, renewed the tradition of federal patronage by authorizing the Secretary of the Treasury to seek designs for public buildings through competition. Local governments soon followed; and from the Minnesota State Capitol of Cass Gilbert to the New York Public Library of John Carrere and Thomas Hastings, cities all across the nation took competitive entries for new municipal and state houses, museums, libraries, malls, and parks.

Apart from the technical progress made in planning during these years, organizational progress was made as well. The early "city beautiful" planners practiced primarily as consultants to municipalities. As it became more widely recognized that planning was an important function of local government, planning staffs were created with their concomitant planning commissions. These commissions, first created to insure fairness and objectivity in plan preparation, eventually were criticized as inhibiting creative planning. Most state enabling legislation still requires planning commissions as a prerequisite to adoption of comprehensive plans. The commission structure in planning is currently under evaluation in the literature, with numerous authors calling for planning to be more of a staff function, modeled after a corporate planning staff.

Zoning vs. Planning

Edward M. Bassett, a major participant in the preparation of the 1916 Building Heights Ordinance, defines zoning as ". . . the regulation, by districts under the police power of the height, bulk, and use of buildings, the use of land, and the density of population."[16]

The first study that led to the consideration of this subject was made by the Commission on Heights of Buildings in New York City. Originally appointed by the Board of Estimate in 1914, the commission was charged with investigating the relation of skyscrapers to the health and welfare of the community. It submitted recommendations that were formally adopted in July 1916. As discussed in Chapter 2, zoning had its first major legal test in 1926, when the Supreme Court, in <u>Euclid v. Ambler Realty</u>, upheld the constitutionality of zoning as a legitimate extension of the police power. Within several years of that decision, planning became widely accepted as a legitimate interest of local government.

In the many cases that followed <u>Euclid</u> v. <u>Ambler Realty</u>, the courts recognized the power to zone vacant land. This, of course, is the primary method for shaping urban growth. In a 1937 ruling, however, the courts definitively upheld the municipality's power to plan for growth and development. The following year, ruling in the case of <u>Mansfield and Swett</u> v. <u>Town of West Orange</u>, the New Jersey Supreme Court gave complete recognition to municipal planning under the police powers:

> . . . And it is essential to adequate planning that there be provision for future community needs reasonably to be anticipated. . . . To challenge the power to give proper direction to community growth and development in the particulars mentioned [the court earlier refers to traffic flow, building lines, street widths and location, and housing] is to deny the vitality of a principle that has brought men together in organized society. A sound economy to advance the collective interest in local affairs is the primary aim of municipal government.[17]

Thus, the municipal power to zone, and to use zoning as a tool for shaping urban growth, was recognized as proper and essential. In 1922 the U.S. Department of Commerce published "A Standard State Zoning Enabling Act," and in 1928 "A Standard City Planning Enabling Act."

Development of the Planning Profession

The noted planner Charles Mulford Robinson gave almost complete attention in his book to street systems, traffic, and the platting of lots for various uses.[19] Most far-reaching in the work, however, is his recognition that planning must be an ongoing process. In the "Conclusion" he states:

> The street, then, is to be thought of, not as a line in a drawing, not as a mark on a map; but as a living thing. . . . This quality of it, which adds so vastly to the interest

of the problem, adds also to its difficulty. For it requires
that our plans not be too rigid. . . .

Apparently, most planners either disagreed with Robinson or
did not read the "Conclusion" of his book, for planning, as it evolved
in the early part of the twentieth century, became a static process.
Owing largely to the nature of the consultant-client relationship of
early planning, it involved the expenditure of large sums within a
relatively short period of time and the attitude that the plan presented
by the consultant was, in itself, the desired objective.[20] Indeed, the
"city beautiful" movement left behind a legacy of monumental structures
and classical civic centers that could accommodate change and growth
only through encroachment on the open spaces or, as has happened in
Washington, D.C., moving of activities to entirely new locations.

However, one significant exception of the era came about when
the Commercial Club of Chicago invited Daniel Burnham to prepare a
master plan. The resulting product was hailed as a milestone in planning. The major contribution of this effort was the scope and extent
of the plan. Burnham gave consideration to railroads, highways, parks,
forests, and bathing beaches.[21] But perhaps the greatest significance
was his development of the city as part of the development of the region.
Chapter III of his plan shows a diagram of the location of Chicago with
regard to the seven central states. The outline for the chapter shows
its broad scope: "Chicago the Metropolis of the Middle West; Reason
for Expecting Continuous Growth; A Lakeside Drive Along Lake
Michigan; Connections Between Outlying Cities; The Building of Good
Roads."

The Chicago Plan was unique and, according to some, "has not
yet found its equal."[22] The country was rapidly changing, however,
and the emerging planning profession would have to accommodate the
new directions. Henry Ford made his first Model T in the year the
Chicago Plan was published, and the well-to-do were deserting the
city for the suburbs.[23] The automobile soon became available to all,
and the "city efficient" obscured the importance of the "city beautiful."[24]

Automobile registration grew from 458,000 in 1910 to over
8 million in 1920. By 1930 there were almost 23 million vehicles
registered in the United States. The Plan of Rochester summarizes
the new developments in the planning profession:

> For the past two decades there has been more or less
> constant study and accomplishment, during which time the
> practice of city planning has passed through the many
> vicissitudes that usually accompany a great transformation
> in ideas and methods of dealing with a structure so complex

as the modern American city. . . . More recently, the
enormous increase in the use of the automobile has concentrated public attention upon the problems of street
design to meet the needs of the motor age.[25]

During the first two decades of the twentieth century, the professional planning consultants had established their identity. Although most of the planning efforts of the era were carried out through private groups, such as the Commerce Club in Chicago and the Regional Plan Association in New York, American cities had claimed planning as a proper function that was carried out through the semi-autonomous planning or zoning commissions. The effectiveness of such arrangements, however, seems questionable. Writes William Alonso:

Seldom prepared with sufficient understanding of the
structural relationships, its [the plan's] administration
consisted of a joyful or reluctant granting of variances
and exceptions so that it soon became riddled with holes.[26]

Lacking funds for permanent planning staffs, the commissions hired consulting planners to prepare master plans that would then be "sold" to recalcitrant political leaders.[27] After hundreds of examples during the first three decades of the twentieth century, the plan began to take on an all-too-recognizable look—"Streets and Thoroughfares, Parks and Recreation, Zoning and Civic Appearance." Once the zoning ordinance was adopted, planning for all intents and purposes was completed, and the commission would do little except "offer the bromide that the Master Plan should be kept up to date."[28]

Indeed, planning, as it evolved through the 1920s, did not heed the earlier pleas for flexibility. Robert Whitten, secretary to the Committee on City Plan of the New York Board of Estimate and Apportionment, is quoted as stating that the building of a city cannot be approached as an architect would approach the design of a large structure,

. . . even of one of those great cathedrals, whose construction extends over a century or more. The great
difference is this—the city is never completed. No limit
can be set to the growth and expansion of the city. No
amount of planning can avoid the necessity for a considerable amount of reconstruction and change. The plan must
develop and change. . . . City planning to be effectual
must be sustained and continuous. It is never completed.[29]

FOUNDATIONS OF MODERN CITY PLANNING

Some foundations were laid in the 1920s that formed the basis for later more dynamic and comprehensive planning. New academic disciplines in urban sociology and geography were becoming recognized. In addition, research in economics furnished a more rigorous basis for later planning.[30]

Three important events in 1929 were indicative of new emphases in planning. First was the completion of Radburn, New Jersey, with its innovative neighborhood designs. Second was the creation of the first school of city planning at Harvard. This signaled entrance into the planning field through professional education in planning itself rather than in allied fields such as architecture or engineering. The third event was the publication of the <u>Regional Plan of New York and Its Environs</u>, which differed from the stereotyped plans of the period in that it relied heavily on social science research and gave new treatment to public finance, government services, and the economic base of the city.[31]

The 1930s were marked by new directions in city planning. The Commission on Urbanism produced several significant reports. Partly as the result of WPA projects, municipalities increased their planning efforts, especially in the retention of permanent planning staffs. And, finally, the Depression caused new government efforts in housing and construction.

New Directions in the 1930s

As the newly gained governmental power to undertake planning became defined and developed, the planning commission was seen as the logical and necessary organization to insure that decisions were not made arbitrarily. However, the commission method of doing business has been assailed by numerous writers in recent years. Paul Davidoff, for example, questions the "propriety of independent agencies far removed from public control."[32] In addition, he argues, the failure to place planning decisions in the hands of elected officials has resulted in a weakened planning staff.

William Alonso notes that early proponents of planning were deeply suspicious of governmental corruption and, hence, advocated independent commissions that would keep clear of politics.[33] He further states that early zoning and planning reflected the values of upper- and middle-income groups.

There is sufficient evidence to support the contention that planning commissions in the 1920s and 1930s consisted primarily of professional and business leaders, and hence they reflected a biased set of values. The composition of the commissions reflected the origins of planning as a civic movement that relies upon men with status and income to obtain public support.[34]

Instead of the semi-autonomous planning commission, Walker argues, planning should be placed in the organizational structure of the municipality as a staff for the executive. By relying on the planning commission, the identity of the planning function is denied.[35] Thus, in order to improve planning, it must first be established as a functional element in the municipal organization. This will lead to a more continuous form of planning, or at least, as Branch calls it, "continuous master planning."[36]

Through the 1930s, more and more municipalities were moving to organize planning staffs. In a 1936 survey conducted by the National Resource Committee, 274 respondents, out of a sample of approximately 1,100 cities, had made some appropriation in their budget for a planning staff.

The consultant-client relationship, so common in the early days of architect/planners, was giving way to paid professional staffs to carry out the regular planning functions. Although consultants were (and are) still called upon to do major plans, the existence of the staff insured some degree of continuity in the planning process. The growing use of regular planning staffs created a need for an increasing number of urban planners with a greater diversity of background.

Under the sponsorship of the WPA and other governmental programs, urban research extended to areas other than physical planning. For example, work relief projects in St. Louis and Boston published municipal cost-revenue studies.[37] Numerous cities undertook comprehensive real property inventories, capital improvement plans, recreation studies, industrial resource studies, and housing studies.

In addition to the new directions established through government and university research, the report of the Urbanism Committee of the National Resource Committee had a significant impact on the role and scope of the planning function.[38] The commission began its report with a comprehensive inventory of urban resources, including population analyses, migration, health, public safety, and housing. Next it discussed the forces that contributed to the tremendous rise in urbanism. Finally, the report dealt with a broad range of metropolitan problems, from family and community disorganization to duplication of local and state government services, and delinquency and crime.

After World War II, there was a dynamic expansion in local government planning that followed the new directions set during the 1930s.[39] Government involvement in urban problems became more widespread, with planning considered a governmental function at all levels. The Housing Act of 1954 established the comprehensive planning grants (Section 701) that enabled thousands of municipalities to establish planning staffs and develop master plans. More important,

FOUNDATIONS OF MODERN CITY PLANNING

the legislation established the "workable program" requirements of citizen participation. Thus, the federal government gave recognition not only to the importance of planning but also to the importance of the process.

Finally, development of the computer enabled the processing of large quantities of data that is necessary for such large-scale analyses as the Chicago Area Transportation Study (CATS). Electronic data processing not only enabled such analyses but also permitted, for the first time, a rapid method for examining the effects of different strategies—in the case of the transportation study—and the effects on land use of different transportation networks.

CONCLUSION

In its infancy, modern planning stressed mainly the aesthetic and civic aspects. Early but lasting principles and concerns evolved from the environment of the nineteenth-century industrial city. Landmark legislation and legal decisions during the 1920s and early 1930s firmly established zoning and planning as a legitimate enterprise of municipal government. From a consultant/client organization, the planning process evolved into a recognized function of local government, encompassing not only the physical aspects of growth but economic and social considerations as well.

Continuing research in economics, sociology, and demography enabled planning to acquire broader jurisdictions. From its early concerns with aesthetics and appearance, the profession soon directed its attention to physical designs to accommodate the mechanical age and the automobile. After World War II, there was increasing emphasis on the human element in planning.

The changing social and political climate of the 1960s added new dimensions to planning: pluralism and citizen participation. The combined forces of computer hardware and a new planning environment prompted the search for tools that could meet the needs of the newly emerging planning climate. The old tools, which in essence had not changed for centuries, consisted primarily of maps, drawings, and architectural scale models. They were not only cumbersome and static,[40] they reflected only a physical model in an era that was, at least analytically, capable of conceptualizing and modeling economic constructs, demographic and sociological characteristics, and fiscal processes.

From the search for planning principles and dictates in the early part of the century, the literature of the 1960s moved to a search for tools to evaluate the desirability of plans. In addition to the emphasis on evaluation, the search included flexible administrative and technical machinery to help implement the new planning processes in an age of rapidly changing political, cultural, and fiscal policies.

NOTES

1. John Kouwenhoven, <u>Adventures of America: A Pictorial Record from Harper's Weekly</u> (New York: Harper Brothers, 1938).
2. Henry George, <u>City and Country</u>, III (New York: Doubleday and McClure, 1898).
3. John Griscom, "The Sanitary Conditions of the Laboring Population of New York (1845)," in Charles Glaab and T. Brown, eds., <u>A History of Urban America</u> (New York: Macmillan, 1967), p. 117.
4. State of New York, "Report of the Select Committee Appointed to Examine into the Conditions of Tenant Houses in New York and Brooklyn," Assembly Doc. 205, 1857. Glaab and Brown, op. cit., p. 267.
5. Arthur Gallion and Simon Eisner, <u>The Urban Pattern</u> (Princeton, N.J.: D. Van Nostrand, 1963).
6. Jacob Riis, <u>How the Other Half Lives: Studies Among the Tenements of New York</u> (New York: Charles Scribner's Sons, 1890).
7. Benjamin Flower, <u>Civilization's Inferno</u> (Boston, 1893), reprinted in L. W. Dorsett, ed., <u>The Challenge of the City</u> (Lexington, Mass.: D. C. Heath, 1968).
8. Gallion and Eisner, op. cit., p. 75.
9. Robert Walker, <u>The Planning Function in Urban Government</u> (Chicago: University of Chicago Press, 1941), p. 10.
10. Jane Jacobs sarcastically dubbed the movement "city monumental." Jane Jacobs, <u>The Death and Life of Great American Cities</u> (New York: Random House, 1961).
11. Ibid., p. 16.
12. Lord James Bryce, "The Menace of Great Cities," in <u>Housing Problems in America. Proceedings, Second National Conference on Housing</u> (Cambridge, 1912).
13. Victor Gruen acidly commented: "In Broadacre City every family would live on a large rectangular plot, presumably finding escape from boredom in long automobile trips." Victor Gruen, <u>The Heart of Our Cities</u> (New York: Simon and Schuster, 1964), p. 180.
14. Jacobs, op. cit., p. 20.
15. Christopher Tunnard and Henry Hope Reed, <u>American Skyline</u> (New York: New American Library, 1956), p. 138.
16. Edward M. Bassett, <u>Zoning</u> (New York: Russell Sage Foundation, 1946), p. 45.

17. 198 Atl. 229 (1938).

18. See Edward M. Bassett, F. Williams, A. Bettman, and R. Whitten, Model Planning Laws (Cambridge, Mass.: Harvard University Press, 1935), pp. 31-47.

19. Charles Mulford Robinson, City Planning (New York: G. P. Putnam's Sons and Knickerbocker Press, 1916).

20. Walker, op. cit., p. 209.

21. Daniel H. Burnham and Edward Bennett, Plan of Chicago, 1909 (repub. New York: Da Capo Press, 1970).

22. Tunnard and Reed, op. cit.

23. Ibid.

24. Ibid.

25. Harland Bartholomew and Associates, A Major Street Plan for Rochester (St. Louis, 1929), p. 6.

26. William Alonso, "Cities and City Planners," Daedalus 92 (Fall 1963): 825-26.

27. James Coke, "Antecedents of Local Planning," in William Goodman, ed., Principles and Practice of Urban Planning (Washington, D.C.: International City Managers' Assn., 1971), p. 24.

28. Ibid.

29. Robinson, op. cit., p. 294.

30. Coke, op. cit., p. 25.

31. Ibid.

32. Paul Davidoff, "Advocacy and Pluralism in Planning," in Wentworth Eldredge, ed., Taming Megalopolis (Garden City, N.Y.: Doubleday, 1967), p. 609.

33. Alonso, op. cit., p. 825.

34. Walker, op. cit., p. 151.

35. Ibid.

36. Melville Branch, "Delusions and Diffusions in City Planning," Management Science 16, no. 12 (August 1970): B-714.

37. "St. Louis—Income and Cost of Municipal Services," WPA Entry no. 3436 (1937).

38. Our Cities, Their Role in the National Economy (Washington, D.C.: National Resource Committee, 1937).

39. Coke, op. cit., p. 27.

40. Branch, op. cit.

CHAPTER 4

THE NEW PLANNING

The dictates and practices that influenced the planning profession during the first half of the twentieth century had strong bases in the desire of such early planners as Frederick Olmstead and John Nolen to alleviate undesirable and blighted conditions of the industrial city of the late nineteenth century. Planners during the 1920s and 1930s searched for new physical forms that would give expression to the popularly conceived desire for open space, privacy, and country greenery.

Clarence Stein and Henry Wright designed the new town of Radburn, New Jersey, for example, on the principle of the superblock and the cul-de-sac. The minor residential streets acted only as service roads, with no through traffic. The houses faced the rear of each lot, looking onto gardens and pedestrian paths.[1]

Variations of the garden city concept, as first described by Ebenezer Howard, were evident in designs other than Radburn. Some of the best-known examples are Garden City and Sunnyside, Long Island, and the Resettlement Administration projects: Greenbelt, Maryland, Greenhills, Ohio, and Greendale, Wisconsin.

Whether the planning principles employed in these designs were in fact viable, offering solutions to the urban problems of the day, may be questionable, depending on one's academic and intellectual leaning. That the plans were static prescriptions for what is essentially a dynamic, ongoing system, however, is a criticism that finds wide support. Thus, while there may be no agreement on what forms are proper or desirable, there seems to be a consensus in recent literature that the process of planning needs closer scrutiny and further development.

THE NEW PLANNING   37

Contributions to the "new planning" seem to fall into several categories. First are those authors, notably Paul Davidoff and Jane Jacobs, who question the traditional planning practices and look to pluralism and advocacy planning as solutions. Second are the practitioners interested in delineating the process of planning and improving or rationalizing it. This second group includes Melville Branch, Herbert Simon, William Alonso, Martin Meyerson, Edward Banfield, and Harvey Perloff. A third group, interested in representation of urban structure, includes Britton Harris, Ira S. Lowry, and Jay Forrester. Alan Altshuler, Morris Hill, and Nathaniel Litchfield are among those working in the area of goal setting and plan evaluation, while Walter Isard, William Alonso, Anthony Downs, and Charles Tiebout are concerned with economic and fiscal processes.

It is difficult to pinpoint the originators of the "new planning" and the date of its first appearance in the literature. Certainly the publication of Stuart Chapin's book in 1957 contributed toward formalizing the use of various analytic techniques in planning.[2] The book's comprehensive treatment of economic analysis and population and transportation analyses signaled a change in the tools that planners would bring to bear in solving urban problems. Jane Jacobs' polemic work, which appeared in 1961, raised numerous fundamental questions regarding the planning heritage.[3] Jacobs criticizes the perceptions that most planners have of urban structure and urban problems, and attempts to show that their solutions are ill-conceived, serving to promote rather than inhibit the decline of cities.

In 1965 the <u>Journal of the American Institute of Planners</u> published two significant issues. The May issue contained a series of articles, edited by Britton Harris, that discussed the progress made in developing computerized urban simulation models.[4] Included in the series are Ira S. Lowry's opportunity-accessibility model, a land-use plan design model, and discussions of the Pittsburgh and San Francisco urban renewal models (the former based on the TOMM model).[5]

The November issue of the <u>Journal</u> featured a series entitled "Process Planning: Symposium on Programming and the New Urban Planning." The topics of the articles included goal setting, comprehensive planning processes, and social planning. The editor's introduction describes the prevailing environment:

> Recent developments in the social sciences are producing an awareness that problem orientation toward the urban condition requires a new way of thinking. . . . Solutions and guidance require bodies of knowledge about urbanism presently without operative unity in the standard writings of the academic fields or in the minds of the professionals.[6]

It appears from this statement that urban planning as a problem-solving, scientific pursuit had finally been recognized, if not formalized. The urban designer's monopoly on planning had ended; and the arena was to be shared with social scientists, economists, systems analysts, and operations research practitioners.

PLURALISM AND CITIZEN PARTICIPATION IN PLANNING

Citizen Participation

Title I of the Housing Act of 1949 (as amended) requires that communities submit a "workable program for community improvement." The program must present an integrated plan for renewal that combines seven interrelated elements, including neighborhood analysis, survey of building codes and ordinances, financing plans, and citizen participation structures. The Demonstration Cities and Metropolitan Development Act of 1966 further increased community participation in the planning and goal-setting process.

Evaluation of the Model Cities citizen participation process is still ongoing; and though no final verdict is available, it does appear that the experiment was less than a total success. Survey work indicates that citizen participation panels were involved in, and raised numerous issues of concern to, the community.[7] It is possible that these issues would not have surfaced had planners been working in isolation from the community. It appears, however, that the citizen panels were not successful in assisting in the implementation of programs or the development of policies. In an analysis of six planning-period functions in eleven cities (66 entries in all), the professional staff is shown to have dominated in 41 of the 66 cells. The functions were shared equally in 16 cases, while community dominance emerged in only 9 entries.[8]

A separate analysis of the relative strength of citizen boards shows that "vociferous" panels may have had a worse effect on the planning process than the "weak" panels. For example, of cities with "strong" community influence, 35 percent produced "best" comprehensive development plans (CDP), while 65 percent produced "worst" CDP's. Ironically, in cities having "weak" citizen influence, 62 percent produced "best" CDP's and only 38 percent produced "worst."[9]

In terms of citizen influence on Model Cities spending patterns, the results also are somewhat paradoxical, with 44 percent of the "strong influence" cities being categorized as "low" spenders and

THE NEW PLANNING

22 percent as "high" spenders. This analysis, however, does demonstrate that the greatest proportion of "high" spending cities is found where the planner-citizen relationship is one of parity.[10]

In offering an explanation for the performance of participation panels in the Model Cities experiment, it may be surmised that strong-influence citizen groups, being of divergent backgrounds and interests, serve to hamper the planning process and make it inefficient. Group dynamics no doubt is an important element in a successful citizen-planner collaboration, and the divergence of expertise between planner and resident can lead to resentment by the nonprofessional, and to severe conflict.[11] A second important requisite for successful resident involvement in planning is the availability of information in proper form to assist in decision-making. Supplying "market facts" to the decision-makers, both private and public, would enhance the development process significantly.[12]

However, these data must be presented in such a fashion that decision-making information can be derived from them. The principal concern of this work is to present tools for providing decision-making information rapidly, thus enhancing the planning process. Such a tool will be discussed in detail in the following chapters.

Advocacy in Planning

Jane Jacobs poignantly puts forth the "citizen knows best" argument for pluralism by relating the attitude of tenants of a Harlem housing project who had come to despise a large lawn area amid the high-rise apartments:

> Nobody cared what we wanted when they built this place. They threw our houses down and pushed us here and pushed our friends somewhere else. We don't have a place around here to get a cup of coffee or a newspaper even, or to borrow fifty cents. Nobody cared what we need. But the big men come and look at that grass and say, "Isn't it wonderful! Now the poor have everything!"[13]

Advocacy planners perform two functions for their "disadvantaged constituency": they provide technical expertise, and they represent the constituency's interest vis-a-vis other groups, such as city hall or governmental agencies.[14] Such a system can lead only to a planning process that is partisan and overtly political.[15]

Recognizing that planning cannot be prescribed from a position of value neutrality, Davidoff proposes that planners prepare several alternative plans that can be evaluated by different interest groups.[16] The process could be taken one step further, with different groups preparing their own plans. Davidoff thus sees an era in which planners will seek employment with agencies and citizen organizations that support their own value systems.[17] The advocacy of alternative plans by interest groups outside government would stimulate city planning by better informing the public of the choices open, by forcing public agencies to compete with other planning groups to win political support, and by forcing critics of the establishment to produce better plans and not just criticism of existing plans.[18]

While there is no question that the municipal planner has the responsibility for taking divergent opinions into consideration, the Model Cities experience has demonstrated the difficulty of mediating the desires of various local pressure groups. If the process were extended to involve the preparation of different plans by numerous groups, planning could well be brought to a halt unless rapid and simple techniques were available for evaluating alternative plans and reaching a consensus plan without undue delay. The research described in subsequent chapters addresses this issue by providing quantitative techniques for evaluating alternatives and establishing objectives for community development.

THE PLANNING PROCESS: OBSERVATIONS, DEFINITIONS, AND PRESCRIPTIONS

Martin Meyerson and Edward Banfield compare the planning process to the parlor game in which each player adds a word to a sentence that is passed around the table.[19] Each player acts as if words that are handed him were planned and does his part to sustain the illusion. In the particular case the authors studied, the planning of a housing program for Chicago, the city was already bound by previous moves—"the sentence was largely formed when it was handed to it."[20] Congress, the Public Housing Administration, the Illinois Legislature, the State Housing Board, and the mayor had largely formed the policy by the time planning was undertaken. Rational planning is hardly possible in such an environment.

In <u>Administrative Behavior</u>, Herbert Simon defines the rational decision-making process as one that involves several steps. First, the decision-maker considers the alternative courses of action open to him within the constraints of the situation and the ends he seeks to satisfy. Next he identifies and evaluates the consequences of each alternative, and finally he selects the alternative whose anticipated consequences are most preferable in terms of the most valued ends or goals.[21]

In practice, the planning process has not been rational, for planners have not presented meaningful alternatives for consideration and, in fact, have tended to confine their planning to extensions of existing development patterns.[22] Thus, the urban master planner has concentrated too much on the future state of the city without providing, for himself and others, the means with which to determine policies in a rational manner.[23]

Russell Ackoff and others have studied the corporate planning process.[24] Because of the success of this process in developing complex missile systems, weapons, and similar physical objects, some systems analysts and operations researchers are attempting to transfer the sophisticated methodology to the municipal government.[25] They are finding, however, that the strategies are not easily applied because they require a "measure of goal consensus, a hierarchy of command and a degree of control that do not exist in the normal context of public affairs."[26] While it is true that large corporations or even military establishments hold multiple goals, they are nonetheless simpler and more singular than the multitude of goals and policies being pursued by the numerous interest groups within a city.[27]

Some of the analytic tools, developed principally in military contingency planning, are applicable to the urban environment. Certain military questions, such as the outcome of a battle, are extremely complex and, in order to answer them, assumptions must be made regarding strategy, terrain, the response of field commanders, and the availability of supplies. In order to formulate the problem for analysis, a series of assumptions normally is made. This assumption matrix is usually so comprehensive that it leads to evaluation of the problem within very closely defined limits. This technique of simulating complex problems within severe constraints usually is referred to as scenario analysis.[28]

In the case of a military battle, the particular scenario may describe such elements as terrain, gun location, size of opposing force, and weather. Thus the decision-maker, although unable to obtain the answer to his basic question—"Who will win the battle?"—can at least obtain an answer under a particular set of circumstances. Using his intuition and experience, he can then formulate a set of circumstances most likely to occur (for instance, the terrain in Western Europe consists of low hills and forests) or least likely to occur; and the analysis may be undertaken for the most probable scenario and least probable scenario. This technique, based on corporate and military planning models, forms the basis for the approach presented in chapter 5.

In observing the municipal planning process, numerous authors delineate its deficiencies. In an often-cited paper, Martin Meyerson sees the deficiencies as the following:

1. Failure to provide timely and meaningful information to support rational and coherent private and public action
2. Failure to translate an abstract master plan into operative, action-oriented objectives
3. Failure to induce planning at the operational level that will lead to accomplishment of long-range goals and policies
4. Failure to evaluate the consequences, both intended and unintended, of previous actions [29]

Melvin Webber criticizes the planning profession for its concern with "end-stating" as opposed to rational planning, and proposes a tactic of programming (not program-making or plan-making).[30] It would utilize decision-aiding processes, on a continual basis, which would never result in a formalized plan but, rather, would support incremental decisions and actions.

Melville Branch defines various types of planning and differentiates between comprehensive planning, functional planning, and physical planning.[31] According to Branch, comprehensive planning is "the continued formulation of guidance of its affairs towards their attainment." Functional planning "focuses on an element of the total problem. In business, this might be manufacturing or finance, and in government it might be highway planning or forest conservation." Physical planning is defined as being concerned with the "location, arrangement, and characteristics of three-dimensional objects on the land. Although cost and many other factors are involved, spatial design is the central form of the analysis, and the end product is an areal pattern embodying engineering-architectural solutions."

Branch observes that most urban planning in the past has been physical master planning, which has been so broad and vague that it has had little, if any, impact on the actual urban "fact or form."[32] He further notes that implicit in master planning, an essentially static technique, are a number of questionable assumptions:

1. That the needs and state of a complex urban system can be projected or foreseen twenty-five years into the future
2. That the community's goals and objectives are sufficiently well known and fixed to permit long-range projection
3. That planners are capable of performing such projections
4. That the community wishes to commit itself twenty-five years into the future

THE NEW PLANNING

5. That no externalities will occur that will make it imperative to alter the predetermined plan once it has been adopted

6. That it is possible for a planner to analyze all the important elements and aspects of the city, project them in concert, identify and quantify their interactions, and explain the results and any significant alternatives clearly enough to permit intelligent reaction and decision

7. That the above complete analysis can be accomplished quickly enough so that the data on which it is based are still valid at the time of the final decision.

Numerous writers agree with Branch's critical description of "brochure planning." Ira Robinson stresses the need for an ongoing planning process with a new type of city planner who has training in model-building, systems analysis, and economic pressures.[33] John Friedman notes that the numerous critiques of the planning profession have served to "shatter the image of planning."[34] Though he does not quite yield to the challenge put forth by the "new planners," he does propose that planning responsibilities be divided into two areas in the municipal organization—one office for urban design, and one for the administration of the master plan and for coordination with other planning offices.

In general, Branch, Webber, and the other "new planners" agree that the planning process must have the following characteristics:

1. There must be a statement of goals, perceived as constantly shifting rather than stable.[35]

2. The goals must be translated into measurable objectives.

3. The planning process must be a continuous one. It is never complete; the master plan is never "complete." The decision-makers continually take incremental actions and then reappraise the situation through feedback mechanisms.

4. The process is fast enough to be of real-time significance. Changes in goals and in urban characteristics occur rapidly. Thus the process must be able to yield results while data are still significant. (Branch cites a case where the master plan took 31 years to develop.)

5. The planner's role does not involve preparing and recommending a single plan. Rather, it is his responsibility to prepare a number of meaningful alternatives that can be evaluated in the planning process. As Webber

puts it, his emphasis must be on process, not on "end-stating."

6. The process provides decision-making information (market facts) regarding the anticipated likely consequences of pursuing a particular alternative. Webber proposes an idealized urban "intelligence" center capable of using simulation techniques to predict what would happen if a certain course of action were undertaken.[36]

GOAL SETTING

As discussed in the previous section, the planning process can be rationalized within the framework of the scientific method.[37] However, planning differs significantly from problem solving in one important respect. In scientific problem solving, goals are given either explicitly (for instance, design a new widget that will equal the performance of other models but will sell at half the price") or are implicit to the problem itself (for instance, "determine why the toaster does not work"). In planning, the determination of goals assumes equal importance with the design that is meant to achieve them.[38] Unfortunately, much planning has been accomplished by planners who have worked toward goals that were more a part of their creed than the result of rational inquiry.[39] Chapters 2 and 3 have traced the development of planning, and particularly the evolution of the planning "axioms" that have served as master-plan goals.

Davidoff was among the first to recognize that while goals could not be prescribed from a position of value neutrality, the process of goal setting must, nonetheless, be rational, taking this factor into account.[40] Indeed, F. S. Chapin notes that goals have been at the forefront of planning thought since the very early literature. However, only in the very recent past has the identification of goals become an integral part of the technical work of planning.[41]

In general, goal statements have not been functional because they are either too broad and vague to be operational or too specific to have any overall direction. Thus, there exists the dichotomy of ill-defined, idealized expressions, on the one hand, and detailed objectives such as "construct X number of low-income housing units," on the other.[42] This dichotomy has led Meyerson to call for a "middle range planning bridge"[43] to produce operational objectives and functions in planning. Altshuler notes that truly comprehensive goals are elusive and tend not to provide any basis for evaluating concrete alternatives. It is thus difficult to plan rationally for their achievement.[44] In addition, certain goals are not well accepted in our society.[45] Socioeconomic goals are resisted because of their association with socialism and dictatorships.[46]

During the last decade, there has been renewed interest in goal setting for public and private entities, and a serious operational difficulty has been the translation of lofty ideals, which can only serve as guidelines, into objectives that can serve as measurable end-states. Robert C. Young gives an interesting illustration.

Assume that a goal is set, through some means, to achieve full employment. This goal in itself has no quantitative meaning and hence a standard or definition must be chosen, such as "full employment implies a maximum unemployment level of 4 percent." This quantitative standard can now be applied to population forecasts, and employment and economic factors, to arrive at a specific number of jobs that must be provided in order to meet the goal. The number of jobs becomes the objective of the plan, and various proposals involving such factors as land use and tax policy can be proposed and evaluated.[47]

As opposed to such a formalized procedure, in which goals are translated into measurable objectives (ends) and various plans (means) are put forth to achieve these ends, goal setting is generally accomplished under a different model. Often plans merely express the author's opinion of a desirable future state.[48] But even if some procedure for goal setting is adopted, instead of adjusting means to ends, ends usually are chosen that are appropriate to the available means.[49] In effect, this describes the satisficing planner who does not strive for innovative or unique goals, but merely attempts to achieve objectives that "will do."[50]

An interesting paradox in goal setting is the fact that while it is easy to reach consensus in the goal statement, conflict often arises in the implementation of goals. Thus, while everyone is interested in lower taxes and better schools, for example, these points often lead to bitter controversy. Differences arise when there is a lack of agreement as to the relative value that should be assigned to an end goal.[51] An examination of the structure of goal sets serves to explain further the cause of controversy surrounding the implementation of goals that are widely accepted.

Goals form a hierarchy of desires that split in pyramid fashion, with the highest aspirations at the peak.[52] For example, let us propose a goal to which there can be little objection—maintaining a low tax rate.[53] This goal can immediately be "split" into two subgoals that will achieve the primary goal. (See diagram below.)

```
                    Low Tax Rate
                   /            \
   High Municipal Income    Low Municipal Expenditures
```

Two groups of advocates will subsequently emerge, one perceiving low municipal expenditures as an end in itself, and the other seeking high municipal income. An industrial development commission, for example, is likely to pursue high municipal income, to the detriment of low municipal expenditures. A finance or budget committee, on the other hand, would see its foremost responsibility as keeping expenditures down, perhaps to the detriment of attracting industry.[54]

A second split introduces further points of conflict. (See diagram below.) Although any of the secondary divisions (such as high unit value) satisfies the subgoal from which it was split, a number of inconsistencies will exist and controversy could easily develop.

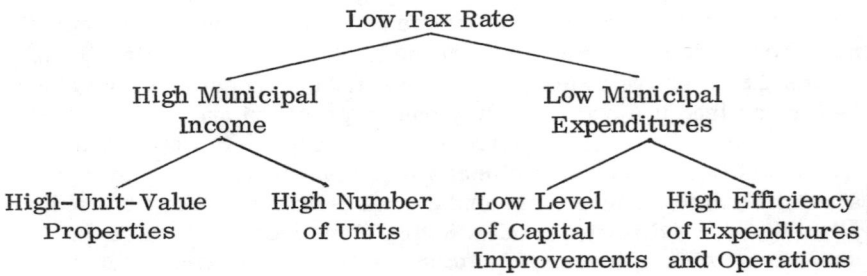

For example, a high level of units (residential or other) is incompatible with a low level of capital improvements. Advocates will argue in favor of one policy over the other and lose sight of the fact that they both achieve the overall goal of maintaining a low tax rate.

In order for goal statements to be operational, they must strike the "middle bridge" between abstract ideals and molecular considerations. Planners must assist in the development of objectives by translating goals into workable and quantifiable policy measures. Goals are prescribed with certain value judgments, which must be recognized and included in a rational goal-setting process. Goal setting has always been an implicit part of the planning process, with goals being offered as a planner's conception or opinion regarding the desired end state. In order to make planning a more viable and scientific endeavor, the development of goals must become an explicit, technical part of the planning process.

Homer Perkins posed the critical question "How do people want to live?"[55] William Alonso, taking the role of the economist, also argues for rationality by pointing out that certain widely lamented urban transitions, such as the decline of the central city, are not in themselves "bad."[56] Thus, planners must appraise the values upon which planning objectives have been set, and improve the rational process through which workable planning goals are determined.

REVIEW OF EXISTING PLANNING MODELS

In response to calls for new planning methods and tools, large-scale decision-aiding computer models have been developed. The construction of computer models as aids in planning was done to meet the need for analyzing the impact of alternative highway configurations on the growth of the urban area and, to a more limited extent, for evaluating alternative urban renewal proposals. Although there are many more models in the former group, those more relevant to community development fall into the second category.

The Community Renewal Program, enacted by Congress in 1959 as an amendment to the Housing Act of 1949, provided the foundation that permitted cities to explore new planning techniques.[57] Although at first the provisions of this act went almost unnoticed, by 1965 it was being used by about 125 cities; and in several of them, it had been recognized as a major new approach to urban renewal and a radical new departure for city planning.[58]

The material that follows briefly discusses several well-published planning models. An excellent critique of the subject has been presented by Garry Brewer.[59]

The Pittsburgh Urban Renewal Simulation

This sytem consists of a complex chain of models including TOMM (Time-Oriented Metropolitan Model), which was developed with federal funding by the University of Pittsburgh, CONSAD Research Corporation, and the Pittsburgh City Planning Department.[60] For its simulation of urban growth, the system relies on the Lowry construct.[61]

The basic features of the urban simulation are the following:
- Employment opportunity is a basic driving force for development.
- Basic employment is site-oriented, and can be allocated heuristically.
- Secondary employment is residentially oriented.

As an aid to planning renewal programs, the system employs three modules:
- Development of alternative plans for renewal
- Computing impacts or consequences of each alternative
- Selecting the preferred alternative.

The computer models assist by presenting the impacts of each of the alternatives that are fed in as spatial plans. These impacts are presented in terms of the following output for each census tract:

- Population by type
- Employment (40 SIC's)
- Land use by category
- Social indexes
- Direct impact of renewal project on its census tract
- Personal income
- State of industrial, commercial, and residential markets
- Blight indexes.

In addition, the following outputs are given on a city-wide basis
- Municipal revenues by type
- Municipal expenditures by type
- Project-oriented information.

The simulation model (TOMM) proved to be cumbersome and expensive to operate. As an aid for testing policy alternatives, its application was thus limited.[62] A given policy is prepared as an input and entered into the model. The policy alternative, however, is actually formulated as a linear program external to the simulation. Thus, for example, a policy of minimizing blight is formulated as "maximize the number of sound housing units in each tract, subject to the cost of upgrading or maintaining housing units in each tract."

In order to evaluate the impact of alternative development plans on the city, thorough and detailed studies are necessary. Wilbur Steger describes the data requirements as burdensome, since an external linear program is required to evaluate policy alternatives.[63] The model is unmanageable and, as a consequence, only a few alternatives can be evaluated. Kilbridge contends that federal funding expired prior to completion of the model's development, and that although the city continued the project on a much lower scale at its own expense, it was finally abandoned when, in an experiment, it allocated population in a nonsensical pattern.[64]

It appears that the TOMM model, though a significant contribution proved unmanageable even for a sophisticated staff of planners and consultants. In a small municipality, such a complex model is not only unwieldy but unnecessary. The lack of technical expertise usually available in the smaller city, combined with the excessive data requirements of the TOMM model, would make its application impractical. In addition, a small city may contain only a few census tracts, and any error in allocation of land-use activity would be greatly magnified. In any case, the small municipality, because it is geographically compact, does not have as great a need for spatial forecasting as does a large city. Finally, development opportunity in the smaller city is more explicitly defined and constrained. While there may be 100 suitable locations for an industrial park in Pittsburgh, a smaller municipality may have only one or two.

THE NEW PLANNING

The San Francisco Urban Renewal Model

This model was developed for use in the San Francisco Community Renewal Program by Arthur D. Little, Inc.[65] Its orientation is somewhat different from that of the TOMM model, in that it neglects any transportation or accessibility considerations. Essentially, the model simulates the housing market dynamics. The effect of various public policies on this market can then be tested. Demand for housing is generated exogenously by projecting household types from the 1960 census. The housing stock is "aged" and projected forward. Consumers of housing are then matched with appropriate housing types; any increase in demand without concomitant increases in the housing stock is reflected through higher rents, which in turn makes investment more attractive. In a like manner, public policies that result in a housing surplus would have a detrimental effect on investment. In simulating the dynamics of the housing market, the model adds more housing when market conditions indicate that development will be profitable.

Spatial considerations enter the process only to the extent required by socioeconomic factors. For example, certain family types will not settle in certain neighborhoods or tracts because of unavailability of suitable housing, or because of discrimination. The "fract," the basic unit of land use in the model, is nonlocational within a neighborhood or tract.

Among the policy alternatives that can be used as inputs are changes in zoning, code enforcement, tax rate changes, various rent subsidy and mortgage insurance programs, construction of public housing, leasing of public projects to private investors, and building demolition.

The outputs of the model consist of a series of fiscal indicators, socioeconomic indicators, and condition of the housing market (rents, surplus or deficit supply).

The San Francisco model gives detailed consideration to the workings of the residential sector. It is not applicable as a general planning and goal-setting aid because it disregards industrial and commercial development and their impact upon the city.

A Land-Use Plan Design Model

The model is prescriptive in nature. In the author's view, the urban complex is a subject for design, not prediction or scientific explanation; and the plan is a "conscious synthesis of urban form to meet human needs."[66]

Kenneth Schlager defines the land-use plan design problem as follows:

1. Given design requirements expressed as:
   a. a set of design standards in terms of restrictions on land-use relationships that may exist in the plan
   b. a set of needs or demands for each type of land use based on forecasts of future activity
2. Synthesize a land-use plan design that satisfies both the land-use demands and design standards considering the current state of natural and man-made land characteristics, at a minimal combination of public and private costs.

The problem can now be transformed into an ordinary linear programming formulation: "Minimize public plus private development costs, subject to demand for various land-use types and design standards."

The linear programming model produces a singular output—public and private development costs. It would seem that this is an insufficient criterion for evaluating the desirability or preferability of alternative spatial configurations. In addition, from a technical viewpoint, the model has serious difficulty not only with nonlinear objective functions but, more significantly, with nonlinear constraints. "When a design model is not able to provide satisfactorily for a design standard, it loses much of its usefulness."[67]

The linear program formulation implies that the objective is to produce the cheapest plan (in terms of development costs) that will meet the design criteria. It is not at all clear that such an objective has great acceptance. Thus, while factors such as travel time and topography are considered in the constraint relationships, they are merely satisficed at the lowest cost. It is not apparent that planning and planners have the responsibility of minimizing private (or public) development costs or that this is, in fact, a desirable goal.

A Plan-Evaluation Methodology for the Small City

Three urban simulation models have been presented and discussed. While these by no means constitute a majority of the urban models that have been developed, they are a representative sample of existing plan evaluation models. These models were all developed as large-scale urban simulations, and most deal with transportation networks and spatial allocation of activities.

It was pointed out earlier that the applicability of the large-scale model as a planning aid in the small city is impractical for several reasons. Among these are the absence of technical talent and large computer availability, and the significant data requirements. In addition, the spatial allocation features of virtually all the large-scale simulations are unnecessary in the small city. As was discussed earlier, a small city may consist of only a few census tracts, and only a small number of transportation zones could be reasonably assigned. Thus, any allocation error would be crucial. Furthermore, because of the geographic compactness, spatial forecasts are an unneeded luxury in the small city, since they can be made only at the expense of simplicity in the modeling. Development opportunities in the small city are well constrained; and because they fall well within human cognitive capabilities, they can be treated as nonlocational.[68]

In conclusion, Alonso's observation can be paraphrased—the small city is not merely a scaled-down version of the large metropolis.[69] It is both quantitatively and qualitatively different.

The large-scale urban models have proved cumbersome and expensive to operate.[70] Thus, implementation was possible only because of the availability of a sizable technical staff working in a regional or large metropolitan context. The more recent urban-system simulations, such as Jay Forrester's model, while demonstrating considerable methodological skill in developing an operational dynamic model, have not yet found much applicability because little empirical or theoretical justification for the assumptions, the parameters, and the multipliers exists.[71]

What is needed in the small city is a simpler construct, one that can easily test many alternatives and can be comfortably used in a time-sharing mode, since large computer availability is a problem. The input requirements must of necessity be kept low, and the output set must be manageable and comprehensible.

The following chapters describe several approaches and techniques that are useful in evaluating proposed plans in the smaller municipality. The basis of the methodology is a cost-revenue impacts analysis of community development projects. It is the aim of the research to develop a tool to assist decision-makers and planners in the smaller municipality during the first phases of the planning process—goal setting.

NOTES

1. Arthur Gallion and Simon Eisner, <u>The Urban Pattern</u> (Princeton, N.J.: D. Van Nostrand, 1963), p. 128.

2. F. Stuart Chapin, Jr., Urban Land Use Planning (Urbana: University of Illinois Press, 1957; repr. 1965).

3. Jane Jacobs, The Death and Life of Great American Cities (New York: Random House, 1961).

4. Journal of the American Institute of Planners 31 (May 1965).

5. Ira S. Lowry, ibid., 158-66; Kenneth J. Schlager, "A Land Use Plan Design Model," ibid., 103-11; Wilbur A. Steger, "The Pittsburgh Urban Renewal Simulation Model," ibid., 144-50; Ira M. Robinson, "A Simulation Model for Renewal Programming," ibid., 126-34.

6. Journal of the American Institute of Planners 31 (November 1965): 282.

7. The Model Cities Program: A Comparative Analysis of the Planning Process in Eleven Cities (Washington, D.C.: Department of Housing and Urban Development, n.d.).

8. Ibid.

9. The Model Cities Program: A Comparative Analysis of the Participating Cities, Process, Product, Performance, and Prediction (Washington, D.C.: Department of Housing and Urban Development, n.d.).

10. Ibid.

11. Ronald L. Warren, "Model Cities First Round: Politics, Planning, and Participation," Journal of the American Institute of Planners 35 (July 1969): 245-52. Warren characterizes the Model Cities planning process as a "struggle for control of the program between city hall and neighborhood residents." Also see Pierre Clavel, "Planners and Citizen Boards: Some Applications of Social Theory to the Problem of Plan Implementation," ibid. 34 (May 1968): 130-39.

12. William C. Wheaton, "Public and Private Agents of Change," in Melvin M. Webber, ed., Explorations into Urban Structure (Philadelphia: University of Pennsylvania Press, 1964).

13. Jacobs, op. cit., p. 15.

14. Warren, op. cit., p. 251.

15. Lisa R. Peattie, "Reflections on Advocacy Planning," Journal of the American Institute of Planners 34 (March 1968).

16. Paul Davidoff, "Advocacy and Pluralism in Planning," in Wentworth Eldredge, ed., Taming Megalopolis (Garden City, N.Y.: Doubleday, 1967), pp. 596-615.

17. Ibid.

18. Ibid.

19. Martin Meyerson and Edward Banfield, Politics, Planning and the Public Interest—The Case of Public Housing in Chicago (New York: The Free Press of Glencoe, 1955).

20. Ibid., p. 269.

21. Herbert Simon, Administrative Behavior (New York: Macmillan, 1947), p. 67.

22. Corwin R. Mocine, "Urban Physical Planning and the 'New Planning,'" Journal of the American Institute of Planners 32 (July 1966): 234-37.

23. Ibid.

24. Russell Ackoff, A Concept of Corporate Planning (New York: John Wiley, 1970).

25. Melvin W. Webber, "The Roles of Intelligence Systems in Urban-Systems Planning," Journal of the American Institute of Planners 31 (November 1965): 289-96.

26. Ibid., p. 291.

27. Ibid.

28. See Ackoff, op. cit., pp. 17, 25-29.

29. Martin Meyerson, "Building the Middle-Range Bridge for Comprehensive Planning," Journal of the American Institute of Planners 22 (Spring 1956): 58-64.

30. Webber, op. cit., p. 292.

31. Melville C. Branch, Jr., The Corporate Planning Process (New York: American Management Association, 1962), pp. 26-27.

32. Melville C. Branch, Jr., "Delusions and Diffusions of City Planning," Management Science 16, no. 12 (August 1970): Applications Ser., B714-31.

33. Ira M. Robinson, "Beyond the Middle-Range Planning Bridge," Journal of the American Institute of Planners 31 (November 1965): 304-12. Perloff, however, asserts that no academic programs in comprehensive planning exist and that, in fact, planning schools are attempting to catch up with all the developments that have taken place in the allied fields. See Harvey Perloff, Education for Planning: City, State, and Regional (Washington, D.C.: Resources for the Future, 1957).

34. John Friedman, "Comprehensive Planning as a Process," Journal of the American Institute of Planners 31 (August 1965): 195-97.

35. Alan Altshuler, The City Planning Process (Ithaca, N.Y.: Cornell University Press, 1965), p. 300.

36. Webber, op. cit.

37. Simon, op. cit. Also see John W. Dyckman, "Planning and Decision Theory," Journal of the American Institute of Planners 27 (November 1961): 335-43.

38. Robert C. Young, "Goals and Goal-Setting," Journal of the American Institute of Planners 32 (March 1966): 76-85.

39. Ibid., p. 77.

40. Davidoff, op. cit., p. 598. See also Paul Davidoff and Thomas A. Reiner, "A Choice Theory of Planning," Journal of the American Institute of Planners 28 (May 1962): 103-15.

41. F. Stuart Chapin, Jr., "Foundations of Urban Planning," in Werner Hirsch, ed., Urban Life and Form (New York: Holt, Rinehart, and Winston, 1963), p. 225.

42. Young, op. cit., p. 81.

43. Meyerson, op. cit.

44. Altshuler, op. cit., pp. 302-04.

45. Young, op. cit.

46. Branch, The Corporate Planning Process, op. cit.

47. Ibid., p. 78.

48. Webber, op. cit.

49. Charles E. Lindblom, "The Science of Muddling Through," Public Administration Review 19 (Spring 1959).

50. Ackoff compares several planning philosophies. Op. cit., pp. 12-20.

51. Young, op. cit., p. 79.

52. Charles H. Granger, "The Hierarchy of Objectives," Harvard Business Review 42 (May-June 1964): 63-74.

53. This example is provided by Young, op. cit.

54. Norton E. Long characterizes this dilemma: "Local urban decision making is a collection of games in which people play varied roles and virtually no one has the overall community or metropolitan interest at heart." "The Local Community in an Ecology of Games," in Lewis A. Coger, ed., Political Sociology—Selected Essays (New York: Harper and Row, 1966), pp. 146-66.

55. Homer Perkins, "Urban Design and City Planning," in Harvey Perloff, ed., Planning and the Urban Community (Pittsburgh: University of Pittsburgh Press, 1961), p. 179.

56. William Alonso, "Cities and City Planners," Daedalus 92 (Fall 1963): 825-26.

57. Robinson, op. cit., p. 305.

58. Ibid.

59. Garry Brewer, Politician, Bureaucrats and the Consultant (New York: Basic Books, 1973).

60. Maurice D. Kilbridge et al., Urban Analysis (Cambridge, Mass.: Harvard University Press, 1970), p. 36.

61. Ira S. Lowry, A Model of Metropolis, RM-4035 (Santa Monica: RAND Corporation, 1964).

62. Steger, op. cit.

63. Ibid.

64. Kilbridge et al., op. cit.

65. For further discussion, see ibid.

66. Kenneth J. Schlager, "A Land Use Plan Design Model," in David C. Sweet, ed., Models of Urban Structure (Lexington, Mass.: D. C. Heath, 1972).

67. Ibid.

68. Webber, op. cit., raises the issue of cognitive capacities and feels that because of their limitation, certain optima problems will never be solved.

69. Alonso, op. cit., p. 830. Alonso observes that the "metropolis is no mere large-scale model of the older city."

70. Wilbur A. Steger, "Review of Analytic Techniques for the CRP," Journal of the American Institute of Planners 31 (May 1965): 166-72.

71. Jay W. Forrester, Urban Dynamics (Cambridge, Mass.: MIT Press, 1968); Harvey Garn and Robert H. Wilson, A Critical Look at Urban Dynamics, the Forrester Model and Public Policy (Washington, D.C.: The Urban Institute, 1970).

CHAPTER 5

A METHOD FOR ASSESSING THE IMPACTS OF COMMUNITY DEVELOPMENT PROPOSALS

The preceding chapters have outlined the historical developments that shaped the growth of urban America and influenced the major concepts in planning. As has been shown, economic motives have played a major role in the development of land. The fact that the private sector is the dominant force in the land development process cannot be denied or neglected. The major axioms of city planning grew out of the late nineteenth century and the desires of reformers to improve the quality of life in the "city of steam." The planning processes emerged during the first thirty years of the twentieth century, taking the consultant-client form at first, and then changing to the planning commission-planning staff structure.

For the most part, these planning concepts and processes are still widely used in most U.S. cities. The tools consist primarily of the master plan, which in its preparation and presentation uses graphics and other physically oriented media. The process involves preparation of the plan by a planning staff or, more often, an outside consultant, and its implementation through the adoption of the appropriate zoning ordinance by the municipal legislative body.

Maintenance of the plan is relegated to the caretaker planning commission and zoning commission, which, as Alonso has pointed out, grant variances and other exceptions as a political expedient. The power to enforce the zoning ordinance is a major political force in local government and perhaps the primary reason for home rule. It is a power that few state legislatures would want to deny or to usurp for themselves.

During the late 1950s and throughout the 1960s, new concepts in planning were introduced into the literature. Pluralism, advocacy planning, and citizen participation (especially as a result of Model

ASSESSING THE IMPACTS OF DEVELOPMENT PROPOSALS 57

Cities) were discussed and evaluated in chapter 4. The transportation planning studies also provided new forms of data and new tools for analysis. Several large-scale urban models were developed, some for use in urban renewal planning. To a large extent, these models are too complex to provide flexibility and applicability to development analysis in the smaller city. In addition, because of their complexity and cumbersomeness, these models did little to alleviate the static nature of planning, or what some writers have referred to as the "all or nothing" approach. Indeed, incrementalism in planning can be achieved only through the development of tools that will allow rapid evaluation of proposed plans and easy reevaluation in the future.

Thus the need arises, in the smaller municipality, for plan-evaluation tools with the following characteristics:

- Interactive design. In order to meet the need for community participation and to enhance that process, the planning tool must be readily accessible to both citizen and official. In this way, community input is obtained from the start of the process.
- Usable output. The output of any system devised must lend itself to ready evaluation and comprehension.
- Data limitations. As previously discussed, complex models often have not been applicable in the smaller municipality because of overwhelming data requirements. To some extent, these requirements also have hindered the implementation of incremental planning in larger cities. Thus the system proposed must be capable of employing readily available data, such as census material, without relying on extensive survey and local study information. Perhaps the most that should be required in terms of local data are those found in the usual "701" master plan.
- Fiscal outputs. While profit is not, and should not be, the motive in the public sector, the fiscal implications of development are of prime concern to both citizen and politician-administrator. Although by its nature, government must provide service that the private sector cannot or will not undertake, it has become increasingly clear that, on the whole, municipal governments must give careful consideration to their financial viability when planning for the future. In addition to the internal requirements for fiscal data, such outputs provide the market information that is of interest to the developer, and assist and prepare the local officials for the negotiating process.
- Other indicators. The system must be capable of providing other quantifiable indicators regarding the quality of life. Information about the anticipated demographic and socioeconomic characteristics under a given plan are essential in evaluating the merits or desirability of that plan. Certain indicators cannot be predicted with any degree of accuracy, and hence will not be treated. Martin Jones and Michael Flax have utilized measures relating to crime, air pollution, and a

host of other indexes that can be determined only after the fact.[1] However, such basic measures as population size, age, and income distribution can be modeled and predicted, and thus should be presented to the decision-maker to assist in the planning process.

- Ease of implementation. Planning staffs in the smaller city usually suffer from a lack of technical expertise. In addition, as noted above, existing data usually are limited. Thus, a practical system that is designed to assist in the planning process of the smaller city must be easily implementable, usable, and flexible.

COST-REVENUE AS A BASIS FOR PLAN EVALUATION

The earliest reference to municipal cost-revenue analysis is found in the WPA studies of the 1930s.[2] Lately, however, more numerous examples are in the literature, and will be cited throughout the chapter. Without exception, these studies are concerned with the possible impacts of a specific development in a given locality. The prime objective of the cost-revenue study is to determine the fiscal consequences of development for the school system and the municipal budget. In the course of the cost-revenue analysis, other findings are discussed and perhaps evaluated. Major emphasis, however, is given to the "bottom line" result; that is, will a given project pay for itself in terms of school and municipal services?

It is felt that the cost-revenue approach can be generalized and expanded in order to assist in the planning process.

Generalizing the Cost-Revenue Approach

Reports in the literature deal with revenue analyses that are project- and locale-specific.[3] That is, given a certain project in a certain municipality (city, county, or town), an analysis is made to determine the expected tax-base value of the project. Next, using marginal costs* for delivery of municipal and educational service, in conjunction with the amount of service likely to be required by the new project (for instance, the number of schoolchildren), a determination

---

*Such costs are not always available, and average variable cost must be employed.

ASSESSING THE IMPACTS OF DEVELOPMENT PROPOSALS   59

is made as to whether the project will be profitable over the planning period.

The techniques used in such an analysis can be generalized so that the process is transferable to different projects in a given locality, or even in different localities. Of course, to the extent that generalizations are made, certain refinements in the analysis are lost. In a given locality, for example, the tipping point for schools and other municipal plant capacities can be accounted for. This leads to greater precision in the analysis. In the general case, long-run average costs that include capitalized or per-unit fixed costs must be employed.

It has already been noted that marginal cost information is not readily available, especially in the general or typical case. William Baumol presents several reasons for the absence of marginal data in most accounting information, including the fact that it requires only one observation to determine average costs, whereas at least two observations are necessary to derive marginal costs. Therefore, while marginal costs should ideally be used in performing cost-revenue analyses, the well-known relationship between the average and marginal cost curves makes the former an excellent surrogate for most applications, and may be employed if sufficient judgment is exercised. Baumol concludes:

> . . . there is something intermediate between the counsel of perfection which regards anything but marginal data as absolutely useless for decision making and the uncritical calculations which employ average or total figures as they are received from the accountant's records.[4]

Expansion of the Cost-Revenue Approach

The cost-revenue analyses in the literature have had the singular objective of determining whether a given project is capable of paying for itself in terms of additional educational and municipal services that will be required. In order to make that bottom-line determination, numerous other projections are usually developed. Such other information can be provided in the form of indicators to the decision-maker to enable him to base his actions on a broader information base. Such an expanded analysis can be automated (computerized) to relieve the planner of the burden of manually computing a set of data. This is the basis of the Community Development Impacts Model (CODIM). To the extent discussed so far, CODIM replaces the manual analysis required to determine the impacts of development projects.

Cost-Revenue Applied to the Planning Process

Past cost-revenue analyses have attempted to respond to specific development proposals—in the case of a Montgomery County study, a 20-year plan for the Germantown area; in an Urban Institute study, a proposed development in Albemarle County, Virginia.[5] CODIM, however, permits impacts to be calculated rapidly, thus permitting users to conveniently explore alternatives to answer "what if" questions.

Thus, hypothetical development mixes, including various residential and industrial development possibilities, can be successively evaluated until one strategy is found with quantifiable characteristics that satisfy the community and its officials. The process is in keeping with Herbert Simon's rational decision-making and Martin Meyerson and Edward Banfield's rational planning (Chapter 4).

In other words, although CODIM can be applied to respond by quickly evaluating a given development proposal, it also can assist in plan evaluation. In the latter application, development scenarios are postulated and their characteristics (population, income and age distributions, associated tax rates, and so on), which are presented as outputs, are evaluated. Thus, a given scenario may have certain desirable characteristics, such as low densities or open space, but result in a property tax rate that the community considers too high. It would therefore be modified and perhaps reevaluated, each time trading off low density for a reduction in the tax rate. Finally, a development strategy is obtained that satisfices the desires of the decision-makers; that it, it has the proper blend of the two factors used in this example—open space and costs as measured by the property tax rate.

The process is presented schematically in Figure 5.1. In the first block, the scenario or development mix is defined. The definition consists of the number of acres of land that will be devoted to various kinds of residential and industrial uses. (Other inputs that are not exogenously required by the model are discussed in subsequent sections.) For example, a typical scenario might consist of 100 acres devoted to industrial use, 500 apartment units, and 800 single-family dwelling units.

Given the scenario input, CODIM will output various demographic, economic, and fiscal indicators (block 2). These outputs are evaluated by the decision-makers (block 3). On the basis of the evaluation, the scenario is either desirable or undesirable. If it is not acceptable, then the mix is reformulated in order to improve on the various characteristics. To use the previous example, if density is too high, the number of housing units might be reduced.

FIGURE 5.1

Interactive Planning System

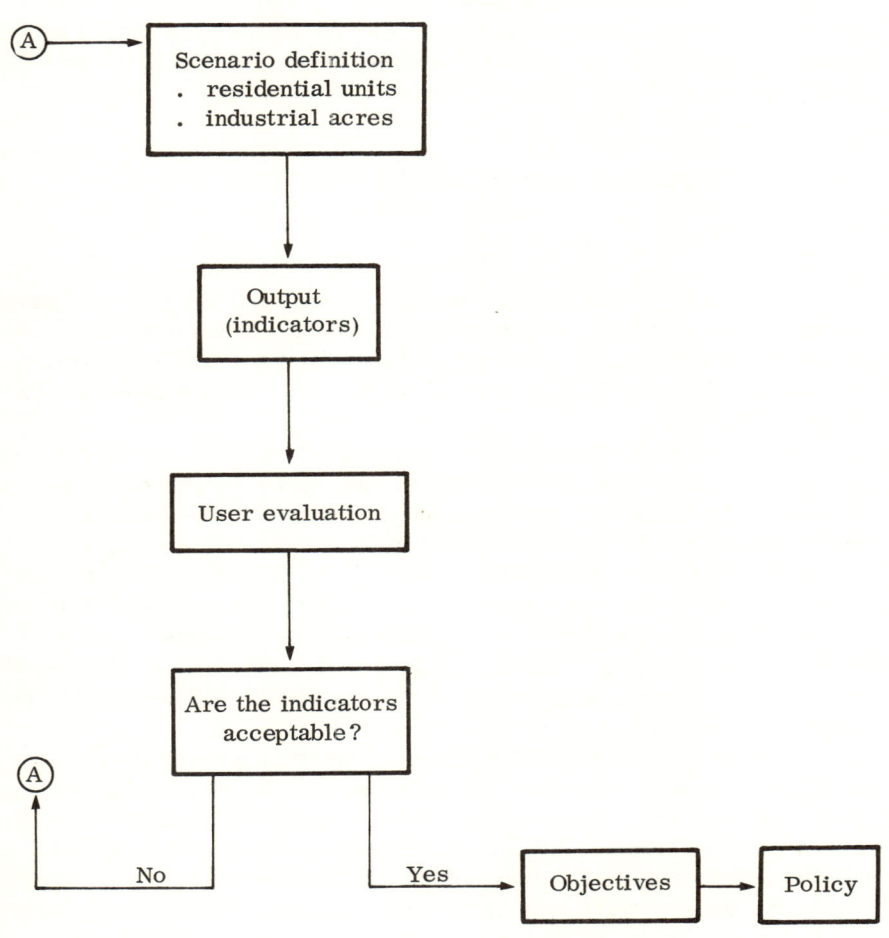

The process converges when an acceptable scenario is found. The indexes or output that accompanies the particular scenario is the objectives of the community, and the particular scenario or mix becomes the policy through which the objectives can be attained.

The use of CODIM "muddles through" in an attempt to find the particular scenario (mix) that will satisfy his value set and desires. While the user may have a well-defined, and perhaps even prioritized, set of objectives he feels a development strategy should fulfill, he may not be able to find the scenario that meets his requirements. If, on the other hand, a satisficing mix has been found, the user still has no guarantee that his solution is in some sense optimal. Explicit treatment of goals and their optimal attainment is discussed in chapter 7.

THE COMMUNITY DEVELOPMENT IMPACTS MODEL: AN OVERVIEW

The CODIM construct is a computerized scheme that calculates the impact of land development proposals using exogenously provided parameter estimates. It represents the state of the art in cost-revenue analysis[6] and forms the basis for normative approaches discussed in chapters 7 and 8.

Aside from the advantages of rapid calculation, CODIM provides a consistent methodology for analyzing and evaluating alternatives. Thus the impacts of a particular development proposal can be compared with other alternatives to form a balance sheet, as suggested by Nathaniel Litchfield and Julius Margolis.[7] Given the uncertainty surrounding many parameters used in cost-benefit analyses, the authors propose that several projects be evaluated and compared, using a consistent methodology. Thus it is the relative outcome of the analysis, as opposed to the absolute results for one project, that are used in the project evaluation.

CODIM accepts a development strategy or scenario as input, and outputs a series of indicators on the impacts of that particular development. The model is composed of modules, each performing a specific series of computations. This modular treatment lends flexibility to the construct. Figure 5.2 summarizes CODIM.

The MAIN routine initializes certain parameter data, and coordinates flow among the subprograms. MAIN determines the kind of scenario a user wishes to input and then directs the sequence of calculations.

The INDUST routine requests only one item of information from the user—the number of acres of industrial development desired. Other values, such as intensity of land use and worker per acre ratios, are initialized within the routine. INDUST computes the square feet

FIGURE 5.2

CODIM Summary Flow Chart

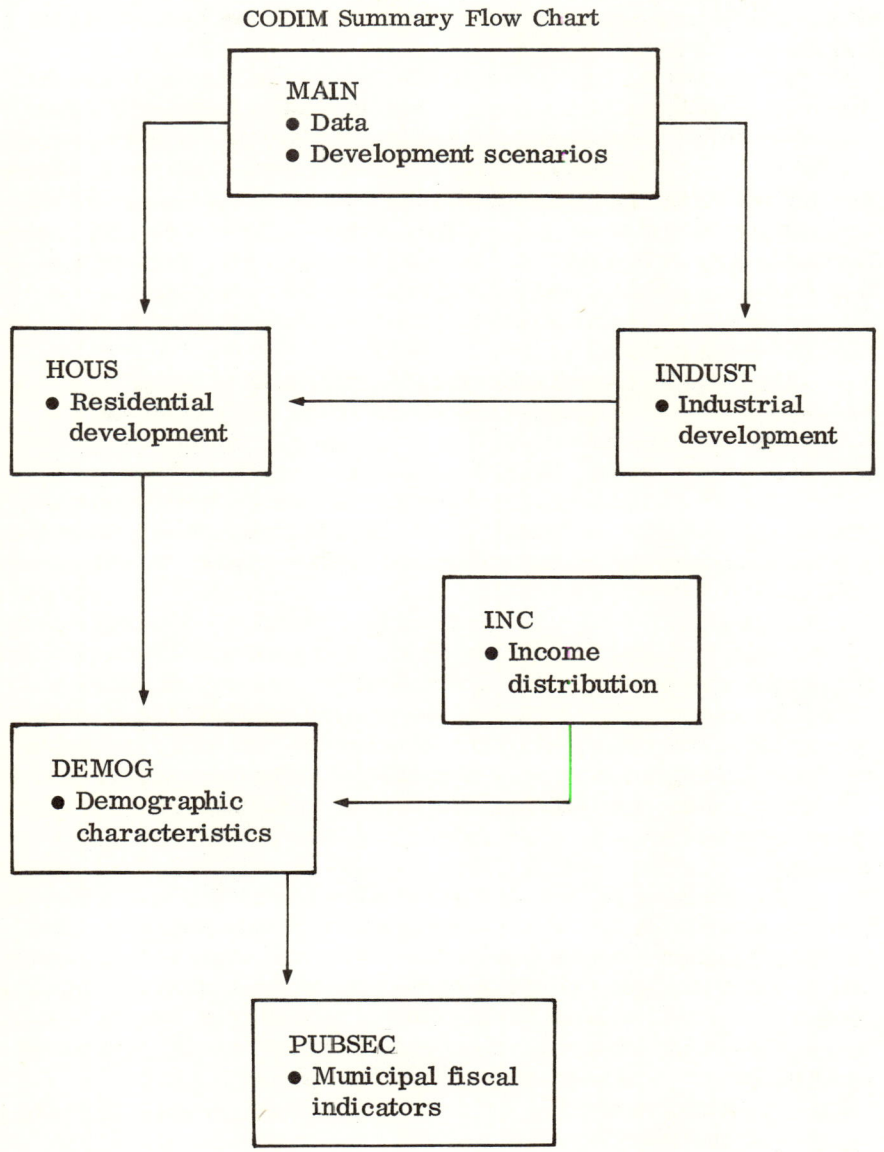

of industrial building space, number of jobs of different types, the anticipated demand for housing as a result of the increase in employment, and the requirements for such public services as roads and utilities.

HOUS asks the user to specify the number of housing units desired. Housing units are broken down into three kinds, with appropriate densities, market values, and land limitations for each. If the original scenario postulated by the user includes industrial development, HOUS incorporates an addition demand computed in INDUST. The routine computes the full value of all new housing units, the overall and specific densities, the total acreage used, the acreage that remains available, and the total number of units resulting from all demands. HOUS prints certain information summaries for the user upon his request and calls DEMOG.

The DEMOG routine takes the information furnished by HOUS and provides certain demographic and socioeconomic characteristics of the population. The function INC is called upon by DEMOG to furnish an income distribution. DEMOG computes an age distribution, size of the population, number of households, number of "new" residents, and anticipated volume of retail sales. The information is produced for the user upon command, and broken down by type of residential unit.

PUBSEC takes information developed so far and computes costs of providing municipal and education services, using exogenously provided cost functions. After accounting for revenues resulting from intergovernmental transfers, it computes a property tax rate. Among the outputs that this routine provides are the total tax base, assessed valuation for school and municipal purposes, property and school tax rates, constitutional debt limits, total municipal and school appropriations, state formula and per capita aid, and nonproperty tax receipts.

The following sections present the links employed in CODIM and a discussion of relevant data. The development is presented in this manner to demonstrate the interaction between construct formulation and data availability. CODIM is a practical application employing fundamental relationships. Its usefulness results from its ability to be readily implemented without overwhelming data needs. The model has been programmed and is operational in an interactive mode. The initial application was made for the city of Cohoes, New York, in the Albany-Schenectady-Troy SMSA.

INDUSTRIAL DEVELOPMENT SUBMODEL

It is the function of this submodel to compute the changes in tax base, employment, and population resulting from industrial development. It also provides data for certain public service requirements, such as utilities and streets.

From a cost-revenue standpoint, industrial development has always been assumed to be desirable. It has been felt that the direct costs of providing service to industrial land users do not begin to approach the great tax benefits that accrue from high-value industrial property. In 1957, for example, Mabel Walker, director of the Tax Institute, wrote:

> More and more items are appearing in the current press to the effect that "x" community badly needs industries in order to keep taxes down, so there appears to be a general belief that industrial expansion will produce higher tax yields and therefore permit a lowering of tax rates. Yet to date, researchers have not been concerned with substantiation of this thesis. There is almost no information on the subject.[8]

More recently, several studies have attempted to determine the cost-revenue implications of industrial development. Woo Sik Kee, for example, points out that in determining the costs and revenues associated with industrial growth, indirect costs must be included.[9] For example, industrial development leads to growth in population and increasing burdens on the school system.[10] This effect must be accounted for in order to properly assess the cost-benefit of industrial development.

Numerous studies have either substantiated or disputed this so-called Margolis effect. Margolis argued that municipalities are mistaken in pursuing industrial and commercial land users for fiscal purposes. After studying the tax structure of 55 San Francisco Bay area municipalities, he concluded that increased industrialization permits low-income workers to bid successfully on residential property, thus reducing the overall per capita tax base.[11]

Robert Coughlin and Walter Isard likewise have noted that although the revenues generated by industrial development often are considerably greater than the additional municipal costs, this apparent advantage may be offset by requirements for sewers and other facilities. "Other things being equal," they conclude, "the larger the industrial development, the greater the decrease in community taxes."[12] However, Coughlin and Isard are quick to note that tax rates may either rise or fall, depending on the number of new residents, the levels of general municipal services, and the amount of unused capacity in the existing municipal infrastructure.[13]

William C. Wheaton has summarized the basic weaknesses of past cost-revenue analyses, specifically with regard to the costs and revenues of industrial development.[14] According to Wheaton, these weaknesses are the following:
- The application of average rather than marginal costs
- Overemphasis on the property tax revenue, to the relative exclusion of nontax revenues
- The unrealistic assignments of charges to residential areas
- The relative neglect of industrial expansion costs.

The use of average rather than marginal costs has already been discussed. CODIM counters the second criticism by considering various nonproperty tax revenues, including state aid and sales tax redistributions. The third point, dealing with the assignments of relative burden for expanded services, is applicable only to cost-revenue studies performed ex post facto to determine the profitability of particular kinds of development.

CODIM does not assign costs to particular sectors of land use, but computes the overall changes in costs resulting from development. The profitability of one kind of development relative to another is determined by the user through the evaluation of different development strategies.

With regard to Wheaton's fourth point, INDUST develops a series of spin-off effects. These are employed by other CODIM routines in the computation of output information. Secondary effects (such as the "Margolis effect") are assumed to exist throughout the system and are incorporated in the analysis.

The industrial development cost-revenue studies cited previously share the luxury of being ex post facto analyses. Their value, then, lies in the fact that they demonstrate some of the quantitative effects of industrial development, both direct and indirect. As such, they serve as models for forecasting.

The following sections discuss various aspects of the INDUST submodel. Input to this submodel consists of the single data element "number of acres devoted to industrial development." The first order of business is to convert this into net land use, from which the remaining relationships are developed.

Gross Acreage and Land Coverage

One of the primary assumptions in the INDUST routine relates to the nature or character of the particular industrial development.

ASSESSING THE IMPACTS OF DEVELOPMENT PROPOSALS

In this analysis it was assumed that the development would consist of a typical light-industry park, including such activities as electronics assembly, printing and publishing (small-scale), warehousing, instrument manufacture, and pharmaceuticals. This assumption can be varied, but accompanying quantitative relationships must also be altered.

Based on the light-industry scenario, it can be determined that one- to five-acre lot sizes are preferred, with a 20 percent to 50 percent lot coverage factor most common. Also, approximately 25 percent of the gross acreage is utilized for passive land uses and transportation. The commonly employed building size is 10,000-50,000 square feet.[15]

The relationship for determining the square footage of industrial development, given the gross acreage desired, is

$$SQFT = ACRESI * NETACR * COVER * K1$$

where

SQFT = square footage of industrial space
ACRESI = number of acres devoted to industrial use (input by the user)
NETACR = net acreage, or the percent of gross acreage remaining after allowance for transportation and passive land uses
COVER = percent of building lot actually covered by construction
K1 = conversion from acres to square feet

Full Value of Industrial Real Estate

From the relationships developed in the preceding section, it is possible to derive the net square footage of building, given a gross acreage devoted to industrial development. It is now necessary to determine the full value of construction in order to derive the tax base implications. Construction cost data do vary. The Means Company publishes a range of $11 to $20 per square foot for the geographic area under investigation. Between one-third and one-quarter of that cost is for mechanical equipment. This range could be narrowed with more stringent assumptions regarding the characteristics of the industrial park.

The Board of Equalization and Assessment of New York State also provides some average figures. For new industrial construction in the Albany area, the Board reports a cost of $14-$15 per square foot for real property, plus $4 to $5 per foot for mechanical components, such as air conditioning.[16] The resultant total cost of $19 per square foot is used by INDUST.

An alternative capitalized-value method for computing likely construction expenditures can be employed. First, a determination is made of obtainable rents. Then, by assuming a given rate of return on investment, the amount a developer will expend on construction is derived.

In CODIM, full value of industrial development is determined through

$$FVAL(I) = COST(I) * SQFT; \quad I = 5$$

where COST = the per-square-foot construction costs. (The variables FVAL and COST are used for other forms of development as well; the index (5) denotes industrial land use.)

Employment Densities

Several studies report the expected number of workers per acre in an industrial site.[17] F. S. Chapin, Jr., shows a possible range, broken down by industry, for three zones in Philadelphia.[18] Table 5.1 presents the data.

Surveys conducted by the New York State Department of Transportation indicate that newly developed light-industry parks generate 15-25 passenger vehicle trips per gross acre per day, with an estimated 1.5 persons per vehicle.[19] Theodore Pasma, in a 1966 study, finds the average number of workers to be 10 per net acre.[20] Pasma also reports on some typical density ranges, in terms of square feet of plant per worker. These range from a low of 680-1200 square feet per employee in chemical plants, to a high of 87 square feet of plant per employee in garment and apparel manufacturing. The median value is 550 square feet of plant per employee, which can be converted to 24 workers per gross acre, using the site-related assumptions of a light-industry park. Thus, given the data available, a consensus figure of 20 jobs per gross acre is deemed reasonable.

The relationship

$$JOBNO = J1 * ACRESI$$

where J1 = jobs per gross industrial acre, is used to determine the total number of jobs (JOBNO).

TABLE 5.1

Illustrative Floor Space and Acreage Standards Used to Determine Industrial Space Requirements by Zone, Philadelphia, 1960

Class of Industry	II Inner Zone		III Outer Zone		V Far Northeast	
	Floor Space per Worker (sq ft)	Workers per Acre	Floor Space per Worker (sq ft)	Workers per Acre	Floor Space per Worker (sq ft)	Workers per Acre
Food	600	109	700	37	1,200	11
Tobacco	250	261	250	105	–	–
Textiles	500	131	500	52	500	26
Apparel	175	373	225	116	–	–
Lumber and furniture	700	93	700	37	700	19
Paper	500	131	500	52	500	26
Printing	400	163	400	65	400	33
Chemicals	600	109	600	44	600	22
Petroleum and coal	–	–	–	10	–	5
Rubber	350	187	350	75	350	37
Leather	375	174	375	70	–	–
Stone, clay, and glass	600	109	600	44	600	22
Primary metals	–	–	1,200	22	1,200	11
Fabricated metals	400	163	600	44	650	20
Nonelectrical machinery	450	145	450	58	450	29
Electrical machinery	220	297	300	87	350	37
Transportation equipment	–	–	400	65	400	33
Precision instruments	350	187	500	52	600	22
Miscellaneous	400	163	400	65	400	33

Source: F. Stuart Chapin, Jr., Urban Land Use Planning (Urbana: University of Illinois Press, 1965), p. 394. Excerpted from Table 7, "The Plan for Industry," in Philadelphia City Planning Commission, Comprehensive Plan for the City of Philadelphia, 1960.

Type of Employment

In order to determine the socioeconomic characteristics of the labor force that will be employed in a new industrial park, it is necessary to project the types of occupational opportunities that will exist. One approach is to assume that any industrial development must capitalize on the existing labor force. Using this assumption, the occupational distribution for the SMSA can be examined. Such an approach, however, tacitly implies that a given industrial park will reflect, in microcosm, the industrial activity of the entire region.

A different technique is to determine the distribution of occupational categories, by industry, for the SMSA. Table 5.2 shows the data sample used for analysis. For each industry, the percent of production (blue-collar) workers and nonproduction (white-collar) workers is computed. As the table shows, the overall distribution is 65 percent production workers and 35 percent nonproduction workers. A sample has been taken of the industry types represented by the table to include industries that are likely candidates for the typical light-industry park. As previously noted, these include electronics assembly, printing, precision instruments, and possibly beverage bottling. The distribution of production and nonproduction workers for this sample, 71 percent and 29 percent, respectively, is used by INDUST.

To summarize:

$$JOBT(I) = XJ(I) * JOBNO, \quad I = 1, 2$$

where $JOBT(I)$ = number of jobs in category I
and $XJ(I)$ = the percent of total jobs in category I.

Capture Rate

The previous sections discussed the techniques applicable to determining the employment that a given industrial development will create by type of job (blue-collar or white-collar). In order to ascertain the full impact of industrial development, however, it is necessary to determine the capture rate for new workers—how many employees of the new facilities will actually move into the city.

There are several reports in the literature on employee migration patterns in response to industrial relocation. One of the early studies on employee proclivity to move was performed by Beverly Duncan, who found that employees who have been with the firm for

TABLE 5.2

Production Workers and Total Workers by Industry, Albany-Schenectady-Troy SMSA, 1967

Industry	Total Number of Workers	Number of Production Workers	Percent of Total	Number of Nonproduction Workers	Percent of Total
All	65,300	42,500	65	22,800	35
Food	5,300	2,700	51	2,600	49
Bakery	1,700	700	41	1,000	59
Beverage	1,000	500	50	500	50
Textile mill production	3,800	2,900	76	900	24
Apparel, other textile products	4,500	4,000	89	500	11
Lumber, wood products	500	400	80	100	20
Paper	4,900	4,000	81	900	19
Printing, publishing	5,300	3,500	66	1,800	34
Newspapers	1,700	800	47	900	53
Books	700	200	28	500	72
Commercial printing	2,700	2,400	89	300	11
Chemicals	3,800	2,300	60	1,500	40
Rubber, plastics	500	400	80	100	20
Stone, clay, glass production	6,200	3,900	63	2,200	36
Primary metal industry	2,900	—	—	2,200	—
Fabricated metal products	1,500	1,200	80	300	20
Metalworking machinery	600	400	67	200	33
Instruments, related products	600	400	67	200	33
Miscellaneous manufacturing	900	700	78	200	22
"Light industry sample": Books, commercial printing, beverage, instruments, and miscellaneous	5,900	4,200	71	1,700	29

Source: Capital District Business Fact Book (Albany: New York State Department of Commerce, 1969), p. 8.

TABLE 5.3

Motivating Factors in An Employee's Decision to Move His Residence Closer to His Place of Work

Characteristic	Employee Who Will Be More Prone to Move Residence	Employee Who Will Be Less Prone to Move Residence
Personal attributes	Male Young Not married If married, no children Lives alone Primary worker	Female Old Married Has children, particularly of school age Lives with family Secondary worker
Personal qualities	Has held few jobs Occupationally upwardly mobile Does not own a car No other source of income	Has held many jobs Occupationally static Owns a car Has other sources of income
Relation to work	Has seniority Company has a pension plan Does highly specialized work Close friends or family work in same plant This is his only job High degree of company loyalty Well-paying job Likes company, and feels respected, needed, and important at his job Considers his job permanent	Has no seniority Company has no pension plan Does general work Has no close ties among the other employees Has another job No sense of company loyalty Not a well-paying job Feels company is indifferent to him Considers job temporary, or plans to retire
Relation to residence	Rents home	Owns home
Relation to residence	Rents home Weak or no ethnic or neighborhood ties Can find new home easily Cannot get to new plant site easily Present community expensive to live in Can easily dispose of present home Has recently moved to community	Owns home Strong ethnic or neighborhood ties Cannot find new housing easily Can get to new plant site easily Present community inexpensive to live in Cannot easily dispose of present home Has lived in the community a long time

Source: Louis K. Loewenstein, "The Impact of New Industry on the Fiscal Revenues and Expenditures of Suburban Communities," National Tax Journal 16, no. 2 (June 1963): 133.

ASSESSING THE IMPACTS OF DEVELOPMENT PROPOSALS   73

some time tend to live further from their jobs than do recent employees.[21] Duncan's survey showed that the average distance traveled to work by white males employed in manufacturing was 4.7 miles. The distance increased as the tenure of employees increased.

Louis Loewenstein surveyed industrial plants that relocated from Philadelphia to several suburbs and found that for one firm the number of employees who migrated with it was 90 percent. In another case, 375 out of 450 employees remained with the firm when it moved to suburban Radnor.[22] In summing up the results of his findings for the three townships he studied, Lowenstein states that local industrial activity had "some, but not an undue" effect on employees' residences.[23]

This finding corroborates the results of other surveys that indicate that only a minority of workers change places of residence when a firm relocates and that their prime motivation is a desire to improve the quality of their place of residence. Another Philadelphia study, for example, indicates that only 9 percent of all recent movers changed their residence because of a change in employment, and only 5 percent moved in response to a locational change by their employer.[24]

None of the studies provides a definitive statement on employee proclivity to migrate. Even Loewenstein's own findings vary widely. Table 5.3 presents some of the qualitative factors attributable to workers' decisions to move their place of residence.

There are alternative methods for deriving a community's "capture rate" for new employees. One technique, suggested by the Center for Urban Policy Research (CUPR), uses the ratio of locally employed persons to the total labor force, and assumes that this ratio remains constant with industrial expansion.[25] Another measure is the ratio of number of jobs to the total population.[26] Again, it is assumed that this ratio remains constant with expansion.

TABLE 5.4

Industrial Employment and Total Population

	1958	1963	1967
Number of Establishments	47	50	45
Number of Employees	2,737	2,507	2,700
Population*	20,359	19,674	19,000
Employees/Total Population	.1755	.129	.1355

*Interpolated from decennial census.
Source: Capital District Business Fact Book (Albany: New York State Department of Commerce, 1959, 1967, and 1972).

This method (jobs/population) is used by INDUST. Table 5.4 shows the pertinent data for the test city. As indicated, industrial employment has remained a relatively constant percentage of total population. The value for "capture rate" in CODIM is set at 15 percent.

Housing Demand by Type of Dwelling

Using the number of jobs resulting from industrial development and the capture rate, it is now necessary to determine the demand for new housing by housing type. This demand, purely the result of industrial development, is computed in the INDUST routine and then stored for use by the housing subroutine.

Several studies that deal with the nature and character of new development in a community are available. However, the most broadly based survey of household characteristics appears to have been undertaken by the CUPR.[27] The survey, parts of which were conducted over a 10-year period, encompassed some 3,600 garden apartments, 1,700 townhouses, 1,600 high-rise apartment units, and 600 single-family units in numerous localities throughout New Jersey. In the absence of local surveys, the CUPR findings can be used to estimate demand for particular housing types, given an occupational distribution.

Table 5.5 presents the occupational distribution of residents in various types of dwelling units.

TABLE 5.5

Occupational Distribution by Dwelling Type
(percent)

Dwelling Type	Blue Collar	White Collar	Other*
Townhouse	8.0	81.5	10.6
Single-family	32.4	60.8	6.8
Garden apartment	15.8	60.8	20.3
High-rise	2.0	83.7	14.3

*Includes retired, students, and unemployed.

Source: Adapted from George Sternlieb, Housing Development and Municipal Costs (New Brunswick, N.J.: Center for Urban Policy Research, Rutgers University, 1973), p. 59.

TABLE 5.6

Dwelling Distribution by Occupational Type
(percent)

Dwelling Type	Blue-collar	White-collar
Townhouse	17.0	39.5
Single Family	24.4	10.2
Garden Apartment	58.6	50.2

Source: Adapted from George Sternlieb, Housing Development and Municipal Cost (New Brunswick, N.J.: Center for Urban Policy Research, Rutgers University, 1973), pp. 58-60.

The available data can be rearranged to show distribution of dwellings by occupational type. Table 5.6 presents this distribution. High-rise units have been deleted, since this type of dwelling is not considered feasible in the test city.

Now, given the total job opportunity derived by INDUST and the distribution of the available jobs, it is possible to estimate the demand for particular types of dwelling units. As will be discussed in the residential submodel, CODIM currently handles three types of dwelling units. Using the dwelling distribution by occupational type (Table 5.6), the housing demand resulting from industrial development can be derived.

$$FAM(I) = CAP * \sum_{J=1}^{2} DD(I,J) * JOBT(J); \quad I = 1, 2, 3$$

where

$FAM(I)$ = the number of families demanding housing type I
CAP = capture rate
$DD(I,J)$ = the percent of families whose wage earner holds type J job that will demand type I housing
$JOBT(J)$ = number of jobs created by type J.

Summary of the INDUST Submodel

Input to the INDUST model consists of a single data element: the number of acres devoted to industrial development. Previous cost-revenue analyses of industrial development have been criticized for their failure to consider the secondary effects of industrial growth, such as in-migration. The INDUST model develops information necessary to compute these indirect effects (such as increased school costs) by other routines of CODIM.

Given the data input, INDUST determines the net square footage of industrial building and the lengths of new streets. From the net land utilization, full value of real estate is derived. Next, employment opportunity is calculated, using standard densities for light-industry parks. From a survey of occupational distributions in appropriate industries, the employment opportunity is defined in terms of blue-collar jobs and white-collar jobs. Finally, a capture rate is applied to find the number of new residents resulting from the industrial development.

The above outputs are provided for the user on the terminal, and also are stored internally for use by other subroutines. The INDUST model then calls the housing subroutine.

EXHIBIT 5.1

Sample Input and Output of the INDUST Model

INPUT NO. OF INDUSTRIAL ACRES(USE DECIMAL)?137.

RESULTS OF INDUSTRIAL DEVELOPMENT
JOBS CREATED   959 NON-PROD.   1781 PROD.
HOUSING DEMAND   143 HIGH   108MOD   338APT

SQ. FT. OF INDUSTRIAL SPACE- 1808400.

Exhibit 5.1 summarizes the input and output to the INDUST model. The input is 137 acres. The output shows that this results in 959 white-collar jobs and 1,781 blue-collar jobs. The housing demand resulting from the industrial growth by three types of units is 143, 108, and 338. The acreage input yields a net development of 1,808,400 square feet of industrial plant space.

ASSESSING THE IMPACTS OF DEVELOPMENT PROPOSALS

HOUSING SUBMODEL

Input to the housing submodel (HOUS) consists of the number of dwellings to be constructed, by type of unit. The routine applies density rates, vacancy rates, and unit construction costs, and develops physical characteristics that are displayed for the user and stored to be employed by subsequent routines.

There are three ways in which input data enter the routine, depending on the type of development specified by the user. When using CODIM, it is necessary to specify whether the development strategy to be evaluated consists of industrial development only, residential development only, or a combination of industrial and residential development. The three ways in which input data are supplied to HOUS are as follows (see Figure 5.2):

- User has specified industrial development only; input to HOUS comes directly from INDUST (expressed as number of families, FAM(I), demanding housing type I) and no user input is required.
- User has specified residential development only; input to HOUS must be entered through the keyboard. Appropriate queries are printed to assist the user.
- User has specified both industrial and residential development; input to HOUS is supplied from INDUST (the housing demand resulting from industrial development), with the remaining input supplied by the user as in preceding item.

Characteristics of Residential Development

HOUS differentiates among several types of residential units, each being typical in its category. The characteristics of the units are specified a priori, and relate to such factors as lot size and unit cost. Both single- and multiple-family units may be considered. The following list is an example of dwelling types used in the test city:

- High-priced single-family units (HIGH). This category represents the typical suburban four-bedroom dwelling on a 10,000-12,000-square-foot lot (100-foot frontage). The average 1970 price for this type of dwelling in the Capital District (Albany-Schenectady-Troy SMSA) was $35,000.[28]
- Moderate-priced single family units (MOD). This category represents a three-bedroom dwelling such as may be purchased by the younger family or a family of moderate means. Assumed sales price is between $27,500 and $30,000.[29] The

typical moderate unit is built on an 8,000-square-foot lot (80-foot frontage).
- Garden apartments (APT). The APT category represents two- to three-story garden apartments with a gross density of approximately 20-25 dwelling units per acre. Monthly rents are assumed to begin at $175 for a one-bedroom unit.

Computation of Physical Development Characteristics

HOUS employs straightforward relationships to compute the overall density of residential development, number of acres used, and full value of construction. In addition, new street and sewer requirements are determined. Although the capital costs for such improvements generally are borne by the developer, maintenance (such as paving and snow removal) is done by the municipality. These costs are computed in the PUBSEC routine.

The first task accomplished by the HOUS routine is the computation of the total number of units. This is simply the sum of the units input by the user plus any housing demand resulting from industrial development as computed by INDUST. The computation can be represented as

$$U(I) = NU(I) + FAM(I)/(1 - VACR(I)); \quad I = 1, 2, 3$$

where

$U(I)$ = the total number of units of type I
$NU(I)$ = the number of units of type I entered by the user
$FAM(I)$ = number of families demanding housing type I as the result of industrial development
$VACR(I)$ = the vacancy rate for type I dwellings, measured as the percent of all units of type I that are vacant or on the market at a given time.

The index I is used as shown below.

I	Housing Type
1	High-priced single-family (HIGH)
2	Moderately priced single-family (MOD)
3	Garden apartments (APT)

TABLE 5.7

Lot Sizes and Dwelling Densities

Dwelling Unit Type	Lot Dimensions per Dwelling Unit (feet)	Net Density[a] Dwelling Units/Acre
Detached houses	100 × 200	2.0
	90 × 120	3.0
	80 × 160[b]	3.5
	70 × 140	3.3
	60 × 125	4.3
	500 × 100	6.5[c]
Semidetached houses	30 × 125	8.7
(outmoded housing type)	26 × 125	10.0
Townhouses, two-story	20 × 100	16.1[d]
	16 × 100	20.4[e]
Garden apartments, two-story		10-20
Garden apartments, three-story		20-35
Apartments, multiple-story, to 12 stories		50-85

[a]Net density represents the number of dwelling units per acre of land, excluding land for streets, parking, playgrounds, and other passive uses. Deduct 25 percent of the site for allocation to streets, park, and recreation areas.
[b]Not a realistic lot size; do not use.
[c]Possible only with a strictly grid layout, which is outdated and should not be used.
[d]Denser type of row housing.
[e]Does not represent a salable density.

Source: The Community Builder's Handbook (Washington, D.C.: Urban Land Institute, 1968).

TABLE 5.8

Lot Areas and Dwelling Densities

Dwelling Unit Type	D.U.'s per Net Acre*	Assumed Average Sq Ft of Lot per D.U.
Single-family	1	32,000
Single-family	2	16,000
Single-family	3	11,000
Single-family	4	8,000
Two-family (outmoded)	5	6,000
Townhouse	10	3,000
	14	2,000
Garden apartment	18	1,600
Multistory apartment	50	

*Acreage exclusive of thoroughfares and passive land usage.
Source: Community Builder's Handbook (Washington, D.C.: Urban Land Institute, 1968).

As the above equation indicates, the industrial housing demand is converted to actual number of units, under the assumption that a given vacancy rate will exist. Thus, more units are constructed than are demanded.

After determining the total number of units by dwelling type, HOUS computes overall acreage used, based on exogenously supplied residential densities. Determining gross densities is straightforward and can be accomplished with the aid of a simple sketch plan and some assumptions regarding the widths of lots and public rights of way. Table 5.7 shows the relation between various lot dimensions and net density (streets excluded). Table 5.8 gives guidelines for relating lot size to dwelling unit densities.

The following gross densities* are considered representative for the dwelling unit types discussed earlier:

<pre>
HIGH   2.5 units/acre
MOD   3.25 units/acre
APT   25   units/acre.
</pre>

*Gross density is the number of dwelling units divided by total available acreage, including thoroughfares and passive land uses.

ASSESSING THE IMPACTS OF DEVELOPMENT PROPOSALS   81

The total acreage used for residential developments is given by

$$\text{ACRES}(I) = U(I)/\text{DENS}(I); \quad I = 1, 2, 3$$

where DENS(I) is the exogenously given gross density, by dwelling type. Logical checks are included in the routine to insure that actual available acreage is not exceeded.

The full value of real estate is taken as the purchase price (or the capitalized value of rents, in the case of apartments) and is computed as

$$\text{FULVAL}(I) = U(I) * \text{COST}(I); \quad I = 1, 2, 3$$

where COST(I) is the exogenously supplied average purchase price for a given type of unit.

Summary and Sample Output

Given the input—the number of dwelling units of different kinds desired by the user and/or resulting as a spin-off from industrial development—HOUS performs several straightforward computations. At the command of the user, the output is produced on the terminal keyboard. All values are stored for use by subsequent routines.

Exhibit 5.2 shows the input requirements to the routine and the output produced. NO. UNITS includes the number of units input

EXHIBIT 5.2

Sample Input and Output of the HOUS Submodel

```
INPUT NO. HIGH, MOD, & APTS?100,100,50

PRINT RESIDENTIAL DEV. DETAILS? (YES-NO;1-0)?1
```

	RESIDENTIAL ZONE TYPE		
	HIGH	MODERATE	APTS.
NO. UNITS	243	208	388
ACRES USED	97.	64.	8.
TOTAL ACRES	100.	300.	16.
FULL VALUE ($MIL.)	8.50	6.24	3.10
UNITS/ACRES (OVERALL)	2.43	0.69	24.25

---

directly into HOUS by the user, plus the spin-off units resulting from industrial development. (See Exhibit 5.1.) TOTAL ACRES indicates the total acreage available for a particular kind of residential development and is based on present zoning. UNITS/ACRE is the gross density, determined by dividing the total available acreage in each category by the number of dwelling units. Note that all densities are below the exogenously given "upper bound" densities.

DEMOGRAPHIC SUBMODEL

The demographic submodel (DEMOG) accepts the outputs generated by HOUS and derives the resultant demographic characteristics. In addition, it calls on the INC submodel to determine the total income of persons and an income distribution for households. The following output is produced by the DEMOG routine:
- Population
- Number of households (families and unrelated individuals)
- Distribution of household income
- Distribution of age of head of household
- Total retail sales volume
- Number of public school pupils

Total Population and Age Distribution

Two methods for projecting the size and age distribution of the population for a given set of development inputs are presented and evaluated. The first method is that of cohort survival analysis.[30] The second technique involves projections based on housing availability.

Projecting the total population and age distribution is important for several reasons. First, such data provide a demographic indicator that can be evaluated by the user. The expected age distribution of the population under a given development strategy is of interest to the local policy-makers because it provides a "feel" for the nature of the city's residents. Second, size of the population and its age distribution is an important determinant of municipal expenditure. For example, total education expenditure is related to the number of pupils, and certain social service costs may be dependent on the number of elderly persons in the community.

The Cohort Survival Technique for Projecting an Age Distribution

This procedure involves an aging of the population over the planning period, taking into account births, deaths, and migration. The analysis usually is performed separately for males and females, and proceeds as follows.

Assume that a projection of the size and age distribution of the population for 1980 is desired. First, the age-specific death rates and fertility rates are obtained for the period 1960-70. Using the 1960 population and age distribution (obtained from the census) as a basis, the population is aged to 1970 (Table 5.9).

The aging process consists of several components. First, persons in the age group 0-4 in 1960 will be in the age group 10-14 in 1970. Of course, certain adjustments need to be made. These consist of accounting for any births and deaths occurring within the age group during the decade. The number of births is estimated either from crude birth rates or age-specific female fertility ratios. Death rates used are age-specific and are obtained from state and county health authorities.

The analysis is performed for all age groups (births affect only the first age group), and the results of this analysis are compared with actual 1970 census data. Any discrepancies are attributed to migration. Now, using the 1960-70 birth and death rates, in conjunction with the migration rates established, a projection is made to 1980.

The cohort survival technique is well suited to projections for large regions, but numerous problems arise in the smaller geographic area. One of these relates to the "law of averages" or central limit theorem.[31] Practically speaking, the implication of the central limit theorem is that the smaller the population to which the birth and death rates are applied, the more tenuous the analysis.

A second and more significant criticism deals with the migration patterns. When cohort techniques are applied to an entire nation or a state, migration can be determined with a fair degree of accuracy. However, in a small municipality, particularly one undergoing change, migration patterns cannot be expected to hold. Where significant community development is anticipated, it is of little value to make population forecasts using previous migration rates.

In view of the complexity of the cohort analysis technique and its severe limitations with regard to changing migration patterns, it was discarded as a potential tool for forecasting population and age distributions.

TABLE 5.9

Sample Work Table Illustrating Forecast Procedure by Cohort Survival Method
Using Five-Year Intervals, for Females

Year	Age Group													Total
	0-4	5-9	10-14	15-19	20-24	25-29	30-34	35-39	40-44	45-49	50-54	55-59	60-64	65-69 etc.	
1960	256	231	283	315	395	373	287	275	228	183	144	133	100	66	3340
1965		XXX Survivors ±XX Net migrants													
1970			XXX Survivors ±XX Net migrants												
1975				XXX Survivors ±XX Net migrants											
1980					XXX Survivors ±XX Net migrants										

Source: F. Stuart Chapin, Jr., Urban Land Use Planning (Urbana: University of Illinois Press, 1965), p. 205.

ASSESSING THE IMPACTS OF DEVELOPMENT PROPOSALS

Demographic Projections Based on Housing Availability

The basic purpose of the community development impacts model is to determine the impact of residential and industrial development in the small municipality. Given particular development strategies as inputs, demographic projections can be made on the basis of housing availability, by matching the characteristics of households with available housing. In order to accomplish this analysis, several factors must be determined for various types of units. Among these are the population per dwelling unit, the age of the head of the household, and the vacancy rates. The next two sections will discuss the data necessary to project population and age distribution based on a household-housing match.

Population Per Unit

The present population per unit or its historic trend is of little value since, with new development, characteristics of in-migrants will be different from those of the existing population. In order to determine appropriate populations per unit, selected census tracts can be reviewed. A crude figure for population per unit can thus be obtained by carefully selecting census tracts whose character is similar to that of the anticipated development.

Other sources of data do exist, however. The National Association of Home Builders, for example, has compiled a study of

TABLE 5.10

Household Size by Housing Type

Dwelling Type	Household Size
Single family	
4-bedroom	3.72
3-bedroom	3.31
Garden apartment	
1-bedroom	1.90
2-bedroom	2.80

Source: George Sternlieb, Housing Development and Municipal Costs (New Brunswick, N.J.: CUPR, 1973), p. 4.

TABLE 5.11

Distribution of Household Size by Housing Type and Number of Bedrooms

		Number of Bedrooms (percent distribution)			
Household Size	Efficiency	One	Two	Three	Four
Garden apartment					
1	3.3	59.7	35.4	1.6	0.0
2	12.1	78.6	9.3	0.0	0.0
3	0.2	71.8	27.7	0.4	0.0
4–6	0.0	39.8	58.9	1.3	0.0
7 or more	2.5	12.1	76.5	8.9	0.0
Townhouse	0.9	85.9	0.0	14.1	0.0
1	0.0	5.2	36.8	51.8	6.1
2	0.0	35.9	49.7	14.4	0.0
3	0.0	12.5	53.1	33.8	0.6
4–6	0.0	0.2	44.9	50.3	4.4
7 or more	0.0	0.0	18.5	69.1	12.4
High-rise	0.0	0.0	7.9	92.1	0.0
1	12.1	42.3	32.5	13.1	0.0
2	43.4	46.9	9.4	0.3	0.0
3	2.4	58.3	34.2	5.1	0.0
4–6	2.2	18.0	64.5	15.3	0.0
7 or more	0.0	1.2	33.7	65.1	0.0
Single-family	0.0	50.3	0.0	49.7	0.0
1	0.0	0.0	3.3	56.8	39.9
2	0.0	0.0	0.0	80.6	19.4
3	0.0	0.0	6.2	69.4	24.4
4–6	0.0	0.0	7.1	66.4	26.6
7 or more	0.0	0.0	1.2	50.9	47.9
	0.0	0.0	0.0	32.4	67.6
All units	3.8	36.3	32.2	22.3	5.4

Source: George Sternlieb, Housing Development and Municipal Costs (New Brunswick, N.J.: CUPR, Rutgers University, 1973), p. 90.

ASSESSING THE IMPACTS OF DEVELOPMENT PROPOSALS   87

residential occupancy characteristics.[32] The CUPR survey of 6,700 households conducted in 1972-73 also provides useful data on population per dwelling unit.[33] Table 5.10 presents a summary of average population per household for different dwelling types.

Table 5.11 presents a detailed distribution of household size according to dwelling type and the number of bedrooms.

From the available data it is possible to estimate average values for household size for use in the DEMOG submodel. The values below were used in the initial application.

Unit Type	Population per Unit
HIGH	4.0
MOD	3.5
APT	2.0

Age Distribution of the Household Head

A second factor used in making demographic projections under the housing-household match concept is the age distribution of the household head. As in the case of population per unit, simply knowing the existing distribution is insufficient, since any new in-migrants will most likely have an age distribution that is independent of the present distribution in the municipality. It can be assumed, for example, that in-migrants taking up residence in new homes and apartment units will have an age distribution similar to that of a newly developing and growing suburban community, as opposed to a small city. One method of estimating age distribution of in-migrants, therefore, is to choose data from selected appropriate census tracts and use them as representative distributions. It is desirable to have the age distribution available by type of housing unit, but this technique yields only a crude distribution.

In order to obtain a detailed age distribution by type of housing, survey data are necessary. Table 5.12 presents the results of such a survey.

As is indicated by the table, the age distribution of household heads occupying four-bedroom, single-family units (HIGH) peaks in the 36-49 age bracket. This is to be expected, since it is then that a family is largest and income is high. The distribution for MOD peaks at an earlier age bracket, and survey data further indicate that the trend for home ownership among younger household heads increased from 1960 to 1970.[34] The dwelling type having the highest

TABLE 5.12

Age Distribution by Housing Type
(percent)

Dwelling Type	Age of Household Head				
	15–26	26–35	36–49	50–64	65+
HIGH	8.4	21.3	54.1	12.3	3.9
MOD	16.6	60.2	17.7	4.4	1.1
APT	22.8	34.8	14.3	13.1	15.0
Current residents	5.0	20.9	20.4	25.7	28.0

Sources: George Sternlieb, Housing Development and Municipal Costs (New Brunswick, N.J.: Center for Urban Policy Research, Rutgers University, 1973), p. 62; Cohoes Housing Study (Cohoes, N.Y.: Planning and Development Agency, 1971).

percentage of elderly is the garden apartment. This likewise makes sense. As the family grows older and children leave, the larger home is no longer needed and parents move to apartments.

Computations

Having estimated the population per household and the age distribution by housing types, it is possible to make basic demographic projections. In making them, the estimates for the in-migrants that result from community development are combined with exogenous projections for the present city population. (See Table 5.12.) Further data on the existing population of the city studied will be found in chapter 6.

The new population by housing type is given as

$$POP(I) = U(I) * PPU(I) * (1 - VACR(I)); \quad I = 1, 2, 3$$

where

$POP(I)$ = population in housing type I
$U(I)$ = number of dwelling units of type I
$PPU(I)$ = population per unit in dwelling type I
$VACR(I)$ = vacancy rate for dwelling type I.

ASSESSING THE IMPACTS OF DEVELOPMENT PROPOSALS

Total population is computed through

$$POPT = \sum_{1}^{4} POP(I)$$

where
- POPT = total population of the city at the planning horizon
- POP(4) = the exogenous population projection for all present residents.

Computation of the age distribution of the new population is

$$NOFAM(I, J) = U(I) * AGEDIS(I, J); \quad \begin{array}{l} I = 1, 2, 3 \\ J = 1, \cdots, 5 \end{array}$$

where
- NOFAM(I, J) = the number of new households residing in dwelling type I, whose household head falls into age group J
- AGEDIS(I, J) = percent distribution (Table 5.12) of age of household by dwelling type and age group

AGEDIS(4, J) is reserved for the distribution projection of present city residents, and must be accomplished exogenously.[35] This leads to a direct computation for the number of existing families by age group, NOFAM(4, J).

By summing over dwelling types (I = 1, 2, 3) and including the exogenous projection for the present households, an overall age distribution is obtained:

$$NOF(J) = \sum_{I=1}^{4} NOFAM(I, J); \quad J = 1, \cdots, 5$$

where NOF(J) is the number of households with household head in age group J.

The percentage distribution is found by dividing the numerical distribution by the total number of families:

$$FNOF(J) = NOF(J) \Big/ \sum_{J=1}^{5} NOF(J)$$

where FNOF(J) is the percent of all households whose head is in age group J.

The overall number of households by dwelling unit type is found by

$$NOFH(I) = U(I) * VACR(I); \quad I = 1, 2, 3$$

where NOFH(I) is the number of households occupying dwelling type I, and NOFH(4) is the present number of households externally projected to the horizon year. Therefore,

$$NOFAMT = \sum_{I=1}^{4} NOFH(I)$$

where NOFAMT is the total number of households at the horizon year.

Summary and Sample Output

Exhibit 5.3 shows output from the DEMOG routine, using the sample case already presented in Exhibits 5.1 and 5.2.

EXHIBIT 5.3

Sample Output of the DEMOG Submodel

	DWELLING TYPE			
	HIGH	MODERATE	APTS	'OLD'
NO. OF HOUSEHLDS	231	202	349	6560
POPULATION	923.	706.	698.	16600.
HOUSEHOLD INCOME	17624.	13184.	11985.	8453.

```
NEW POPULATION       2328.
TOTAL POPULATION    18928.
PUB. SCHOOL PUPILS   2935
TOT. H'SHOLD INCOME  66.343($ MIL.)
AVG. H'SHOLD INCOME  9036.
RETAIL SALES($MIL.)  32.581

PRINT AGE DISTRIBUTION? (YES-NO;1-0)?1

AGE OF HOUSEHOLD HEAD
   15-25    26-35    36-49    50-64    65+
   471.    1683.    1562.    1776.   1907.
    6.4     22.9     21.3     24.2    26.0     (PERCENT)
```

ASSESSING THE IMPACTS OF DEVELOPMENT PROPOSALS 91

The output is interpreted as follows:

- NO. OF HOUSEHOLDS—the number of households by dwelling type, NOFH(I)
- POPULATION—population by dwelling type, POP(I)
- HOUSEHOLD INCOME—discussed below
- NEW POPULATION: $\sum_{1}^{3} POP(I)$
- TOTAL POPULATION—population at the horizon year (POPT)
- PUB. SCHOOL PUPILS—discussed below
- TOTAL AND AVERAGE H'SHOLD INCOME—discussed below
- RETAIL SALES—discussed below
- AGE OF HOUSEHOLD HEAD—the number, NOF(J), followed by the percent distribution FNOF(J).

Number of Schoolchildren

The most straightforward technique for estimating the public school loading resulting from residential development is to use school-age-children multipliers. Previous studies have published multipliers on the basis of type of dwelling unit and number of bedrooms.[36]

George Sternlieb breaks down the results of his survey by student educational level as well as dwelling type.[37] A comparison of the various published multipliers reveals some variability, which is attributable to unique characteristics of each of the samples. Table 5.13 shows the public school pupils by dwelling type and number of bedrooms, as reported in different studies.

The table shows that the largest variation among the reported multipliers appears in the garden apartment category. Some of this variability can be explained by the fact that apartment samples had different distributions with regard to the number of bedrooms, and only the CUPR reports its figures based on apartment size.

For the purpose at hand, the stability of the multipliers as a neighborhood ages is perhaps of greater interest than the actual value of the multipliers themselves. Earlier it was argued that a major deficiency of the cohort survival model was its inability to handle migration well. Proponents of cohort technique would argue, however, that through the aging process of a neighborhood, the age distribution of the residents, and hence the number of school-age children, will change over time. There appears to be some intuitive validity to that contention. As any observer realizes, it is possible to deduce the age

TABLE 5.13

Public School Pupils, by Dwelling Type and Number of Bedrooms, as Reported by Six Surveys

Dwelling Type	CUPR[a]	ASPO[b]	NAHB[c]	Fairfax County[d]	Montgomery County[e]	Albemarle County[f]
Single-family						
HIGH (4-bedroom)	1.293	.94*	.80*	1.3	1.27	1.05
MOD (3-bedroom)	0.626			1.1	.85	.90
Garden apartment						
1-bedroom	.046	.30*	.11*	.21*	.42*	.43*
2-bedroom	.344					

*Does not differentiate among different number of bedrooms.

Sources: [a]George Sternlieb, Housing Development and Municipal Costs (New Brunswick, N.J.: Center for Urban Policy Research, Rutgers University, 1973); [b]American Society of Planning Officials, School Enrollment by Housing Type, Planning Advisory Report no. 210 (Chicago); [c]National Association of Home Builders, Garden Apartments and School Age Children (Washington, D.C., 1962); [d]Fairfax County Planning Division, Student Contribution from Apartments and Mobile Homes (Fairfax, Va., 1966); [e]Maryland National Park and Planning Commission, Population and Household Growth Forecast (Silver Spring, Md., 1972); [f]Thomas Muller and Grace Dawson, The Fiscal Impact of Residential and Commercial Development: A Case Study (Washington, D.C.: The Urban Institute, 1972).

of a neighborhood through such simple factors as style of architecture, or maturity of the trees and vegetation.

With an increasing pattern of national migration, however, it can be argued that a neighborhood regenerates itself, and hence over time takes on a fairly stable distribution that is a function only of the type of dwelling units. Sternlieb presents some empirical evidence to support this hypothesis. For two-bedroom garden apartment units, the school-age-children multiplier changed less than 4 percent between 1963 and 1972. For one-bedroom apartments, the change was about 13 percent. In view of the data, he concludes that "consistency over time is more than adequate for local-planning purposes."[38]

The DEMOG routine therefore computes the number of schoolchildren according to the straightforward formula:

$$\text{PUPILS} = \text{NP} + \sum_{I=1}^{3} U(I) * \text{PUPH}(I)$$

where
$\quad U(I)$ = number of units of type I
$\quad \text{PUPH}(I)$ = student multiplier for unit type I
$\quad \text{NP}$ = exogenous projection of the number of pupils for the horizon year, for the current city population.

For income forecasts, DEMOG calls the subprogram INC, which is discussed next.

HOUSEHOLD INCOME SUBMODEL

Input to the INC routine is provided by DEMOG and consists of the number of households in each of the types of new residential units (NOFH(I)) plus the projected number of families for the present population (NOFH(4)). Output from INC consists of an income distribution, total household income, and average household income. The procedure for computing an income distribution assumes that the distribution for current residents will remain stable over the planning horizon.

Stability of Current Residents' Income Distribution Over Time

INC computes an income distribution by taking the current distribution of the population and inserting new households into the appropriate income category of the current distribution. The technique therefore assumes that the income distribution of current residents remains constant over the planning period.

In order to determine the stability of the current income distribution over time, curves representing the cumulative distribution of income were plotted. The plot of these Lorenz curves remained remarkably stable over the period 1950-70.[39] Using data from the 1950, 1960, and 1970 censuses, the cumulative income was plotted for each year for families and for families and unrelated individuals. The results are presented in Figure 5.3. As the figure shows, there is

FIGURE 5.3

Lorenz Curve: Stability of Income Distribution, 1950-70

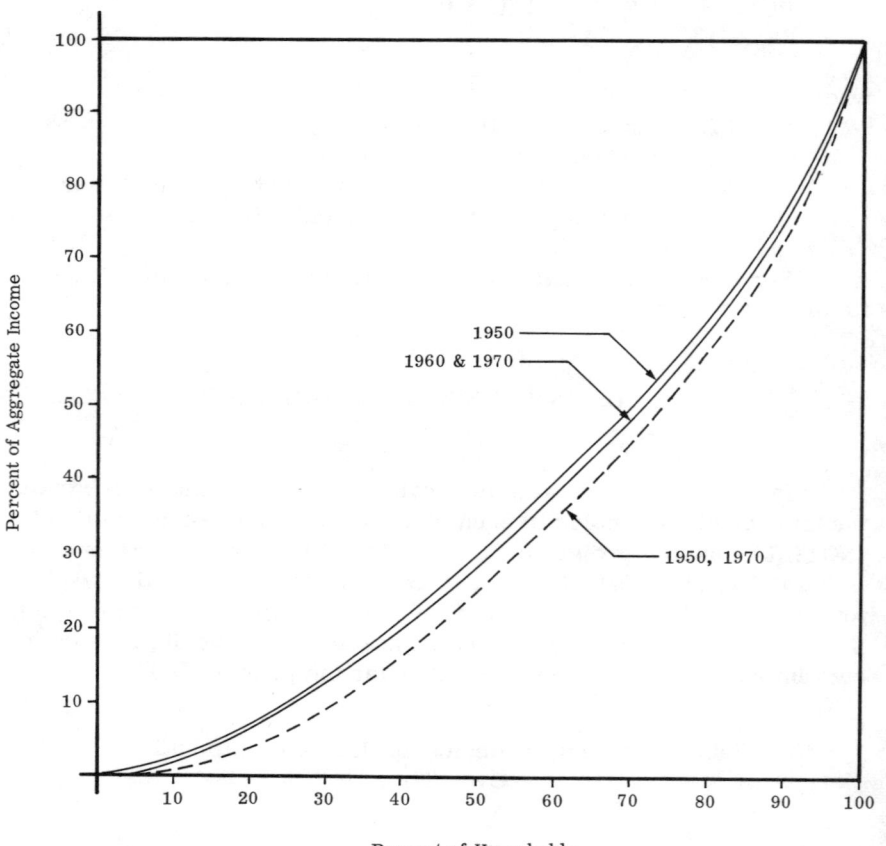

ASSESSING THE IMPACTS OF DEVELOPMENT PROPOSALS 95

the expected disparity between the curves for family only and for families and unrelated individuals.

Over time, the Lorenz curves show a high degree of consistency. In the scale to which the data were plotted, the curve for 1970 family income is indistinguishable from the 1960 family income curve. The 1950 family income curve lies very close to both of these. Likewise, the 1950 and 1970 family and unrelated individuals curves are superimposed. It is thus concluded that income distribution for the present population is stable over time. A new distribution that reflects changes caused by a large number of in-migrants can therefore be constructed by modifying the existing distribution, as explained above.

1970 Income Distribution of Residents

Table 5.14 presents pertinent 1970 income data for five income categories that are aggregated from the fifteen income categories reported by the 1970 census. The column "Category Mean" is the total income for the category divided by the number of families and unrelated individuals in the category.

Income Distribution of "New" Residents

Several methods can be used for estimating the income of new in-migrants. One common method is to relate household income to housing costs. The usual approximation is that the value of an owner-occupied dwelling is 2.5 times annual household income; however, the results of one study[40] show income related to housing value by the formula

$$Y = \$4,964 + .413 * H$$

where
Y = annual household income
H = housing value

The Bureau of Labor Statistics prepares typical budgets for families living in various parts of the United States. Table 5.15 shows the total family budget and the shelter costs for Buffalo, New York. The data in the table could be used directly to determine the income of renters, given the monthly rent. Income of homeowners would have

TABLE 5.14

1970 Income: Families and Unrelated Individuals

Category (in dollars)	Number in Category	Percent of Total	Category Mean	Total Income for Category (in dollars)
0–4,999	2,004	30.2	$ 2,548	5,107,500
5,000–9,999	2,378	35.9	7,635	18,158,000
10,000–14,999	1,586	23.9	12,211	19,366,000
15,000–19,999	357	5.4	17,104	6,106,000
20,000+	301	4.5	24,213	7,288,000
Total	6,626	100.0		56,025,000

Source: Adapted from Capital District Business Fact Book, Part II (Albany: New York State Department of Commerce).

TABLE 5.15

Annual Costs of Living for a Four-Person Family,
Buffalo, N.Y., Spring 1967

	Budget		
	Low	Moderate	High
Total Budget			
Renter families	—	$ 8,842	$12,815
Homeowners	—	9,885	13,832
Combined[a]	$ 6,083	9,624	13,679
Shelter Costs			
Renter families	1,010	1,279	1,745
Homeowners	—	2,097	2,467
Combined[a]	—	1,892	2,359
Shelter/Total Budget[b]	16.6	19.6	17.3

[a] Weighted average, renters and owners.
[b] Ratio of combined costs to combined total budget (in percent).
Source: Bureau of Labor Statistics, Monthly Labor Review, April 1969.

to be computed by using a capitalized value of property (mortgage payments) plus estimated property taxes.

In view of the necessary compatibility between earned income and prevailing housing costs in an area, it is possible to determine the income distribution of new in-migrants by surveying different dwelling types. This approach, being straightforward, was used to develop an income distribution by dwelling type for use in the INC routine.

Table 5.16 presents a percent distribution of total household income by housing type. Using the number of new residential units by type, it is now possible to derive a modified income distribution by combining the existing distribution (current residents) with the appropriate distributions of residents in HIGH, MOD, and APT housing.

The formulation is as follows:

$$NOFI(K) = \sum_{I=1}^{4} NOFH(I) * INCDIS(I,K); \quad K = 1, \cdots, 5$$

where

TABLE 5.16

Household Income Distribution by Housing Type
(percent)

Housing Type	Under $5,000	$5,000–9,999	Income Category $10,000–14,999	$15,000–19,999	$20,000+
HIGH	2.1	4.7	22.9	37.5	32.8
MOD	1.9	27.3	36.2	25.4	9.2
APT	11.7	26.6	31.3	21.6	8.8
Current residents*	30.2	35.9	23.9	5.4	4.5

*1970 census.

Source: Adapted from George Sternlieb, Housing Development and Municipal Costs (New Brunswick, N.J.: Center for Urban Policy Research, Rutgers University, 1973).

NOFI(K) = the number of households in income group K

NOFH(I) = the number of households in dwelling type I

INCDIS(I, K) = the percent of households residing in dwelling type I that fall into income group K (see Table 5.16).

A percent distribution is obtained through

FNOFI(K) = NOFI(K)/NOFAMT; $K = 1, \cdots, 5$

where NOFAMT is the total number of families.

The total income of households is obtained by multiplying the average income of each category, K, by NOFI(K), the number of households in that income category. The average household income is found by dividing total household income by NOFAMT.

Output of the INC Routine

Upon command, the INC submodel displays the income distribution, total income, average household income, and the total number of households. The total income and average income per household also are stored for further use by the DEMOG routine.

Exhibit 5.4 shows sample output, using the previous example.

EXHIBIT 5.4

Sample Output of the INC Submodel

```
PRINT INCOME DISTRIBUTION? (YES-NO; 1-0)?1

    CAT.      NO.FAM.         %
    $0-5      2033.          27.7
    -10       2513.          34.2
    -15       1806.          24.6
    -20        566.           7.7
    20+        423.           5.8

TOT. INCOME ($M) -  66.343
NO. OF FAM.  -  7342.
AVG. FAM. INC.-    9036.
```

The INC routine returns to the DEMOG submodel and transmits the total income of households and the average income per household. These data are used by DEMOG to determine the effects of new development on retail sales volume.

Assessing the Impacts of Development on Retail Sales

Retail sales can be estimated by using the average income of households and the aggregate residential income. Spending on retail goods is a direct function of available disposable income. In the case of a small city located within an SMSA, however, attention must be focused not on total retail spending, but on expenditures for convenience goods.

Paul Samuelson, for example, shows that with a household income of $10,000, approximately $2,000 will be spent on convenience goods.[41] A survey for the city being investigated revealed that approximately 19 percent of total household income was spent within the city.[42] The survey further showed that a significant volume of sales was generated by consumers from outside the city.

Retail sales are computed in DEMOG through

SALES = SPEND * AGGINC + SR

where

SPEND = percent of household income spent within the city
AGGINC = total income of households
SR = retail sales generated by demand from outside the city.

AGGINC is derived through

$$AGGINC = \sum_{K=1}^{5} XMEAN(K) * NOFI(K)$$

where XMEAN(K) is the average household income for income group K.

This information is printed on the display unit along with the other output of the DEMOG routine. (See Exhibit 5.3.) DEMOG stores appropriate data and calls the public sector submodel.

ASSESSING THE IMPACTS OF DEVELOPMENT PROPOSALS 101

PUBLIC SECTOR SUBMODEL

The public sector (PUBSEC) routine takes all pertinent data previously generated by other CODIM submodels and computes various municipal fiscal information.

Among the inputs provided PUBSEC by the other routines are
- Number of residential units, by type
- Square footage of industrial development
- Full value of all new real estate
- Number of public school pupils
- New roads and utilities
- Total population.

These factors have been discussed in previous sections. PUBSEC uses these data to compute
- Total tax base
- Nonproperty tax revenues
- Municipal expenditures
- Expenditures for education
- State aid for education
- Property and school tax levies required to balance the budget.

Municipal Tax Base

Two components are used to derive the municipal tax base (the assessed value of taxable property). One consists of the projected value of existing real estate. Added to this is the growth in tax base resulting from residential and industrial development. Historic trends are used to project the value of the existing tax base, and published equalization ratios are used to convert from assessed value to full value of real property.

In New York State, the Board of Equalization and Assessment regularly appraises a sample of properties in each municipality to determine their full value. On the basis of the sample, an equalization rate (assessment ratio) is published.[43] It is the statutory conversion factor between assessed value and full value:

$$\text{full value} = \frac{\text{assessed value}}{\text{equalization rate}}$$

In the absence of municipal reassessment, a declining equalization rate from one year to the next reflects increasing property values. Table 5.17 shows the recent trends in assessed value and full value for the test city.

TABLE 5.17

Tax Base Trends, Cohoes, N.Y., 1967-71

Year	Assessed Value	Equalization Rate (percent)	Full Value
1967	$18,922,840	39	$48,520,102
1968	18,653,100*	37	50,413,784
1969	18,713,436	37	50,576,854
1970	18,757,858	37	50,696,913
1971	18,797,858	34	55,287,818

*Decrease due to introduction of property-tax exemptions for persons over 65 years of age.

Source: State of New York, Office of the Comptroller, Special Report on Municipal Affairs (Albany, 1968-72).

The growth in full value of real property is the result of the combined effects of increasing property values (as indicated by a decreasing equalization rate) and a small amount of new construction (as indicated by the increase in assessed value).

The effects of industrial and residential development, as input to CODIM by the user, must be added to the existing tax base in order to project the total full and assessed value of real estate. As discussed earlier, it is assumed that full value of new construction is equivalent to the costs of construction. This full value is converted to an assessed value through use of the equalization rate. In addition to an overall rate, the assessment ratio is available by type of land use (residential, industrial, and so on).

Using the information developed so far, the new tax base can be determined through

$$TAXBN = \sum_{L=1}^{4} FULVAL(L) * EQRATE(L)$$

where
$FULVAL(L)$ = full value of new construction for land use of type L
$EQRATE(L)$ = equalization rate (assessment ratio) for land use of type L

ASSESSING THE IMPACTS OF DEVELOPMENT PROPOSALS

The land-use index, L, is given the following definitions:

L	Land Use
1	HIGH
2	MOD
3	APT
4	Industrial

The total tax base at the end of the planning period is determined through

$$\text{TAXB} = (1 - \text{EX}) * \text{TAXBN} + \text{TAXBO} * (1 + \text{XA}) ** \text{NYEARS}$$

where

EX = percent of new property exempt from municipal taxation[44]
TAXBO = 1970 tax base (Table 5.17)
XA = growth rate of existing tax base (from Table 5.17)
NYEARS = number of years in the planning period
TAXB = total assessed value at the planning horizon.

The PUBSEC computations discussed so far are presented to the user as shown in Exhibit 5.5.

EXHIBIT 5.5

PUBSEC Output Pertaining to Tax Base

```
        MUNICIPAL FISCAL DATA($ MIL.)
     NEW TAXBASE    -   17.313
     TOT. TAXBASE   -   38.080
     SCHOOL TAXBASE-    38.963
     FULL VALUE        113.288
     STAUTOTRY DEBT LIMIT -    7.930*
```

*For cities whose population is under 125,000, the New York State constitutional debt limit is 7 percent of the full value of real property.

Sources of Revenue: State Revenue Sharing and Sales Taxes

New York State returns 9 percent of its income tax revenue to municipalities. This revenue sharing consists of two categories: per-capita aid to cities and formula aid.

Per-Capita Aid to Cities

Half of the total revenue sharing is distributed on a per-capita basis to cities in the state. For any given year, the per-capita assistance is a constant.

Formula Aid

The remaining half of the state revenue-sharing allocation is disbursed to all municipalities under a formula using full value of real property and total population. For cities the formula is as follows. If the full value of real property per capita exceeds $8,000, the municipality receives $8.60 per person. For every $100 below $8,000, $0.05 is added to the subsidy. The formula aid can therefore be expressed as

$$FAPCAP = Max[\{(\$8.60)\} ; \{\$8.60 + (\$8,000 - FVALT/POPT) * .005\}]$$

where

FAPCAP = formula aid per capita
FVALT = full value of real property = TAXB/EQR
   (EQR is the overall equalization rate)
POPT = total population.

Based on the input data received by PUBSEC, a computation of the per-capita and formula aid is made. This forecast is produced on the display terminal and will be exhibited later along with other output.

An additional source of revenue for municipalities in New York State is the sales tax. For the city investigated, sales taxes are levied by the county and distributed to the municipal jurisdictions within the county on a per-capita basis. In order to compute the redistribution, a forecast of county-wide sales is made. Table 5.18 shows the volume of retail and service activity in the county.

For the period 1954-67, the dollar volume expanded at an annual simple rate of 4.1 percent. For the more recent period 1958-67, the simple growth was 6.8 percent annually.

ASSESSING THE IMPACTS OF DEVELOPMENT PROPOSALS

TABLE 5.18

Volume of Trade in Retail Activity and Selected
Services in Albany County, 1954-67

Year	Dollar Volume ($1,000)
1954	$384,520
1958	423,940
1963	522,696
1967	689,859

Source: Compiled from Capital District Business Fact Book (Albany: New York State Department of Commerce, 1969).

Computation of Nonproperty Tax Revenues

The sales tax and state aid represent the major sources of municipal revenues aside from the property tax. Since these revenues cannot be directly controlled through municipal policy, they will be referred to as fixed revenues.

PUBSEC computes the sales tax redistribution on the basis of expected population and county-wide taxable business activity. State aid is computed by using existing statutory formulas. The two components of state aid plus the sales tax are combined to yield total fixed revenues:

$$STAID = (CAPAID + FAPCAP) * POPT * (1 + XGS) ** NYEARS$$

where
  STAID = total state aid at the planning horizon
  CAPAID = 1970 per-capita assistance to cities
  FAPCAP = 1970 formula assistance per capita
  XGS = growth rate in state aid
  NYEARS = number of years in the planning period.

Now

$$FIXREV = STAID + ST * POPT * (1 + XGC) ** NYEARS$$

where
> FIXREV = total nonproperty tax revenues
> ST = 1970 per-capita sales tax redistribution
> XGC = growth rate in county-wide retail and service activity.

Municipal Expenditures

In the cost-revenue studies previously cited, several techniques are employed for determining and apportioning municipal expenditure. Among the most straightforward is to take major expenditure categories and find a per-person average value. This procedure is deemed unsatisfactory for the case of a municipality undergoing growth, since a substantial portion of costs usually are fixed costs for existing infrastructure. Thus, residential growth may require the addition of a police patrol, for example, but the administrative and other overhead costs for police protection will remain relatively constant.

A second difficulty of using simple per-capita rates of present spending is that not all municipal costs are attributable to a particular sector, such as residential land users or industrial land users.[45] Some studies have apportioned present expenditure to various land users on the basis of the proportion of assessed value that a particular land-use category represents. Using this approach, if 70 percent of the total assessed valuation in a municipality consists of residential land, then 70 percent of the cost of such community-wide services as fire protection and financial administration is allocated to the residential sector.[46] This technique makes the tenuous assumption that various sectors consume services in proportion to the value of real estate.

Other techniques have been used, and Table 5.19 shows the results of one analysis in which expenditures were allocated to the residential sector, using more subjectively determined proportions.

Although it is generally recognized that assessed value is not necessarily a good measure of services actually consumed, the use of this approach in most studies is necessary in order to avoid complex cost analyses. Some investigators have suggested categorizing costs as "people-related" and "property-related" to get a more meaningful allocation.[47] The results could then be applied to a particular development. Table 5.20 shows an analysis in which municipal service costs are applied to a subdivision under various development densities. This approach forms the basis for estimating public expenditures in the PUBSEC routine.

TABLE 5.19

Unit Costs of Municipal Services and Their Allocation to the Residential Sector

Service	Unit of Activity	Unit of Cost (in dollars)	Unit of Time	Unit of Incidence	Residential Portion (percent)	Unit of Residential Cost
Police patrol	Patrol car beat	51,264	Annual	15,000 people	50	$25,632
Detective	Per patrol car beat	8,635	Annual	15,000 people	50	4,318
Fire station	Pumper company	72,182	30 years	10,000 people	75	54,137
Engine	Pumper company	20,623	10 years	10,000 people	75	15,467
Equipment	Pumper company	34,339	10 years	10,000 people	75	25,754
Company	Pumper company	48,802	Annual	10,000 people	75	36,602
Fire alarm						
Boxes	Box	155	30 years	—	100	155
Circuit	Wire-mile	150	30 years	—	100	150
Traffic signs						
Initial	Sign	12	4 years	—	100	12
Replacement	Sign	5	4 years	—	100	5
Street paving	Street-mile	22,295	15 years	—	100	22,295
Paved street maintenance						
Resurfacing	Street-mile	10,388	15 years	—	100	10,388
Other	Street-mile	398	Annual	—	100	398
Street signs	Sign	18	10 years	—	100	18
Garbage collection	Collection route	11,139	Annual	750 houses	100	11,139
Street cleaning	Street-mile	61	Annual	—	100	61
Building inspection	—	—	—	—	—	—
Street lighting	Lamp	22	Annual	—	100	22

Source: F. Stuart Chapin, Jr., Urban Land Use Planning (Urbana: University of Illinois Press, 1965), p. 324.

TABLE 5.20

Annual and Amortized Capital Costs for a Hypothetical Subdivision,
Assuming Minimum Varying Lot Sizes
(square feet)

Annual and Amortized Periodic Costs	6,000		9,000		18,000		36,000	
	Subdivision Total*	Average per House*	Subdivision Total*	Average per House*	Subdivision Total*	Average per House*	Subdivision Total*	Average per House*
Annual costs								
Police patrol	5,991	6.41	4,544	6.41	2,288	6.41	1,314	6.41
Detective	1,009	1.08	765	1.08	385	1.08	221	1.08
Pumper company	12,833	13.73	9,732	13.73	4,901	13.73	2,815	13.73
Street maintenance	2,974	3.18	2,872	4.05	2,114	5.92	1,691	8.25
Garbage collection	13,887	14.85	10,530	14.85	5,302	14.85	3,045	14.85
Street cleaning	456	.49	440	.62	324	.91	259	1.26
Street lighting	1,607	1.72	1,430	2.02	902	2.53	660	3.22
General activities	3,004	3.21	2,349	3.31	1,257	3.52	775	3.78
Total annual costs	41,761	44.66	32,662	46.06	17,473	48.94	10,780	52.59
Amortized capital costs, Years 1-4								
Fire station	633	0.68	480	0.68	242	0.68	139	0.68
Fire engine	542	.58	411	.58	207	.58	119	.58
Fire equipment	903	.97	685	.97	345	.97	198	.97
Fire alarm boxes	62	.07	52	.07	41	.11	47	.23
Fire alarm circuit	15	.02	15	.02	14	.04	11	.05
Street signs—initial	117	.13	96	.14	66	.18	30	.15
Street paving	11,105	11.88	10,727	15.13	7,895	22.11	6,316	30.81
Street signs	97	.10	88	.12	49	.14	36	.18
General activities	1,044	1.12	973	1.37	686	1.92	534	2.60
Interest	184	.20	140	.20	70	.20	40	.20
Total, years 1-4	14,702	15.72	13,667	19.27	9,615	26.93	7,470	36.43
Grand total	56,463	60.39	46,329	65.34	27,089	75.88	18,251	89.02

*In dollars.

Source: F. Stuart Chapin, Jr., Urban Land Use Planning (Urbana: University of Illinois Press, 1965), p. 326.

ASSESSING THE IMPACTS OF DEVELOPMENT PROPOSALS

A Method for Estimating Municipal Expenditure Increases Resulting from Development

As was noted at the beginning of this chapter, an analysis of marginal costs and revenues is ideally desirable. It was also noted, however, that marginal values are difficult to obtain, especially when the cost-revenue model is generalized. PUBSEC computes additions to the municipal budget on the basis of a priori estimates of expenditure for certain hypothetical scenarios. These estimates are developed by using existing costs for public services.

Estimates of future costs are always subject to uncertainty, and usually are based on the assumption that current levels of service will not be changed.[48] In reality, the level of service for municipal functions can be largely controlled by the local chief executive. Thus absolute projections will necessarily be tenuous. However, where various alternatives are evaluated and compared, the consistency of the methodology makes those comparisons valid, even when the absolute value of the projection suffers from risk and uncertainty. (This will be demonstrated in chapter 9.) It will be shown that when expenditure (or revenue) estimates are varied by as much as 25 percent, the ranking of alternatives does not change.

The method for estimating costs presented was found to be useful in the test city. Other estimates and techniques for calculating municipal and educational costs (or revenues) can be used instead without affecting the applicability of the descriptive construct or the optimization model presented in subsequent chapters.

The analysis for determining these costs was carried out as a preliminary to the development of CODIM. Several initial development options were defined. The associated municipal costs were then determined with the aid of local officials. The initial development options (scenarios) each represented only one kind of land-use development (such as residential), thereby simplifying the cost-estimating procedure. The initial scenarios consisted of zero action, maximum residential development, and maximum industrial development.

Zero Action Scenario

This "do nothing" alternative assumed that present trends in the city would continue without any concerted effort on the part of government or private groups to promote change. Aside from providing a bench mark against which to evaluate various development alternatives, this initial scenario yields valuable information that may be considered as the intercept on a plot of municipal expenditure versus size. This

110   POLICY EVALUATION FOR COMMUNITY DEVELOPMENT

often overlooked factor in cost-revenue analyses is the change in municipal expenditures when population remains stable (or declines).[49]

A major contributing factor to an increasing budget under stable population conditions may be inflation. Increases in level of service, however, as represented by both quality and diversity, also add to the municipal burden. In the city investigated, the municipal budget doubled between 1966 and 1971. Federal categorical grants to some extent served to inflate the budget; but even when these funds were excluded, the budget still exhibited a compound annual growth rate of approximately 15 percent. During 1966-71 the city actually experienced a small decline in population. Using the historic trends and making allowances for inflation (as represented by the Consumer Price Index of the Bureau of Labor Statistics), an estimate of the increases in municipal expenditure for a relatively constant population was made. This real growth rate is included in PUBSEC expenditure computations.

Maximum Residential Development

There are about 600 vacant acres in the city, two-thirds of which lie in several large contiguous parcels. The residential development scenario postulated full development of these parcels in conformance with existing zoning. Table 5.21 shows the development potential of the sites and present zoning.

TABLE 5.21

Residential Development Potential

Site	Zoning	Number of Acres	Maximum Number of Units
A	S.F.[*]	80	270
B	both	64	550
C	S.F.	60	170
D	S.F.	29	80
E	S.F.	130	365
F	apartment	2	35
G	apartment	8	100
H	S.F.	43	100
Total		416	1,620

[*] Single-family, R-1 and R-2 zoning.

Source: Cohoes Planning and Development Agency, *Cohoes Housing Study* (1971).

ASSESSING THE IMPACTS OF DEVELOPMENT PROPOSALS

A map was prepared showing the eight sites and the potential number and type of units on each. This map was presented to various municipal departments heads, who were asked to assist in estimating cost increases if the sites were developed instantly.

With the aid of detailed budgets for each of the major city departments, costs were separated into fixed and variable categories. Each department head, considering his budget items, detailed any expenditure increases. The public safety commission, for example, after inspecting the map, felt that the addition of one police patrol (three shifts per day) would adequately serve the new residents. The commissioner of public works, after being informed of the linear miles of new streets likely to be constructed, was able to estimate increases in his expenditures for street maintenance and sanitation, and administration of his department.

The estimates described above were first made assuming full development, and subsequently, assuming that two-thirds full residential development would occur. In some cases the costs did not change significantly. In the public safety category, for instance, it was felt that an additional patrol would still be required even if the eight sites were developed only to two-thirds of capacity. The resulting estimated 1970 budget, omitting federal programs, is presented in Table 5.22.

Since the number of residential units by type is known for each of the scenarios, the expenditure estimates shown in Table 5.22 can be converted to per-capita estimates using the population per unit. This leads to the results shown below.

Scenario	Population	Total Expenditure	Expenditure per Capita
"Current" (1970)	18,600	$2.905 million	$156.20
Two-thirds residential development	22,600	3.395 million	150.22
Full residential development	24,600	3.616 million	146.99

The figures above show the expected trend in per-capita spending. As city size increases, existing infrastructure, currently underutilized, becomes more fully used, causing the average total costs to decrease over the population range 18,600 to 24,600. This suggests the following model for computing expenditures:

$$y_p = b_0 - b_1 p$$

where

TABLE 5.22

Estimated Municipal Expenditures Under Two Development Scenarios

Category	"Old" (current)	"New" (estimated) Two-Thirds Development	"New" (estimated) Full Development
Legislative	$ 19,245	$ 20,000	$ 21,000
Judicial	18,747	22,000	24,000
Executive	27,761	29,000	30,000
Staff	270,147	271,000	274,000
Public safety	856,722	911,000	942,000
Streets and sanitation	367,689	449,000	493,000
Public health	7,100	8,000	9,000
Recreation	99,742	150,000	160,000
Youth bureau	25,939	30,000	35,000
Library	31,200	50,000	65,000
Sewer district*	81,000	100,000	110,000
Water*	295,390	394,000	444,000
General	349,340	360,000	365,000
Debt service	415,881	555,000	605,000
Total	$2,904,400	3,395,000	3,616,000

*This item consists of user charges and was later deleted.

y_p = per capita expenditure

p = total population. This model reflects a linear decrease in per-capita spending as population increases.

Now, if we set $y = y_p p$, where y is the total expenditure, the relationship

$$y = a_0 p - a_1 p^2$$

is derived. This model was applied to the cost estimates shown above with resulting values

APPR = 183.9 * POPT - .0015 * POPT ** 2

where APPR is the total municipal expenditure.

The function was found useful for the test city over the population range 18,600 to 24,600. In other municipalities different functions may prove more applicable, depending on the characteristics of the municipality (such as older, declining city or new suburb).[50] Next, the expected real budget growth under stable population conditions is included to yield total municipal expenditure at the horizon year:

APPRT = APPR * (1 + XGR) ** NYEARS

where

APPRT = municipal appropriations at the horizon year

XGR = real growth rate in expenditures.

Maximum Industrial Development

This scenario postulates that acreage, currently vacant and suited for industrial use, be fully developed. As was done for the residential development scenario, a map outlining the sites and their development potential was prepared; and department heads were asked to assist in estimating expenditure increases under the assumption of instant development.

Again, two cases were considered: development of all acreage, and development of two-thirds of the acreage. As a result of analyzing the above two cases, it was estimated that industrial development would lead to increased expenditure at the rate of $750 per acre developed. This expenditure consists primarily of street maintenance and fire protection. It was assumed that costs for items such as snow removal, security, and utilities would be borne entirely by the developer.[51]

The additional public expenditure resulting from combined residential and industrial development is taken to be the sum of the two increases,

APPRT + 750 * ACRESI

where ACRESI is the number of industrial acres developed.

While there may be some overlap in the expenditure increase when both industrial and residential development are undertaken, it is felt that this overlap is minor, primarily since the costs associated with industrial development are small.

In conclusion, the scenario approach to estimating anticipated increases in municipal expenditure has been found to be more straightforward and representative than cost techniques discussed earlier. The greater the number of estimated budgets for particular type of development, the greater the reliability of the cost function. The cost function for residential development can be further improved by relating the estimated budgets to different types of dwelling units rather than just to population. Finally, preparing scenarios that combine different types of land use development would eliminate the difficulty of overlapping costs encountered in their analysis.

Expenditures and Revenues for Education[*]

Cost-revenue studies previously cited employ a common method for computing education expenditure. Current average per-pupil costs are multiplied by the projected number of pupils to arrive at a total cost. Any state assistance for education is then subtracted to arrive at the local share for education.[52] PUBSEC utilizes these basic techniques in determining education costs. As is the case with the municipal budget, increasing school expenditures due to rising costs or expanded services must be included. This growth rate is derived from historic trends.

Using historic data on educational expenditures and student population, a cost per pupil is derived. Since this cost includes appropriations for current operations as well as debt service, the computations used by PUBSEC to determine a school budget may lead to inflated results when the additions to the student population are small. The average cost approach to estimating school expenditures is commonly used, however; and some improvement in the estimation can be made by differentiating among the kindergarten, elementary school, and

---

[*] In New York State, cities with a population under 125,000 may form city school districts that function independently of the municipal budget. The tax levy of such districts (for operating purposes) may not exceed 2 percent of full value of taxable real estate.

ASSESSING THE IMPACTS OF DEVELOPMENT PROPOSALS

high school populations. The New Jersey Education Association has adopted a system of weighting average costs of education for the three levels. The weighted relative costs are shown below.

Level	Relative Cost
Kindergarten	0.5
Elementary	1.0
Secondary	1.3

Per-household student multipliers have been published that distinguish among public school pupils in different levels.[53] The use of the more specific multipliers in conjunction with refined cost data may lead to more reliable projections of expenditure.

State Aid for Education

The major source of nonproperty tax revenues for the school district is state aid. This aid is given for numerous allowable expenditures that include capital improvements. The state formula relates public school enrollment to the tax base in the following manner:

$$SCHAID = 1 - .51 * \frac{FVALT(K)/WADA(K)}{\Sigma \, FVALT(K)/\Sigma \, WADA(K)}$$

where

SCHAID = fraction of school expenditures reimbursed by state

FVALT(K) = wealth of school district K as measured by the full value of real property

WADA(K) = enrollment in school district K as measured by the weighted average daily attendance

and the summation applies over all districts in the state. For the purposes under discussion, the denominator of the formula is assumed to remain constant over the planning period.* Thus, the higher the value of real property per pupil, the lower the state aid to education.

---

*At the time this was being written, the State Legislature was considering revising the above formula at the recommendation of its Education Task Force. If the assumption is made that education costs are a function of the number of students, it can be shown that the amount of state aid is independent of the number of pupils, and related only to municipal wealth.

Property Tax and School Tax Rates

The previous sections have dealt with the techniques used in computing expenses and revenues for both the municipal and school budgets. The difference between the expenses and the nonproperty tax revenues (fixed revenues) is the amount that must be raised through the property tax levy. In New York State, both municipal corporations and school districts must prepare balanced annual budgets.*

Political considerations do enter into the budgetary process; and expenditures are trimmed, when deemed appropriate, in order to yield an acceptable tax rate. In the case of the city studied, a review of recent tax levies shows a marked decline during the 1971 election year. Some investigators have overlooked such political realities, or else have considered the tax rate (and hence the tax levy) to be constant.[54] While this may be true in the larger city, it does not appear to hold in the budget-making process of the smaller municipality.[55]

Although political and organizational considerations are recognized, it is outside the scope of this work to model the budgetary process. Hence, the property tax levy required to balance the budget is taken simply as the difference between appropriations and nonproperty tax revenues. The total levy required is divided by tax base to yield the tax rate per $1,000 of assessed value.

Output of the PUBSEC Routine

In addition to the output already shown in Exhibit 5.5, PUBSEC displays the information shown in Exhibit 5.6.

The property and school tax rates are in dollars per $1,000 of assessed value. Other items are explained below:
- MUN. APPROPRIATION (million dollars)—municipal expenditures at the end of the planning period
- FIXED REVENUES (million dollars)—nonproperty tax revenues, the sum of state aid and sales tax revenues
- SALES TAX REDIST.—county sales tax redistribution
- SCHOOL APPROP. (million dollars)—total expenses for education
- STATE AID RATE (ED.)—state aid for education as a percent of total expense

---

*Debt may be incurred only for items for which a probable useful life (capital items) has been established.

ASSESSING THE IMPACTS OF DEVELOPMENT PROPOSALS

EXHIBIT 5.6

Output of the PUBSEC Routine

```
PROP. TAX RATE-       $61.43
SCHOOL TAX RATE       $67.00

MUN. APPROPRIATION-   3.713
FIXED REVENUES    -   1.374
SALES TAX REDIST. -   0.748

SCHOOL APPROP.    -   5.009
STATE AID RATE(ED.)   47.878%
LOCAL SHARE       -   2.611

MUN. APPROP./CAPITA   $155.51
STATE AID(MUN.)   -   0.626
NO. OF PUPILS     -   2935
```

- LOCAL SHARE (million dollars)—total education expenses less state aid
- STATE AID (MUN.) (million dollars)—the sum of per-capita and formula state aid.

SUMMARY

CODIM uses cost-revenue analysis as the basic framework. In addition to fiscal data, it computes demographic and socioeconomic indicators of municipal activity. The model has been programmed in a modular structure that makes it convenient to change specific elements or to insert new ones. Coupled with the fact that its data requirements are small, this feature makes it a versatile tool that is simple to implement.

CODIM is operational in a conversational mode. As such, it is readily accessible to evaluate the impacts of given development projects. In addition, the user may input hypothetical growth strategies. This provides a consistent methodological framework for evaluating land development strategies. While community goals are not an explicit input to CODIM, evaluation of alternatives provides the user with an insight as to how development will affect the city. This insight yields the basis for a more explicit treatment of goal setting, which will be discussed in the goal-programming formulation of the community development problem.

CODIM uses public expenditure estimates derived from several initial scenarios. Other estimation techniques may be employed where appropriate.

Throughout this chapter, reference was made to the test city, Cohoes, New York. This was done for ease of understanding. Chapter 6 compares the results of a cost-revenue study performed for three specific residential projects in this city with the results obtained from CODIM.

NOTES

1. Martin Jones and Michael Flax, The Quality of Life in Metropolitan Washington, D.C. (Washington, D.C.: The Urban Institute, 1970). Also see Raymond Bauer, ed., Social Indicators (Cambridge, Mass.: MIT Press, 1966).

2. "St. Louis—Income and Cost of Municipal Services," WPA Entry no. 3436 (1937).

3. One recent publication proposes some generalized constructs. See Housing and Suburbs: Fiscal and Social Impact of Multifamily Development (Trenton, N.J.: County and Municipal Government Study Commission, 1974), pp. 137-58.

4. William J. Baumol, Economic Theory and Operations Analysis (3rd ed.; Englewood Cliffs, N.J.: Prentice-Hall, 1972), pp. 34-36.

5. Montgomery County Planning Board, Fiscal Impact Analysis, Germantown Master Plan (Silver Spring, Md., 1974); Thomas Muller and Grace Dawson, The Fiscal Impact of Residential and Commercial Development: A Case Study (Washington, D.C.: The Urban Institute, 1972).

6. An evaluation of cost-revenue analysis methodologies is given in Phillip S. Schaenman and Thomas Muller, Measuring Impacts of Land Development: An Initial Approach (Washington, D.C.: The Urban Institute, 1974).

7. Nathaniel Litchfield and Julius Margolis, "Benefit-Cost Analysis as a Tool in Urban Government Decision-Making," in Howard G. Schaller, ed., Public Expenditure Decisions in the Urban Community (Washington, D.C.: Resources for the Future, 1963), pp. 118-46.

8. Mabel Walker, Business Enterprises and the City (Princeton, N.J.: Tax Institute Inc., 1957), p. 37.

ASSESSING THE IMPACTS OF DEVELOPMENT PROPOSALS

9. Woo Sik Kee, "Industrial Development and Its Impact on Local Finance," Quarterly Review of Economics and Business 8 (1968): 19-24. Also see Werner Z. Hirsch, "Fiscal Impact of Industrialization on Local Schools," Review of Economics and Statistics 46, no. 2 (May 1964): 191-99.

10. See Louis K. Loewenstein, "The Impact of New Industry on the Fiscal Revenues and Expenditures of Suburban Communities," National Tax Journal 16, no. 2 (June 1963): 113-36. Also see Harold M. Groves and John Riew, "The Impact of Industry on Local Taxes," ibid., 137-46.

11. Julius Margolis, "Municipal Fiscal Structure in a Metropolitan Region," Journal of Political Economy 65, no. 3 (1957): 236.

12. Robert E. Coughlin and Walter Isard, Municipal Costs and Revenues Resulting from Community Growth (Wellesley, Mass.: Chandler-Davis, 1957), p. 44.

13. Ibid.

14. William C. Wheaton, "Application of Cost Revenue Studies to Fringe Areas," Journal of the American Institute of Planners 25, no. 4 (1959): 170-73.

15. The Community Builder's Handbook (Washington, D.C.: Urban Land Institute, 1968), pp. 449-67; William N. Kinnard, Industrial Real Estate (Washington, D.C.: Society of Industrial Realtors, 1967); "Industrial Districts—Principles in Practice," Urban Land Institute Technical Bulletin no. 44 (1962).

16. Conversation with Leon Kaplan, Board of Equalization and Assessment, Albany, New York.

17. A Land Use Plan for the Roanoke Valley Region (Roanoke, Va.: Department of City Planning, 1963); Industrial Areas (Cincinnati: City Planning Commission, 1946), p. 46; Dorothy A. Muncy, "Space for Industry, an Analysis of Site and Location Requirements," Urban Land Institute Technical Bulletin no. 23 (1954).

18. F. Stuart Chapin, Jr., Urban Land Use Planning (Urbana: University of Illinois Press, 1965), p. 394.

19. Conversation with Earl Herschenhorn, Capital District Transportation Study, Albany, New York.

20. Theodore Pasma, "Characteristics of 63 Modern Industrial Plants," Industrial Development (March-April 1970).

21. Beverly Duncan, "Factors in Work-Residence Separation," American Sociological Review 21 (February 1956): 53.

22. Loewenstein, op. cit., pp. 119-20.

23. Ibid., p. 130.

24. Ibid., p. 132.

25. George Sternlieb, Housing Development and Municipal Costs (New Brunswick, N.J.: Center for Urban Policy Research, Rutgers University, 1973).

26. Chapin, op. cit., p. 211.
27. Sternlieb, op. cit.
28. Housing market survey conducted in conjunction with Cohoes Housing Study (Cohoes, N.Y.: Planning and Development Agency, 1971).
29. Ibid.
30. For a detailed discussion, see Chapin, op. cit., pp. 203-08.
31. See Irwin Miller and John Freund, Probability and Statistics for Engineers (Englewood Cliffs, N.J.: Prentice-Hall, 1965).
32. National Association of Home Builders, Garden Apartments and School Age Children (Washington, D.C., 1962). Also see Maryland National Park and Planning Commission, Population and Household Growth Forecast (Silver Spring, Md., 1972).
33. Sternlieb, op. cit.
34. Sternlieb, op. cit.
35. For example, Cohoes Housing Study.
36. Muller and Dawson, op. cit. Also see National Association of Home Builders, "Schools and Urban Growth" (Washington, D.C., n.d.) (mimeo); Fairfax County Planning Division, Student Contribution from Apartments and Mobile Homes (Fairfax, Va., 1966); American Society of Planning Officials, School Enrollment by Housing Type, Planning Advisory Report no. 210 (Chicago); Maryland National Park and Planning Commission, op. cit.
37. Sternlieb, op. cit.
38. Ibid. Also see "The Garden Apartment Development: A Municipal Cost-Revenue Analysis," Urban Land (September 1964).
39. See Paul A. Samuelson, Economics: An Introductory Analysis, 7th ed. (New York: McGraw-Hill, 1967), pp. 109-11.
40. Montgomery County Planning Board, op. cit.
41. Samuelson, op. cit.
42. Planning and Development Agency, Economic and Marketing Study (Cohoes, N.Y., 1972).
43. State of New York, Office of the Comptroller, Special Report on Municipal Affairs (Albany, annual).
44. Computed from ibid. and city tax records.
45. Chapin, op. cit., p. 323.
46. For example, see Ruth Mace and Warren Wicker, Do Single-Family Homes Pay Their Way?, Research Monograph no. 15 (Washington, D.C.: Urban Land Institute, 1968).
47. See Chapin, op. cit., p. 324.
48. See, for example, Eugene P. McLoone et al., Long-Range Revenue Estimation (Washington, D.C.: George Washington University Press, 1967).
49. Richard Spangler, "The Effect of Population Growth upon State and Local Government Expenditures," National Tax Journal 16, no. 2 (June 1963): 193-96.

50. For discussion, see Housing and Suburbs, pp. 14-22.
51. See Community Builder's Handbook, pp. 449-65.
52. See, for example, Muller and Dawson, op. cit., p. 51; and Mace and Wicker, op. cit., p. 20.
53. Sternlieb, op. cit.
54. See J. P. Crecine, Governmental Problem Solving (Chicago: Rand McNally, 1969).
55. Thomas J. Chimura and William A. Wallace, "A Computer Simulation Model of Municipal Budgeting for Small Cities," Socio-Economic Planning Sciences 9 (June 1975): 131-36.

CHAPTER

6

AN APPLICATION OF THE MODEL

CODIM was tested in the small city of Cohoes, New York, while one of the authors was employed by the Planning and Development Agency of that city. This analysis will compare the results from CODIM with cost-revenue analyses performed for three residential development projects currently under construction in Cohoes.[1] Before describing the results of this comparison, an economic and geographic overview of the city and its relationship to the region will be presented.

GEOGRAPHIC AND ECONOMIC OVERVIEW

The City of Cohoes is located in the Albany-Schenectady-Troy SMSA in upstate New York (see Figure 6.1). The SMSA (the Capital District) comprises four counties and the three named central cities. Cohoes is located near the demographic center of the region; but because of the existing transportation networks, it suffers a distinct locational disadvantage. Proposed extensions of existing arterial systems may improve the city's location with respect to Albany, which is the state capital and a major employment center for clerical, administrative, professional, and related service occupations.

Table 6.1 shows the trend of some basic economic indicators for the region, the city, and the city as a proportion of the region.

FIGURE 6.1

Regional Location, Cohoes, New York

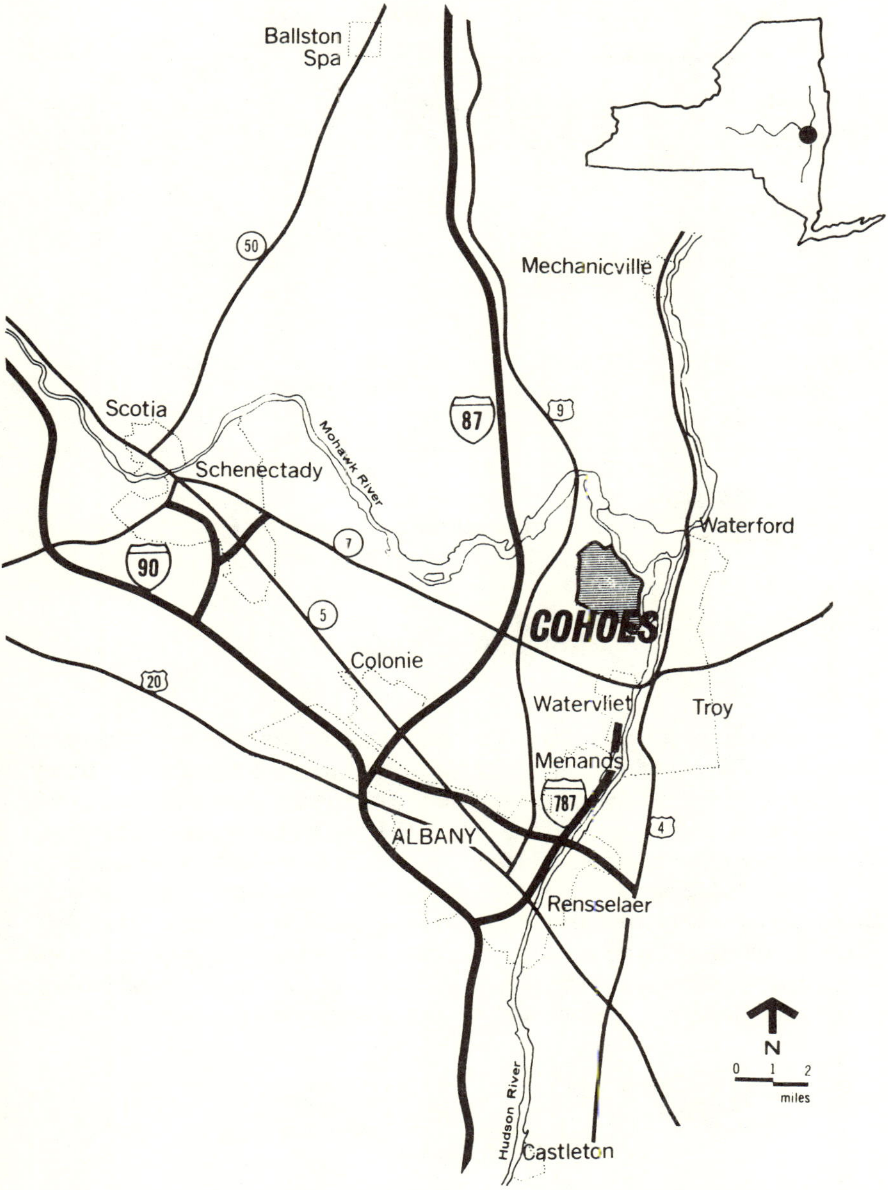

Source: Cohoes Planning and Development Agency, <u>Economic and Marketing Study</u> (1972), p. 6.

TABLE 6.1

Some Economic Indicators, Cohoes Versus Region, 1958-67

Economic Indicator	Percent Increase 1958-67		Cohoes as Percent of SMSA	
	SMSA	Cohoes	1958	1967
Population	(1960-70) 9.6	(1960-70) -7.3	(1960) 3.06	(1970) 2.58
Housing units	(1960-70) 9.8	(1960-70) -1.93	(1960) 3.03	(1970) 2.71
Value-added manufacturing	41.1	20.7	2.62	(1963) 2.93
Wholesaling	59.0	100*	1.18	1.52
Retail trade	21.7	0.3	2.11	1.74

*Estimated.
Source: Compiled by the authors.

HISTORIC OVERVIEW

The city of Cohoes became urbanized in the nineteenth century because of water power and transportation. In the twentieth century, electric power replaced the need for water power and the transportation canals were routed around the city. Cohoes began a steady decline symptomized by population decrease and physical deterioration.

In 1967 Cohoes was designated an All-America City, and in 1968 it received a demonstration grant under the Model Cities Program. As the result of large amounts of federal funding, the city undertook numerous redevelopment programs, including housing, neighborhood improvement, code enforcement, and urban renewal.

DEMOGRAPHIC CHARACTERISTICS

Population

Between 1960 and 1970, the region's population experienced an increase of almost 10 percent. Projections to 1980 indicate an

AN APPLICATION OF THE MODEL   125

18 percent expansion. The city's population, on the other hand, experienced a decline from 20,272 in 1960 to 18,653 in 1970. Projections for the next decade indicate the city will lose another 2,000 persons. Therefore, in addition to the absolute decline in population, the city's share of the regional population has been falling (see Table 6.2).

Coupled with the declining population is an age distribution that is becoming increasingly skewed toward the older age groups. Compared with both national and regional distributions, the city's population shows a proportionately lower number of persons in the category 0-25 years and a proportionately higher number in the categories 50-64 and 65 years and older.

Households

Table 6.3 shows the age distribution of household heads in 1970 for the city and for the region. In addition, projections for the number of households (by age of head) to the year 1980 are presented. The age distribution of household heads for the city is older than the distributions for the region or for the United States as a whole. The smaller average household size for Cohoes (2.89) also indicates that the city has more than its share of older households, many of them consisting of single or unrelated individuals.

The rate of household formation for the region between 1960 and 1970 was 13.0 percent (higher than the rate of population growth). The fact that household size for the region declined from 3.23 to 3.13 persons per household drove the rate of household formation above the rate of population change. This trend toward smaller household size is expected to continue, and is projected to be down to 3.03 persons per household by 1980. The rate of household formation is projected to increase to 15.6 percent for the period 1970-1980.

Households in Cohoes increased from 6,415 in 1960 to 6,423 in 1970. The resultant positive 0.1 percent rate of household formation can be attributed to a steep decline in household size (7.4 percent), from 3.12 in 1960 to 2.89 persons in 1970. This rate was somewhat larger than the decline of 7.1 percent in population.

Closer inspection of the population dynamics reveals that the younger households just attaining the affluence necessary for moderate- and higher-cost housing are migrating out of the city. An underlying cause for this is the inability to match the housing supply to consumer demand.

TABLE 6.2

Population Trends, Cohoes and Capital District, 1900-70

Year	Cohoes Population	Percent Change by Decade	Regional Population	Percent Change by Decade	Cohoes Population as Percent of SMSA
1900	23,910	—	395,209	—	6.0
1910	24,709	3.3	446,094	12.9	5.5
1920	22,987	-7.0	468,627	5.1	4.9
1930	23,226	1.0	520,069	11.0	4.5
1940	21,955	-5.5	531,249	2.1	4.0
1950	21,272	-3.1	589,359	10.9	3.6
1960	20,129	-5.4	657,503	11.6	3.1
1970	18,653	-7.3	721,910	9.6	2.6

Source: Cohoes Planning and Development Agency, Cohoes Housing Study (1971), p. 13.

TABLE 6.3

Number of Households, by Age of Head: Cohoes,
Capital District, and United States

Age of Household Head	1970		1980		Capital District Region (SMSA)		United States	
	Number of Households	Percentage Distribution	Number of Households	Percentage Distribution	Number of Households	Percentage Distribution	Number of Households	Percentage Distribution
15-24	442	6.9	307	5.0	14,944	6.5	4,633,593	7.3
25-34	888	13.8	1,287	20.9	37,882	16.4	11,742,735	18.3
35-44	922	14.4	868	14.0	40,013	17.4	11,775,650	18.6
45-64	2,527	39.3	1,986	32.1	88,685	38.5	23,158,338	36.5
65 and over	1,644	25.6	1,733	28.0	48,960	21.2	12,239,431	19.3
Total	6,423	100.0	6,181	100.0	230,484	100.0	63,449,747	100.0
Average Household Size	2.89				3.04			

Source: Cohoes Planning and Development Agency, Cohoes Housing Study (1971), p. 22.

HOUSING STOCK

Age and Structural Characteristics

The housing stock is overaged, contains an excessive number of oversized rental units, and suffers from a shortage of adequate owner-occupied single-family units. In 1970 there were only 265 units in the city (4 percent of total) that were under 10 years old. These units accounted for only 0.7 percent of housing built in the region during 1960-70. By comparison, 16 percent of the region's housing stock was under 10 years old in 1970.

In the city, 26 percent of the housing units were single-family dwellings in 1970, versus 54 percent for the SMSA. In addition, both contract rent and housing value were substantially lower in Cohoes. The most critical divergence was in contract rent: the city, which contains about 4 percent of the rental units in the region, had 15 percent of the region's units renting for under $60. The housing stock contains a disproportionately large share of rental units with three or more bedrooms (5.3 percent of the regional stock) but a shortage of adequate owner-occupied units with four or more bedrooms.

Between 1960 and 1970, the regional housing stock increased 9.8 percent, to 241,000 year-round units, while the city's housing declined from 6,753 to 6,644 units. This decline is reflected by a drop in the city's share of regional housing from 3.03 percent in 1960 to 2.75 percent in 1970.

Vacancy Rates

Regional vacancy rates in 1960 were 1.3 percent for owner units, 6.2 percent for rental units, and 3.1 percent for all units. By 1970, vacancies had fallen to 0.6 percent for owner units, 5.3 percent for rental units, and 2.3 percent for total housing stock.

Cohoes in 1960 had a gross vacancy rate of 3.3 percent, slightly higher than that of the region. The 1970 census, however, recorded an overall vacancy rate of 1.7 percent, the lowest in the region. Specific vacancy rates that year were 0.2 percent for owner units and 3.1 percent for rental units.

HOUSEHOLD INCOME

Between 1960 and 1970 the average income of families in the city increased 65 percent, from $5,573 to $9,207. The increase for the

TABLE 6.4

Distribution of Family Income, Cohoes and the Capital District Region, 1959 and 1969

Annual Family Income	Cohoes 1959		Cohoes 1969		Capital District Region 1959		Capital District Region 1969	
	Number	Percent	Number	Percent	Number	Percent	Number	Percent
Under $3,000	825	15.2	320	6.3	24,874	14.7	11,335	6.3
$3,000 - $3,999	609	11.2	259	5.1	14,977	8.8	6,094	3.4
4,000 - 4,999	787	14.5	230	4.5	19,949	11.8	6,951	3.8
5,000 - 5,999	855	15.8	317	6.2	23,103	13.6	8,812	4.8
6,000 - 6,999	618	11.4	357	7.0	20,068	11.8	10,292	5.7
7,000 - 7,999	563	10.4	432	8.5	16,905	10.0	12,077	6.7
8,000 - 8,999	418	7.7	533	10.4	12,762	7.5	12,992	7.2
9,000 - 9,999	223	4.1	489	9.6	9,635	5.7	13,361	7.4
10,000 - 14,999	420	7.7	1,528	30.0	20,052	11.8	55,993	30.9
15,000 - 24,999	84	1.6	570	11.2	5,643	3.3	34,235	18.9
$25,000 and over	19	0.4	63	1.2	1,647	1.0	8,823	4.9
All families	5,421	100.0	5,098	100.0	169,615	100.0	180,965	100.0
Median family income	$5,573		$9,207		$6,095		$10,655	

Source: U.S. Bureau of the Census, 1960 and 1970 Census of Population and Housing.

TABLE 6.5

Employment by Occupation, Cohoes and the
Capital District Region, 1970

Occupation	Cohoes		Capital District Region (SMSA)	
	Number	Percent	Number	Percent
Professional, technical and kindred workers	692	8.7	52,038	18.2
Managers and administrators, inc. farm	377	4.7	22,578*	7.9
Clerical and kindred workers	1,849	23.3	66,115	23.1
Sales workers	436	5.5	18,930	6.6
Craftsmen, foremen, and kindred workers	1,159	14.6	37,367	13.1
Operatives	2,112	26.7	41,752	14.6
Service workers, exc. private household	914	11.5	31,535	11.0
Private household workers	19	0.2	2,043	0.7
Laborers, inc. farm	382	4.8	13,775	4.8
Total, occupation reported	7,490	100.0	285,138	100.0
Occupation not reported	—	—	—	—
Total employed	7,940		285,138	

*Excludes farm managers.
Sources: U.S. Bureau of the Census; <u>1970 Census of Population</u>.

AN APPLICATION OF THE MODEL

entire Capital District was 75 percent, to $10,655. The income distribution for the region is generally flatter and more skewed to the right than that of the city (Table 6.4). The lower income categories (below $10,000) represent a larger proportion of the distribution for the city than the region. In addition, the median ranges of the distribution are more pronounced.

It is the income categories over $15,000, however, that clearly define the economic position of the city's households vis-a-vis the region. As Table 6.4 shows, the region has nearly twice the share of these families (23.8 percent) as does the city (12.4 percent).

The lack of residents in the higher-paying occupations (professional, technical, managerial) accounts for the difference (Table 6.5). The majority of the labor force falls into the clerical or operatives categories, while the proportion in professional technical occupations is less than half that in the region. Nearly 40 percent of the labor force is employed in manufacturing, twice the regional figure, whereas only 16 percent is employed in services, about half the regional figure.

POTENTIAL FOR RESIDENTIAL DEVELOPMENT

The residential development potential is determined by regional growth and the city's physical capacity. The first indicates the general form of residential development potential in the region, while the latter suggests bounds on development opportunities in the city.

Of the total buildable land area of 1,932 acres, approximately 617 were vacant in 1970. 416 acres of this vacant land lie in several contiguous parcels that are zoned for residential use.

Housing demand for the region over the period 1970-80 has been estimated at 37,000 additional units.[2] Significant development could be achieved in the city even if only 1 or 2 percent of the growth were captured. While Cohoes does not enjoy a particular advantage in accessibility, significant capital improvement in the city makes construction more advantageous to developers. An ongoing water and sewer project, for example, enables potential developers to enjoy considerable reductions in construction costs.

ECONOMIC BASE

Cohoes accounts for a small percentage of regional commerce and has not participated in the region's economic growth. Figure 6.2 shows the trend of commercial activity in real dollars. Between 1954

FIGURE 6.2

Sales Volume, Cohoes, New York
(corrected to 1957-59 dollars)

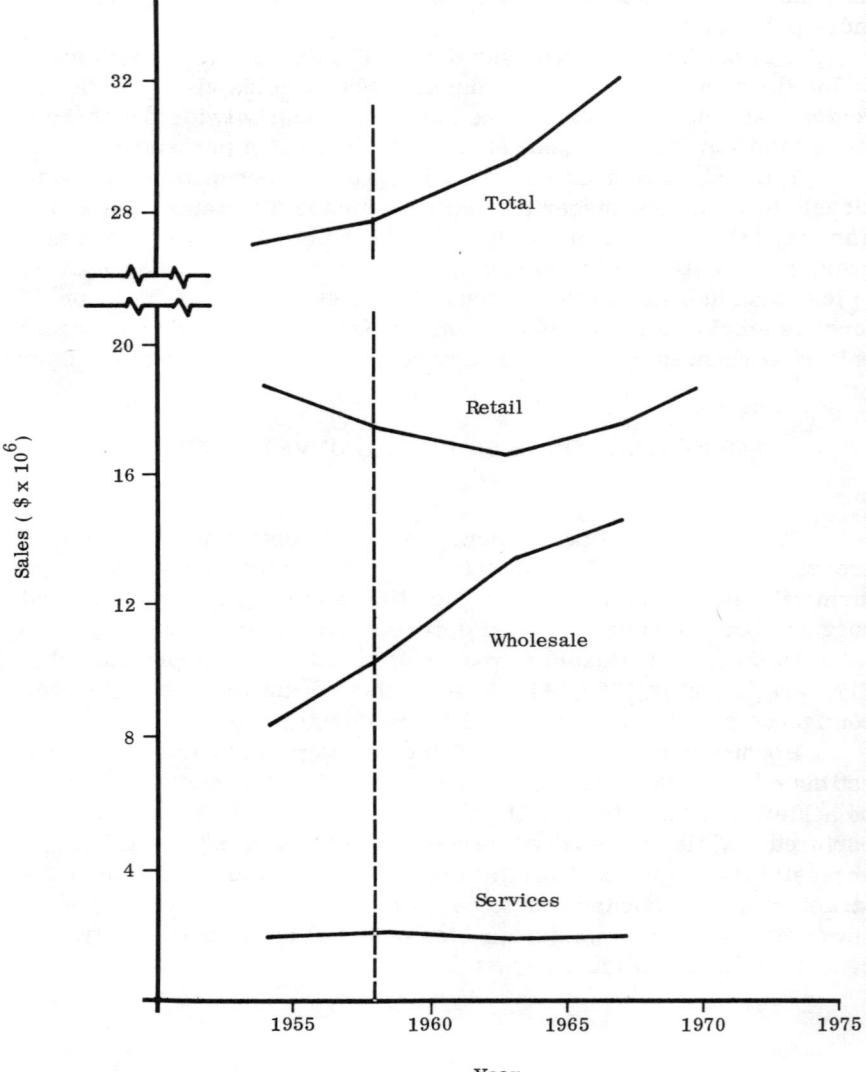

Source: Cohoes Planning and Development Agency, Economic and Marketing Study (1972), p. 11.

AN APPLICATION OF THE MODEL

and 1967, the number of retail establishments dropped from 257 to 184. Thus, while the real sales volume was virtually unchanged between 1954 and 1967, it is fair to presume that what occurred over the period was a consolidation, with the survivors faring better at the end of the period. Approximately 60 percent of the retail demand in the city originates from outside Cohoes, and it is estimated that over 50 percent of the consumption of local residents is from outside sources.[3]

The number of wholesale establishments remained constant over the period 1954-67 (20 establishments), while the real volume showed steady increase. The regional growth, however, was larger.

Value added in manufacture grew by about 20 percent over the period 1954-67, and the payroll of manufacturers exhibited both actual and real dollar growth (44 percent and 28 percent, respectively). During the period the total employment in manufacturing decreased while the man-hours of production increased. This change resulted in higher weekly earnings, with a disproportionate amount of the increase being received by nonproduction personnel.

There is strong interaction between the city and the region in terms of location of place of employment. Sixty-five percent of the city's labor force is employed elsewhere in the region, while 40 percent of the employment opportunity existing within the city is filled from the rest of the region. Thus, while the occupational characteristics of the residents are in the clerical and operative categories (Table 6.5), fairly high mobility with regard to place of employment makes it reasonable to assume that industrial development within the city will attract other skills if they are not available in the city.

COST-REVENUE ANALYSIS OF THREE PROJECTS

Description of the Projects

Three residential projects are currently in various phases of construction. A conventional cost-revenue analysis of the projects was performed by the city's planning staff.[4] The analysis was based on detailed project descriptions (all three projects were under way at the time the analysis was conducted) and included only appropriate marginal increases in service costs for the city. What follows is a summary of the results.

Project A

This development consists of 115 units of single-family unattached housing units on a 30-acre site in the north end of the city. The homes will sell for between $26,500 and $29,500. Assessment for the purpose of municipal and school taxes will be between $5,500 and $6,000 per unit.

It is estimated that 410 persons, with an annual aggregate income of $1,288,000, will occupy these dwellings. The additional school loadings are presented below.

	All Pupils	Public School
Kindergarten	9	7
Elementary school	53	40
Middle school	25	19
High school	28	20
Totals	115	86

The increases in municipal services attributable to Project A are $13,860 per annum, while the anticipated property tax revenue is $41,126. An immediate profit of $27,473 per annum is projected. With the addition of increases in state aid and sales tax revenue, the eventual difference between increased revenues and increased expenditures is about $53,000 per year.

The net variable educational expenditures attributable to the development are $37,840, while the anticipated increase in revenue to the school district is $47,190. After including such additional revenue as the utility tax, the analysis shows the marginal revenue exceeding the marginal education costs by about $10,090.

Project B

This development consists of 110 single-family unattached dwellings on a 37-acre site. The homes will sell for about $30,000, and assessment is assumed to be $6,000 per unit.

It is estimated that 392 persons, with an annual aggregate income of $1,320,000, will occupy these dwellings. The additional school loadings are as follows:

	All Pupils	Public School
Kindergarten	9	7
Elementary school	51	39
Middle school	24	18
High school	26	19
Totals	110	83

AN APPLICATION OF THE MODEL

The increase in municipal services attributable to Project B is $20,020 per annum, while the anticipated property tax revenue from the development is $41,129. The service costs are higher than for Project A, even though Project B consists of fewer dwellings, because the latter has a larger lot size and incorporates nearly one-half mile more in street lengths than Project A. The immediate difference between additional revenue and additional cost is $20,946 yearly. After including state aid and other additional revenues, an eventual difference of $46,000 is projected between marginal revenues and marginal costs.

The marginal increases in educational expenditures are estimated at $36,520 per annum. Revenues from the property tax are expected to be $47,100, which, when added to other additional revenues, shows the difference between marginal revenues and marginal education costs to be $11,400 annually.

Project C

Project C is a garden apartment development consisting of 180 one-bedroom and 60 two-bedroom apartments on an 18.6-acre site. The total development will consist of 240 units with monthly rents between $155 and $175. While assessments had not been set at the time of the analysis, an estimate of between $1,100 and $1,300 was used.

It was projected that Project C would house 390 persons with an aggregate annual income of $2,277,000. School loading resulting from this development are

	All Pupils	Public School
Kindergarten	7	5
Elementary school	22	16
Total	29	21

The increase in annual municipal service cost as the result of Project C is $10,470, and the expected tax revenue is $18,760. After including additional revenues, the difference between revenues and expenditures is about $33,000.

The marginal increase in education expenditure is $9,240. The expected tax revenue for the school district is $20,550. The difference between marginal revenues and marginal costs is estimated at $13,240.

Municipal Cost-Revenue Summary

This section summarizes the results of the planning staff report. Table 6.6 presents residential characteristics for the three development

TABLE 6.6

Summary of Projected Residential Characteristics

Project	Population	Total Annual Household Income	Increase in Annual Sales Volume
A	410	$1,288,000	$250,000
B	392	$1,320,000	$260,000
C	390	$2,277,000	$450,000
Total	1,192	$4,885,000	$910,000

Source: Compiled by the authors.

TABLE 6.7

Increase in Municipal Property Tax Revenue

Project	Number of Units	Assessment per Unit	Total Assessed Valuation	Projected Exemptions	City Tax Revenue
A	115	$5,750	$661,250	$29,900	$ 41,126
B	110	$6,000	$660,000	$28,600	$ 41,129
C	240	$1,200	$288,000	—	$ 18,760
Total per annum city property tax revenue					$101,015

Source: Compiled by the authors.

TABLE 6.8

Total Additional Municipal Revenue

Project	Property Tax Revenue*	Additional State Aid	Additional Sales Tax Revenue	Total Additional Revenue
A	$ 40,833	$15,060	$12,370	$ 68,263
B	$ 40,966	$14,350	$11,820	$ 67,136
C	$ 18,613	$14,380	$11,760	$ 44,753
Total	$100,412	$43,790	$35,950	$180,152

*Includes revenue lost from present tax on vacant parcels.
Source: Compiled by the authors.

TABLE 6.9

Additional Municipal Service Costs by Function

Function	Additional Cost (in dollars)
Public safety	12,520
Waste collection	8,540
Maintenance of streets	6,490
Street cleaning	1,780
Street lighting	5,700
Snow removal	8,820
Total	43,850

Source: Compiled by the authors.

projects. Tables 6.7 and 6.8 show the increases in municipal revenue, and Table 6.9 gives the increased expenditures by type of service.

Additional unitemized expenditure increases are added to the service cost in Table 6.9 to arrive at a total service cost of $50,000 per annum. The difference between the total additional revenue (Table 6.8) and the total additional service costs is approximately $130,000 "profit" for the city annually. This difference, broken down by project, is

Project A	$53,000
Project B	$46,000
Project C	$33,000
Total	$132,000

A slight discrepancy occurs due to rounding.

School District Summary

This section summarizes the results of the staff report with regard to education. The student loadings are given in Table 6.10, while Tables 6.11 and 6.12 give the additional costs and revenues.

TABLE 6.10

Additional Pupil Loading, by Project
(total students/public school students)

Grade Level	Project A	Project B	Project C	Total
Kindergarten	9/7	9/7	7/5	25/19
Elementary school	53/40	51/39	22/16	126/95
Middle school	25/19	24/18	—	49/37
High school	28/20	26/19	—	54/39
Total	115/86	110/83	29/21	254/190

Source: Compiled by the authors.

TABLE 6.11

Additional Educational Costs, by Project

Development	Additional Costs (in dollars)
Project A	37,840
Project B	36,520
Project C	9,240
Total	83,600

Source: Compiled by the authors.

TABLE 6.12

School District Additional Revenue Summary
(in dollars)

	Project			Total
	A	B	C	Development
Property tax revenue	47,190	47,100	20,550	114,845
Revenue replaced	310	180	160	650
Utility tax revenue	1,150	1,000	2,090	4,140
Total additional revenue	47,930	47,920	22,480	118,330

Source: Compiled by the authors.

The aggregate difference between additional revenues for education (Table 6.12) and additional costs (Table 6.11) is $34,730. This difference can be presented, by development, as follows:

Project A	$10,090
Project B	$11,400
Project C	$13,240
Total	$34,730

The following section compares the results of the cost-revenue analysis discussed thus far with output of CODIM.

A COMPARISON WITH RESULTS OF CODIM

Using the three development projects evaluated by the planning agency staff as input, the results of the Community Development Impacts Model were compared with the results of the staff cost-revenue analysis. Project A, which consists of moderately priced single-family homes, was input as 115 units of "MOD"; Project B was input as 110 "HIGH" units; and Project C as 240 "APT" units.

In order to obtain results in a format comparable with the staff report, a base run of CODIM was made first. In this run no development is input (Exhibit 6.1).* The next three exhibits (Exhibits 6.2, 6.3, and 6.4) are the analyses of the individual projects. The marginal values associated with each project can be determined by subtracting the appropriate value in the output from the appropriate value in the base run. For instance, the additional municipal service costs for Project A are $51,000, determined by subtracting the municipal appropriation of the base run ($2,824,000) from the municipal appropriations under Project A ($2,875,000). For some items, the marginal values are presented in the output and no subtraction is necessary. Some examples are "new tax base" and "new population."

Table 6.13 presents a summary of the various indicators from CODIM and the staff report. The values are presented by project, and totals for all three projects. With some exceptions, the totals for each indicator equal the sum of the values for each project. The exceptions are "Additional Municipal Costs," which are not linear with increases in city size, and "Additional Education Costs," which cannot be added

---

*Exhibit 6.1 shows an input of one apartment unit because if the input consists of all zeros, the program goes to a "zero action" mode and output is not comparable.

EXHIBIT 6.1

Base Run

```
     INPUT NO. HIGH, MOD, & APTS?  0   0   1
     PRINT RESIDENTIAL DEV. DETAILS? (YES-NO;1-0)?0


     PRINT INCOME DISTRIBUTION? (YES-NO; 1-0)?0


TOT. INCOME ($M) -  55.467
NO. OF FAM. -  6561.
AVG. FAM. INC.-   8454.


     PRINT SOCIO-ECO. DATA? (YES-NO;1-0)?1

     SOCIO-ECO. CHARACTERISTICS
                         DWELLING TYPE
                    HIGH    MODERATE   APTS      'OLD'
NO. OF HOUSEHLDS     0          0        1       6560
POPULATION           0.         0.       2.     18000.
HOUSEHOLD INCOME     0.         0.   14234.      8453.

NEW POPULATION          2.
TOTAL POPULATION    18002.
PUB. SCHOOL PUPILS   2373
TOT. H'SHOLD INCOME  55.467($ MIL.)
AVG. H'SHOLD INCOME  8454.
RETAIL SALES($MIL.)  28.742

     PRINT AGE DISTRIBUTION? (YES-NO;1-0)?0


   MUNICIPAL FISCAL DATA($ MIL.)
NEW TAXBASE    -    0.001
TOT. TAXBASE   -   18.301
SCHOOL TAXBASE-    19.601
FULL VALUE         55.300
STAUTOTRY DEBT LIMIT -   3.871

PROP. TAX RATE-    $67.09
SCHOOL TAX RATE    $54.59


MUN. APPROPRIATION-    2.600
FIXED REVENUES    -    1.339
SALES TAX REDIST. -    0.712

SCHOOL APPROP.    -    3.400
STATE AID RATE(ED.)   68.531%
LOCAL SHARE       -    1.070

MUN. APPROP./CAPITA  $156.90
STATE AID(MUN.)   -    0.627
NO. OF PUPILS     -    2373
```

EXHIBIT 6.2

Project A

```
INPUT NO. HIGH, MOD, & APTS?    0    115    0

PRINT RESIDENTIAL DEV. DETAILS? (YES-NO;1-0)?0

PRINT INCOME DISTRIBUTION? (YES-NO; 1-0)?0


TOT. INCOME ($M) -  56.964
NO. OF FAM. -  6675.
AVG. FAM. INC.-   8534.


PRINT SOCIO-ECO. DATA? (YES-NO;1-0)?1

SOCIO-ECO. CHARACTERISTICS
                         DWELLING TYPE
                  HIGH    MODERATE   APTS     'OLD'
NO. OF HOUSEHLDS    0        115       0       6560
POPULATION          0.       409.      0.     18000.
HOUSEHOLD INCOME    0.     13221.      0.      8453.

NEW POPULATION       409.
TOTAL POPULATION   18409.
PUB. SCHOOL PUPILS  2459
TOT. H'SHOLD INCOME  56.964($ MIL.)
AVG. H'SHOLD INCOME  8534.
RETAIL SALES($MIL.)  28.996

PRINT AGE DISTRIBUTION? (YES-NO;1-0)?0


   MUNICIPAL FISCAL DATA($ MIL.)
NEW TAXBASE    -    0.660
TOT. TAXBASE   -   19.460
SCHOOL TAXBASE-    20.260
FULL VALUE         58.514
STAUTOTRY DEBT LIMIT -   4.096

PROP. TAX RATE-    $64.03
SCHOOL TAX RATE    $54.60


MUN. APPROPRIATION-   2.614
FIXED REVENUES    -   1.368
SALES TAX REDIST. -   0.728

SCHOOL APPROP.    -   3.443
STATE AID RATE(ED.)  67.867%
LOCAL SHARE       -   1.106

MUN. APPROP./CAPITA  $156.29
STATE AID(MUN.)   -   0.640
NO. OF PUPILS     -   2459
```

EXHIBIT 6.3

Project B

```
INPUT NO. HIGH, MCD, & APTS?  110   0    0
PRINT RESIDENTIAL DEV. DETAILS? (YES-NO;1-0)?0


PRINT INCOME DISTRIBUTION? (YES-NO; 1-0)?0


TOT. INCOME ($M) -  57.387
NO. OF FAM. - 6670.
AVG. FAM. INC.-  8604.


 PRINT SOCIO-ECO. DATA? (YES-NO;1-0)?1

 SOCIO-ECO. CHARACTERISTICS
                        DWELLING TYPE
                 HIGH   MODERATE   APTS     'OLD'
NO. OF HOUSEHLDS  110       0        0      6560
POPULATION        392.      0.       0.    18000.
HOUSEHOLD INCOME 17672.     0.       0.     8453.

NEW POPULATION        392.
TOTAL POPULATION    18392.
PUB. SCHOOL PUPILS   2456
TOT. H'SHOLD INCOME  57.387($ MIL.)
AVG. H'SHOLD INCOME  8604.
RETAIL SALES($MIL.)  29.068

 PRINT AGE DISTRIBUTION? (YES-NO;1-0)?0



 MUNICIPAL FISCAL DATA($ MIL.)
NEW TAXBASE   -   0.660
TOT. TAXBASE  -  19.460
SCHOOL TAXBASE-  20.260
FULL VALUE       58.594
STAUTOTRY DEBT LIMIT -  4.102

PROP. TAX RATE-   $64.43
SCHOOL TAX RATE   $54.68


MUN. APPROPRIATION-   2.620
FIXED REVENUES    -   1.366
SALES TAX REDIST. -   0.727

SCHOOL APPROP.    -   3.438
STATE AID RATE(ED.)  67.784%
LOCAL SHARE       -   1.108

MUN. APPROP./CAPITA  $156.31
STATE AID(MUN.)   -   0.639
NO. OF PUPILS     -   2456
```

EXHIBIT 6.4

Project C

```
     INPUT NO. HIGH, MOD, & APTS?  0   0    240


     PRINT RESIDENTIAL DEV. DETAILS? (YES-NO;1-0)?0

     PRINT INCOME DISTRIBUTION? (YES-NO; 1-0)?0


 TOT. INCOME ($M) -  58.329
 NO. OF FAM. -  6800.
 AVG. FAM. INC.-   8578.


     PRINT SOCIO-ECO. DATA? (YES-NO;1-0)?1

     SOCIO-ECO. CHARACTERISTICS
                            DWELLING TYPE
                   HIGH    MODERATE   APTS     'OLD'
 NO. OF HOUSEHLDS    0         0       240      6560
 POPULATION          0.        0.      389.    18000.
 HOUSEHOLD INCOME    0.        0.     11986.    8453.

 NEW POPULATION         389.
 TOTAL POPULATION     18389.
 PUB. SCHOOL PUPILS    2394
 TOT. H'SHOLD INCOME  58.329($ MIL.)
 AVG. H'SHOLD INCOME   8578.
 RETAIL SALES($MIL.)  29.228

     PRINT AGE DISTRIBUTION? (YES-NO;1-0)?0


  MUNICIPAL FISCAL DATA($ MIL.)
 NEW TAXBASE    -   0.288
 TOT. TAXBASE   -  19.088
 SCHOOL TAXBASE-   19.888
 FULL VALUE        56.734
 STAUTOTRY DEBT LIMIT -   3.971

 PROP. TAX RATE-    $65.13
 SCHOOL TAX RATE    $54.71


 MUN. APPROPRIATION-   2.610
 FIXED REVENUES    -   1.367
 SALES TAX REDIST. -   0.727

 SCHOOL APPROP.    -   3.400
 STATE AID RATE(ED.)  67.999%
 LOCAL SHARE       -   1.088

 MUN. APPROP./CAPITA $156.32
 STATE AID(MUN.)   -   0.640
 NO. OF PUPILS     -   2394
```

EXHIBIT 6.5

All Projects

```
INPUT NO. HIGH, MOD, & APTS?  110   115   240


PRINT RESIDENTIAL DEV. DETAILS? (YES-NO;1-0)?0

PRINT INCOME DISTRIBUTION? (YES-NO; 1-0)?0


TOT. INCOME ($M) - 61.771
NO. OF FAM.  -  7025.
AVG. FAM. INC.- 8793.


  PRINT SOCIO-ECO. DATA? (YES-NO;1-0)?1

  SOCIO-ECO. CHARACTERISTICS
                         DWELLING TYPE
                  HIGH    MODERATE   APTS    'OLD'
NO. OF HOUSEHLDS    110       115     240     6560
POPULATION          392.      409.    389.   18000.
HOUSEHOLD INCOME  17672.    13221.  11986.    8453.

NEW POPULATION        1190.
TOTAL POPULATION     19190.
PUB. SCHOOL PUPILS    2563
TOT. H'SHOLD INCOME  61.771($ MIL.)
AVG. H'SHOLD INCOME  8793.
RETAIL SALES($MIL.)  29.814

  PRINT AGE DISTRIBUTION? (YES-NO;1-0)?0



   MUNICIPAL FISCAL DATA($ MIL.)
NEW TAXBASE      -   1.608
TOT. TAXBASE     -  20.408
SCHOOL TAXBASE-     21.208
FULL VALUE          63.254
STAUTOTRY DEBT LIMIT -   4.428

PROP. TAX RATE-    $59.78
SCHOOL TAX RATE    $56.39


MUN. APPROPRIATION-    2.645
FIXED REVENUES    -    1.424
SALES TAX REDIST. -    0.759

SCHOOL APPROP.    -    3.588
STATE AID RATE(ED.)   66.673%
LOCAL SHARE       -    1.196

MUN. APPROP./CAPITA  $155.12
STATE AID(MUN.)   -    0.666
NO. OF PUPILS     -    2563
```

145

TABLE 6.13

Summary of CODIM Output and Staff Report

	Staff Report	CODIM
Additional population		
Project A	410	409
Project B	392	392
Project C	390	389
Total	1,192	1,190
Additional retail sales		
Project A	$250,000	$254,000
Project B	260,000	326,000
Project C	450,000	486,000
Total	$910,000	$1,066,000
Additional assessed value		
Project A	$661,250	$660,000
Project B	660,000	660,000
Project C	288,000	288,000
Total	$1,609,250	$1,608,000
Additional municipal costs		
Project A	$13,860	$14,000
Project B	20,020	20,000
Project C	10,470	10,000
Total	$44,350[a]	($44,000)
		($45,000)[b]
Additional municipal revenue		
Project A	$68,263	
Project B	67,136	not applicable
Project C	44,753	
Total	$180,152	

New pupils		
Project A		86
Project B		83
Project C		21
Total		190
Additional education costs		
Project A	$37,840	$36,000
Project B	36,520	38,000
Project C	9,240	18,000
Total	$83,600	($92,000)
		$126,000[b]
Additional school district revenue		
Project A	$47,930	
Project B	47,920	not applicable
Project C	22,480	
Total	$118,330	
Municipal revenues less municipal costs		
Project A	$53,000	$59,550
Project B	46,000	51,760
Project C	33,000	37,410
"Unitemized expenses"[a]	6,150	
Total	$138,150	($148,720)
		$149,180[b]
Education revenues less education costs		
Project A	$10,090	$ -2,000
Project B	11,400	-18,000
Project C	13,240	-22,400
Total	$34,730	($-42,400)
		$-38,200[b]

---

[a] $6,150 in "unitemized expenses" is added in the staff report, for a grand total of $50,000.
[b] Column sum different due to nonlinearity of expenditure or revenue. The actual value is based on output for all three projects.

because of the effects of the state aid formula. Therefore, the totals for the last two items of the table are also not equal to the sum of the individual projects. For these four items, the totals must be determined from a run that evaluates the impact of all three projects. Exhibit 6.5 shows the output from such a run.

Additional municipal revenue and additional school district revenue cannot be directly determined from CODIM because, in the staff cost-revenue analysis, the additions in tax levy are determined by multiplying the new tax base by the existing tax rate. Other revenues, such as state aid, are then added in. CODIM, on the other hand, computes the state aid and other nonproperty taxes based on formulas, and then determines the tax rate necessary to balance the budget. While a marginal revenue figure can be obtained from the CODIM output, it would not be comparable with the staff analysis because of the change in the tax rate. The CODIM marginal revenue can, however, be computed from the difference in the total tax levy between the base run and the particular project. The tax levy is found by multiplying the tax rate by the tax base. The difference in fixed revenues must then be added to provide the total marginal revenue.

Since marginal revenue computations from CODIM are not comparable with the staff analysis, the "revenues less costs" (the last two items in the CODIM column) are determined by taking the difference in the tax rates between the base run and the run for each project. This difference is then multiplied by the tax base for the particular project, as described above. Although the product cannot be interpreted as the difference between revenues and costs, it does indicate a measure of dollars saved (or lost) by the municipal residents as a result of development of a particular project.

DISCUSSION OF RESULTS AND RECOMMENDATIONS

On the whole, there is good agreement between the CODIM output and the planning staff report. The differences that exist are due to variations in methodology or assumptions. The discrepancies are discussed above.

CODIM considers income differences between households occupying moderate homes and those in higher-priced homes. The differentiation is not as great in the staff analysis; hence, the income difference between Project A and Project B is not as great. In addition, CODIM uses higher household income figures than does the staff report. Similar spending rates are used by CODIM and the staff analysis. The differences in total sales, therefore, are due to the higher aggregate income computed by CODIM, while the differences in individual projects are caused by greater computational precision in CODIM.

AN APPLICATION OF THE MODEL

CODIM employs per-pupil average costs that include variable cost and fixed costs. In the staff report, average fixed costs are eliminated from the analysis. On the other hand, the staff analysis employs the existing state aid rate, while CODIM performs a more accurate computation that reflects the increased wealth per pupil caused by the developments. These factors serve to explain the difference in the results. The staff report more than likely understates the increases in costs, especially for Project C, because no consideration is given to the added real property wealth in determining the state aid rate.

As for the total effect of all three projects on the education budget, the CODIM output is more representative since it is not possible, because of the nonlinearities introduced by the aid formula, simply to add the costs for all three projects to determine the total result.

As discussed above, the CODIM results for municipal revenues less municipal costs are not actually the difference between revenues and costs, but a saving or loss to the municipal resident. Nonetheless, the figures in the two columns are perfectly compatible. The revenues less costs computed by CODIM are greater than those derived in the manual analysis, even though the additional municipal costs are quite similar. Thus fixed revenue calculations employed in CODIM result in a higher return to the municipality than the computations employed in the staff analysis. Additional sales tax revenue, for example, is determined to be $35,590 by the staff (Table 6.8), while CODIM computes an addition of $47,000. The larger figure results when additional retail sales and additional population are included in the computations. In toto, CODIM and the cost-revenue report compare well. The discrepancy in this item reduces to a difference of approximately $0.50/$1,000 in the tax rate, which ultimately is the significant decision criterion.

The significance of the CODIM values for education revenues less education costs is the same as in municipal revenues less municipal costs. Because of the different techniques used for estimating costs and state aid in the two analyses, the values for the individual projects are different. However, the CODIM total (a loss of $38,200) is more representative than the profit of $34,730 projected in the staff report. As discussed under additional education costs, the state aid rate, when all three projects are considered, is different from the rate resulting from the development of any individual project. The aid rate in Exhibit 6.5 is 66.7 percent, while the rates for the individual projects are 67.9, 67.8, and 68.0 percent, respectively. The overall rate affects the contribution of each of the projects, and the total cannot be obtained through a simple summation of the individual values. Since the total school budget is on the order of $3.5 million, a 1 percent difference in the aid rate is significant.

CONCLUSIONS

This chapter has discussed the application of the CODIM model to analysis of the impacts of three specific development projects in the city of Cohoes. In order to evaluate the construct, its results were compared with a cost-revenue analysis performed manually. The comparison is favorable, and differences can be attributed to variations in approach and assumptions.

The staff analysis is based on much the same data as CODIM. This lends credibility to the CODIM constructs, since there is general agreement between the two analyses. For some of the items discussed, the automated calculations carried out in CODIM are more precise than the manual computations.

For the purpose for which it was designed, the CODIM model provides satisfactory results and meets the criteria established at the beginning of the chapter. As shown throughout this chapter, the model is easily implemented and the output is useful, readily understandable, and provides greater flexibility due to rapid turnaround. Project C has been modified since preparation of the planning staff report. In addition, the selling price of homes in the other two projects has risen for units now being completed. CODIM can provide a reevaluation quickly with only minor changes in data.

Finally, CODIM helps focus the analysis and demonstrates relationships. It is not obvious, for example, that the state aid rate for education is such that individual project contributions cannot be added to find the overall result, or that the addition of new real estate significantly affects the wealth-per-pupil portion of the formula. As shown in the previous section, however, the difference is one between a profit of $34,730 and a loss of $38,200. The capability of the model to focus and demonstrate relationships, coupled with its straightforward application, interactive design, and rapid turnaround, makes it an ideal tool to assist the community in goal formulation. This application is discussed next.

NOTES

1. Cohoes Planning and Development Agency, <u>Fiscal Impact of Equinox Estates, National Homes and Columbia Gardens on the City of Cohoes</u> (1972); and <u>Impact Analysis of Equinox Estates, National Homes and Columbia Gardens on the Cohoes Public School District</u> (1972).

2. Capital District Regional Planning Commission, Housing (Albany, N.Y., 1970).

3. Cohoes Planning and Development Agency, Economic and Marketing Study (1972), p. 13.

4. Ibid. This section draws freely from the reports.

CHAPTER

7

COMMUNITY DEVELOPMENT PLANNING: NORMATIVE APPROACHES

CODIM, presented in Chapter 5, has the capability to respond rapidly to inquiries regarding the impact of various development strategies. As such, it can demonstrate the relationships between the socioeconomic, fiscal, and demographic characteristics of the municipality under different development alternatives. This capability enhances the user's understanding of the trade-offs that must be made among competing desirable end states for the community and, therefore, assists policy-makers in exploring the consequences and implications of development.

Local officials and the community itself may have difficulty in expressing community goals explicitly, much less defining them quantitatively. CODIM helps the user develop a feel for the impacts of development, thereby leading to a better understanding of what the desirable goals might be, including their quantitative value and relative importance. Although it is not possible to explicitly determine the community welfare function, CODIM focuses the issues and parameters that must be considered in deriving a set of goals.

Community development goals consist of measurable end states that describe the condition of the community. Included are desired physical (land use), demographic, socioeconomic, and fiscal characteristics. Once these have been explicitly defined, the problem is to search for a development strategy that will satisfy the goals. CODIM can be used to search for such a policy. The user can "muddle through," successively inputting development strategies until he finds one whose measurable characteristics satisfy the explicitly stated goals. However, in employing CODIM in this fashion, two problems arise.

NORMATIVE APPROACHES 153

First, there is no guarantee that a policy satisfying the goals exists; or, if one does exist, there is no guarantee the user can find it. In either of these cases, the user is forced to satisfice by settling for a strategy that comes close without knowing that he has, in some sense, optimized the attainment of his goals.

Second, CODIM (or any model) does not include all the attributes of urban life that an individual or group would use in deciding on the best development strategy. Examples of attributes not considered are pollution, traffic congestion, and aesthetics. Therefore, the user may find a strategy that is optimal (satisfies the goals) but is not desirable. A desirable policy, therefore, is defined as one that the user feels satisfies factors or attributes, such as political considerations, which are not included in the model. If the user finds an optimal strategy that is not desirable, he would like to search for an alternative optimum that is more desirable. This condition introduces the difficulties previously discussed.

As Charles Lindblom has noted, an individual chooses a policy to attain certain objectives and simultaneously chooses the objectives themselves.[1] In other words, the means by which end states are achieved are as important as the end states themselves. One will, therefore, not settle for an unacceptable policy, even if it results in desired objectives but, rather, will modify the policy. In our case, the policy is the chosen development strategy and the objectives are the indicators produced by CODIM as well as other attributes of the municipality not included in the model.

CODIM permits an interactive evaluation of policies but in no way guarantees optimality. However, it does identify desirable strategies, and the indicators produced can serve as preliminary objectives. The next iteration would entail optimizing the attainment of given objectives within the framework of a desirable policy. Since CODIM does not permit this operation directly, there is a need for a normative approach.

Lindblom's "muddling through" has been criticized because it is not purposeful: there may be no end or convergence to the search. This could well occur with the use of CODIM. Nonetheless, CODIM serves as a link between "muddling through" and the political realities. It presents the implications of alternatives and focuses relationships. An approach that employs a descriptive model such as CODIM in conjunction with normative models may well lead to purposeful incrementalism in the planning process. One could define "purposeful incrementalism" as "muddling through," but with an end guaranteed.

This chapter proposes a framework for analysis of community development strategies that is based upon multiple-objective optimization. Utility theory foundations are briefly described and the concept of efficiency is rigorously presented. An argument is made that in formulating community development policies, a descriptive approach must be used in conjunction with a prescriptive model. Finally, several techniques for multiple-objective optimization are outlined.

UTILITY THEORY AND THE ATTAINMENT-POSSIBILITY FRONTIER

Utility Theory

Utility theory and its more general analogue, social welfare theory, are based on the assumption that the rational individual can, in some manner, assign priorities to or rank his preferences. Early work in utility theory assumed that individual preferences could be cardinally ranked.[2] This assumption implies that utility or preferences are independent and additive. Thus, the pleasures or benefits derived from consuming, for example, soft drinks and hamburgers are independent and can be combined to determine total utility.*

Later work overcame certain objections to the above definition. For example, a person's utility for tires is at least partially related to his automobile ownership. Likewise, his utility for Iranian caviar is a function of the amount of other foods he consumes. Economists such as Francis Edgeworth and Irving Fisher defined total utility as $U(X_1, X_2, \cdots, X_n)$. In other words, the utility derived from the consumption of a certain bundle of goods is a function of the goods involved.[3]

A second source of criticism of the Marshallian utility concept is its assumption that preference is cardinally measurable. The work of Vilfredo Pareto formed the basis for overcoming this difficulty. Pareto's work does not imply that utility is not cardinally measurable. Its value stems from the fact that it is useful with simple rank ordering of preference, and does not rely on cardinal measurement.

---

*The terms "pleasure" and "benefit" are used loosely, and "utility" actually implies neither; consider the fact that the injection of rabies vaccine has a high utility for a person bitten by a rabid dog.

Let U represent utility and let goods 1, 2, $\cdots$, n be consumed in different quantities, $X_1, X_2, \cdots, X_n$. If $U_i(X_i)$, the amount of utility derived from consumption of X units of the ith good, can be determined, then total utility of consuming an entire bundle of goods is $\Sigma U_i(X_i)$.

NORMATIVE APPROACHES

Depending on the problem, it may or may not be possible to define quantitative scales for preferences or to make cardinal rankings.[4] For example, consider an electronics firm producing television sets at a profit of $100 per set and radios at a profit of $10 per set. To the managers of the firm, a television set is ten times preferable to a radio.

Going one step further, management may be indifferent between ten radios and one television set, preferring the bundle "four televisions + four radios" to the bundle "two televisions + thirteen radios" by a factor of 4/3. In this case it is possible not only to define a quantitative scale along which to measure preference (dollars) but, in addition, assuming constant utility of profit over the range $330 to $440, to rank the bundles of goods cardinally.

Next, consider an administrator of a city faced with several alternative proposals for developing a parcel of land, each of the proposals having a different land-use density. Assuming that density is a negative good, the preference of the chief executive can be expressed as "a lower density is preferred to a higher density." The qualitative concept of density can be transformed to a quantitative scale, such as dwelling units per acre or persons per square mile. Now one is able to say that the policy-maker prefers a plan that results in four units per acre to one resulting in six units per acre. This ordinal ranking, however, cannot be converted to a cardinal ranking unless more is known about such factors as the utility of open space. In this example, a quantitative scale is available for measuring objectives, but only an ordinal ranking can be achieved.

Finally, consider the same administrator desiring to adopt a development plan that has a high quality of life. While a composite index for quality of life could perhaps be derived,[5] no direct measurement scale is available. In this case, even a rank ordering would be difficult to achieve.

Objectives can be employed in a meaningful way only when there are scales along which they can be measured. The CODIM model makes the policy-maker aware of such scales. A multiple-objective optimization can assist in choosing among alternative policies where ranking among objectives is difficult to formalize (as where utilities are not known). As will be discussed later, this is accomplished by presenting the policy maker with alternative efficient solutions.

The Concept of an Attainment-Possibility Frontier

Economic theory defines the production-possibility frontier as the locus of efficient production combinations. (The reader not familiar with the economics of welfare and social choice is referred to Appendix A.) If the marginal rates of substitution (the price ratio) and the indifference map of consumers are known, then each production-possibility frontier can be associated with a single utility-possibility frontier representing an infinite number of Pareto-optimal combinations. If, in addition, the social welfare function is known, a single equilibrium (optimum) point can be found on the utility-possibility frontier. However, Kenneth Arrow has shown that this point cannot be reached through a democratic process. Operationally, analytic results are therefore limited to a prescription that defines all Pareto-optimal points (the utility-possibility frontier).

Utility is difficult to measure. A comparison with dollars suffers from the fundamental problem that money is not of constant utility. Interpersonal comparisons involving utility are likewise difficult to make. Finally, when commodities in question involve socially desirable goods such as quality of life, or open space, or socioeconomic balance in the population, the marginal rate of substitution is unknown.[6] In order to combat these difficulties, an approach is proposed whereby an analogy to the production-possibility frontier is established, permitting policy to be set on an empiric basis.

Let us define an attainment-possibility frontier (APF) as a set of efficient points between two objectives (the maximum that can be achieved for one objective, given any level for a second objective). For example, consider the two presumably desirable objectives facing a municipal policy maker: achieving a low tax rate and minimizing the amount of land devoted to heavy industrial use.

The acreage devoted to industrial land use is plotted along the abscissa, with the highest amount possible at the origin. Now minimize the tax rate for different values of the abscissa and plot the results, using an ordinate scale that ranges from the highest possible tax at the origin to the lowest possible tax.[7] Thus, as one moves along either axis, the preference of the policy-maker rises (tax and industrial land use are reduced). Figure 7.1 shows a hypothetical APF for property taxes and industrial land. Confronted with such a locus of efficient points, the policy-maker resorts to his preferences, his notions regarding the utilities (nonadditive) and the marginal rates of substitution of the objectives, and defines a point along the curve at which he chooses to operate.

By presenting the policy-maker with a variety of such two-dimensional APF's, a set of n-dimensional efficient points can be determined. The problem of transitivity is not addressed, nor is the need to deal with n-tuples in more than two dimensions. Although the validity of the approach has not been determined, the construction of APF's is proposed as a way of dealing with utility comparisons for

NORMATIVE APPROACHES

FIGURE 7.1

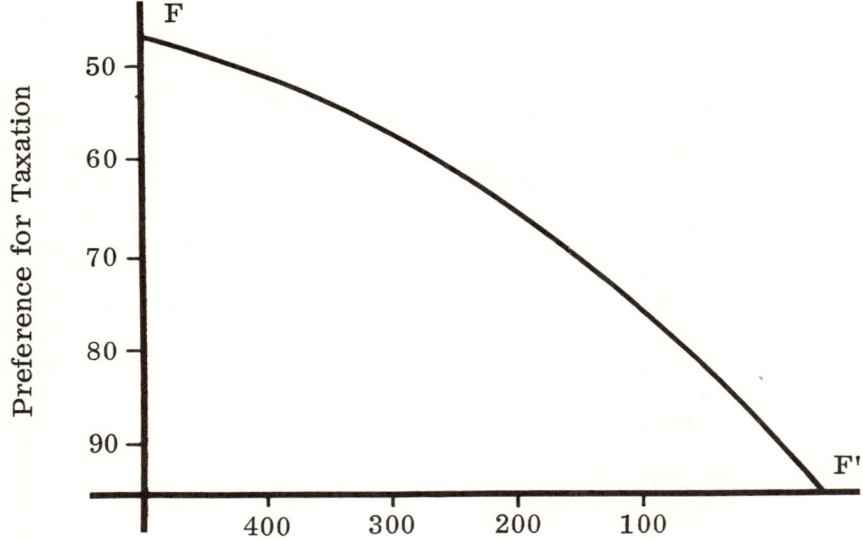

Attainment-Possibility Frontier

dissimilar objectives by focusing and directing the decision-making process.

EFFICIENCY: A MATHEMATICAL APPROACH

One of the earliest works on efficiency is that by T. C. Koopmans, in which economic activity (input-output) is used to develop theorems and definitions regarding "efficient" combinations of inputs in the production process.[8] Koopmans defines an efficient production point as follows:

> A possible point in the commodity space (A) is called efficient whenever an increase in one of its coordinates (the net output of one good) can be achieved only at the cost of a decrease in some other coordinate (the net output of another good).[9]

This can be expressed mathematically thus: A point y in the commodity space is called efficient if

1) it is possible (that is, if y is in (A))
2) there exists no other possible point y' in (A) such that
$$y' - y \geq 0$$

While this definition does state that a point cannot be more efficient than another (if a > b, then only a is efficient), it is not operationally useful for the purposes of multiple-objective or vector optimization. A. Charnes and W. W. Cooper provide a definition that is based on Koopmans' activity analysis and deals more directly with the vector properties of the multiple-objective problem.[10]

Consider a set of vectors that is ordered. Any set $n_1, n_2, \cdots, n_k$ is said to be ordered (or orderable) if relations of the form $n_i \leq n_j$ can be established. It is said to be only partially ordered unless the relation can be established for every i,j pair (i ≠ j), in which case it is said to be completely ordered.

A vector Y_i is said to be <u>efficient</u> if there is no other vector Y_j with the property

$$Y_j \geq Y_i, \quad Y_j \neq Y_i \tag{1}$$

That is, no component of Y_j is less than the corresponding component of Y_i, and at least one component of Y_j exceeds its counterpart in Y_i. The twin conditions of (1) define what Charnes and Cooper call K-efficiency.[11] Some authors term it the vector maximum.[12]

Multiple Objectives

Having recognized that any multiple-objective programming problem is a vector-maximization problem, we can now turn our attention to defining an efficient point in terms of separate objectives. As will be seen, the definition comes directly from the development of efficiency given above. Consider the problem

$$\begin{aligned} \text{max:} \quad & y = ax \\ \text{max:} \quad & z = bx \end{aligned} \tag{2}$$

subject to
$$cx \leq d$$
$$x \geq 0$$

NORMATIVE APPROACHES

Denote:
$$y(\bar{x}) = a\bar{x} \qquad z(\bar{x}) = b\bar{x}$$
$$y(x_i) = ax_i \qquad z(x_i) = bx_i$$

$\bar{x}$ is an efficient solution if there exists no other feasible point x_i such that

$$y(x_i) > y(\bar{x}) \quad \text{and} \quad z(x_i) \geq z(\bar{x})$$
$$z(x_i) > z(\bar{x}) \quad \text{and} \quad y(x_i) \geq y(\bar{x}).$$

By simple inspection, it will be noted that any point, x^*, that is an optimal solution to either of the objectives in (2) will also be an efficient point. This will be discussed further below.

Geometric Representation of Efficiency

Consider a multiple objective problem having the general form

$$\text{min:} \quad a_1 x \tag{3}$$
$$\text{min:} \quad a_2 y$$

subject to

$$C_1 x + C_2 y \leq B$$
$$x; y; a_1; a_2; \geq 0$$

where uppercase denotes a matrix.

A graphic representation of the constraints is given in Figure 7.2.

The illustration shows that only the points connected by the line segment $P_4 P_5$ are properly efficient,[13] since any improvement for one objective can be obtained only at the expense of the other. For the line segment $P_2 P_3$, y can be decreased without increasing x. For segments such as $P_3 P_4$ and $P_5 P_6$, both x and y can be decreased. The points along $P_1 P_2$ can be termed "locally efficient,"[14] since they are efficient within a small neighborhood. However, by moving away from this segment, it is eventually possible to find properly efficient points. As Charnes and Cooper note, a necessary, but not sufficient, condition is that properly efficient points lie on the boundary of the convex set.[15]

FIGURE 7.2

Illustration of Efficient Points

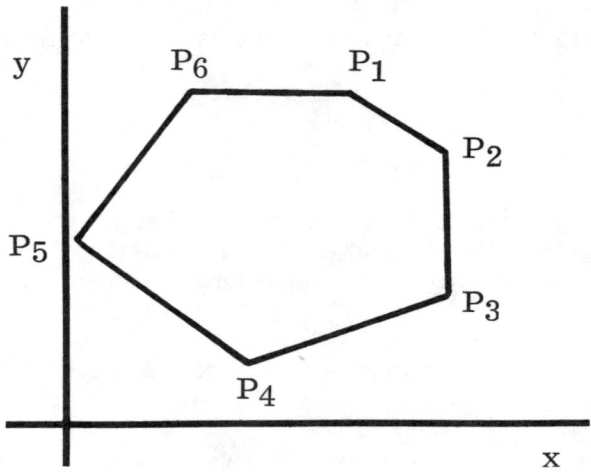

Efficient Points: Computational Assets

It was noted above that any x^* that is a unique optimal solution to either of the objectives of problem (2) is also an efficient point. The reason is that the two objectives

$$\text{max: } y = ax$$
$$\text{max: } z = bx$$

can be rewritten as a single function

$$\text{max: } (a + b)x$$

In general, consider the multiple objective problem

$$\text{min: } f(x) = \{f_1(x), \cdots, f_n(x)\} \qquad (4)$$

subject to: x in the convex set X.

This vector minimum problem is, in effect, the problem of finding efficient points x^* such that there will exist no other point x' such that $f_i(x') \geq f_i(x^*)$ and $f_j(x') \neq f_j(x^*)$. As has been noted by several authors,[16] the computationally equivalent problem is

NORMATIVE APPROACHES

min: $\sum_{i=1}^{n} a_i f_i(x)$

(4a)

subject to: x in the convex set X

and where a_i are nonnegative parameters, such that $\sum_{i=1}^{n} a_i = C$.

It is obvious that an x^* that is optimal in (4a) is also efficient. If some other feasible point can be found that reduces one of the objectives by some value, say V, without increasing one or more of the remaining functions by a total value at least as large as V, then x^* would not be an optimal solution to (4) or (4a). Or, put another way, suppose that x^* is not efficient. Then it would be possible to reduce some f_i without hurting any other f_j ($i \neq j$). But if this were the case (x^* not efficient), then x^* would not be optimal in (4a).

Operationally, therefore, the problem of finding efficient solutions reduces to finding all optimal points. This is accomplished by parametrically varying the a_i in (4a) while maintaining the restriction that $a_i > 0$ and

$\sum_i a_i = C$, where C is often taken as 1.

In the linear case, where constraints form a convex set, the above procedure will yield all efficient points.[17] In the nonlinear problem, the procedure is not guaranteed to yield all efficient points unless there is convexity in the objective function as well (concavity in the maximization case).[18]

Some authors use the term "weightings" with respect to the a_i. Without further qualification, this nomenclature is misleading. Suppose $a_j = 4a_k$. This does not imply that the objective associated with a_j ($f_j(x)$) is given four times the weight of $f_k(x)$. Because of numerics in the objective function itself (numbers of different orders of magnitudes), the weights by themselves do not reflect relative importance and should be taken only as parameters that are varied to locate different efficient points. More attention will be given this matter in a later section.

Anomalies in Vector-Maximization Problems

We can now succinctly state the solution to the vector-maximum problem as follows:

If X is a convex set, and f_i is a concave function, then solving the parametric problem

$$\max: \sum_{i=1}^{n} a_i f_i(x) \qquad (5)$$

will yield all properly efficient points if the a_i are varied subject to the conditions $a_i > 0$ and $\Sigma a_i = C$.[19]

However, a situation can arise where x^* is optimal in the problem; but there exists an x such that for some i, $f_i(x) >>> f_i(x^*)$, where $>>>$ denotes "infinitely larger." If, for the same x, we have a concurrent condition $f_j(x) < f_j(x^*)$, then we are in a dilemma as to how to evaluate the point x.[20] It is this case, however, that led Geoffrion to redefine proper efficiency.[21] A point x^* is said to be a properly efficient solution to problem (5) if it is efficient, and if there exists a strictly positive scalar M such that for each i we have

$$\frac{f_i(x) - f_i(x^*)}{f_j(x^*) - f_j(x)} \le M$$

for some j such that $f_j(x) < f_j(x^*)$ whenever x (which is a feasible point) is such that $f_i(x) > f_i(x^*)$. In other words, if, no matter how large we choose M, an x can be found that will make the above ratio still larger, then x^* is not properly efficient.

Consider the example

$$\max: f_1(x) = x^2$$

$$\max: f_2(x) = -x^3$$

subject to: $x \ge 0$.

If we combine the objectives to form the problem max: $x - x^3$, it can be readily seen that $x^* = 0$ is efficient, since any increase, while resulting in an improvement to f_1, also results in a worsening of f_2. But for sufficiently small positive values of x, f_1 can be made arbitrarily large with respect to f_2. The ratio condition above will not be met unless M = infinity, and hence $x^* = 0$ is not a properly efficient point.

The intuitive logic is that if the marginal gain in f_1 can be made arbitrarily (infinitely) large relative to the marginal loss in f_2, and if the decision-maker's desire for the f_1 objective is not fulfilled at x^*, then x^* certainly is not desirable or properly efficient.

A short illustration will serve to further explain the properly efficient point while demonstrating its relative containment for operational purposes. Suppose $f_1(x)$ refers to the (negative of) the tax rate and $f_2(x)$ relates to the amount of industrial land use. By referring to the attainment-possibility frontier (Figure 7.1), it will be noted that an efficient path for tax rate and industrial land use can be defined.

The usefulness of Geoffrion's concept comes into focus if we assume for the moment that there exists an efficient point x^* somewhere on the FF' frontier (perhaps in the neighborhood of either of the two axes) and, further, that there exists a second point x' such that by moving from x^* to x' along the frontier, we can make the marginal improvement to the tax rate objective arbitrarily (infinitely) large compared with the minor decline we must accept in the industrial land-use scale. If the policy-maker's desire to minimize taxes has not been fulfilled at x^*, then such a point should not be considered properly efficient. The possibility of a situation such as the one described seems remote in practice and the implications, therefore, are limited.

Another interesting anomaly is presented by J. P. Evans and R. E. Steuer.[22] As we have seen, from an operational standpoint the vector-optimization problem is solved by optimizing the sum of the various objectives, each of which is multiplied by a parameter (weight) that is varied to find all efficient points. Evans and Steuer note that this procedure is not fail-safe and, in the case of equal weights, can cause some difficulties. Consider the problem

P_1 max: $2x_1$

P_2 max: $-x_1 + x_2$

subject to: $x_2 = 1; x_1 \geq 0$.

We approach this problem in the usual fashion by summing the objective function ($P_1 + P_2$) to solve the resulting linear program, max: $a_1 x_1 + a_2 x_2$ where a_1 and a_2 are each assigned a value of 0.5.

Observe that the equal-weight objective function is unbounded. The original problem has an efficient point at ($x_1 = 0$, $x_2 = 1$), since any change (increase) from $x_1 = 0$ improves P_1 but worsens P_2. The equal-weighting combined objective does not detect this efficient point and, moreover, will fail to detect the entire unbounded efficient path. This problem is the motivation for the authors' presentation of a linear algorithm that is guaranteed to find all efficient points.

Concluding Remarks

With certain minor exceptions, the general method for solving the vector-optimization problem is useful. Conditions that may lead to improper efficiency, as described by Geoffrion, are limited. Likewise, the example presented by Evans and Steuer reflects some rather unusual conditions. In both cases, an increase in the variable produces definite improvement in one objective while resulting in definite reduction of the second. If x has only positive coefficients in the functional, then the chances for the type of difficulty described above seem to be eliminated.

Solving the optimization problem as a set of successive programs (preemptive ordering) instead of summing the objectives nullifies the entire discussion of anomalies, since the objectives are taken one at a time. Computer codes to perform such optimizations are available for the linear case. Under such an approach, the objectives are ranked with respect to priority, then minimized and constrained to their minimum value before the optimization proceeds with successive objectives From a general standpoint, it may not be possible to view the objectives as having preemptive priorities such that one objective must be optimized prior to optimization of a second objective. More importantly, unless one takes the narrow view that simply meeting the objective is the most or best that the policy-maker hopes for (that is, he is not interested in a solution that is better than the one that simply meets his objectives), the preemptive technique does not yield efficient solutions. That is, it may well be possible to find another solution that meets all the goals and actually improves on at least one.[23]

LINEAR PROGRAMMING AND GOAL PROGRAMMING: PRESCRIPTIVE TOOLS FOR COMMUNITY DEVELOPMENT PLANNING

Optimization Versus Simulation

Chapter 5 discussed the application of CODIM as a tool to assist local decision-makers in finding development policies that meet certain objectives. Figure 5.1 showed the iterative process through which this could be accomplished. The policy-makers formulate a certain development strategy, then test it to see whether its characteristics (indicators) are desirable. After a finite number of iterations, the process converges when

- The policy makers have found a strategy that meets all the requirements, one they consider "best": where the term "best" implies that the results are optimal and the policy is desirable

NORMATIVE APPROACHES

- They are unable to find the "best" strategy and instead satisfice, settling for one that is perhaps desirable but not optimal, or optimal but not desirable
- They are able to find a strategy that is neither optimal nor desirable
- They have converged on several policies, but a consensus for any particular policy cannot be achieved.

A prescriptive model can help in any of the four situations. Generally, where goals have been formulated through some process, a multiple-objective optimization model can take the objectives directly and find a policy (or policies) that maximizes their attainment.[24] This feature, as was noted at the beginning of the chapter, differentiates between the descriptive and optimization approach. In the former, the input consists of a proposed policy. In the optimization, the input consists of the proposed objectives. When these are available, the optimization yields a solution with more desirable characteristics without sacrificing the policy-maker's freedom to evaluate both policies and objectives on a case-by-case basis.

For the four cases presented above, an optimizing construct can be of help.

In the first case, although the simulation process has converged on a policy that the users consider best, it is optimal or efficient only in a very narrow sense. Taking the strategy indicators for the final best policy, it may be possible, for example, to find another policy that meets all the criteria and yet has a still lower tax rate. Such a solution would have to be considered an improvement.

In the second case, an optimal strategy may not exist; in any case, the users are unable to find it with an interactive process. If it does not exist, optimization will provide a strategy that is, in some sense, the closest (as opposed to merely satisficing). If an optimal but undesirable policy is found, then a parametrization of the objective function may yield a solution that is equally optimal but more desirable.

If a best strategy exists for the third case, optimization will insure that it is found. If such a strategy does not exist, optimization insures that the solution comes as close as possible.

In the fourth case, assuming that problems of goal decomposition have been minimized as the result of increased awareness that comes from interaction with the simulation, normative modeling may be able to assist. (See Chapter 4 for a discussion of goal decomposition and other problems inherent in goal formulation.) Where several policies are available but no consensus can be reached, the problem may be one of finding a median strategy that is a compromise from the policy-makers' original respective positions. Thus, while the users may have an inherent view of the trade-offs required, they may not have an explicit understanding of the shape of the attainment-possibility frontier. Since an optimization model treats this problem in direct fashion, it may be possible to find an intermediate solution that requires the minimum amount of compromise. Of course, it may be possible to detect a solution that makes everyone better off than they were with their original best simulation results.

In summary, the simulation allows the users to gain insight into the system and to develop a feel for what the objectives might be. Once the objectives are defined, optimization yields a solution with known characteristics in the most direct manner.

Linear Programming, Goal Programming, and Multiple-Objective Programming

Mathematical programming has received considerable attention as a tool for planning, decision-making and evaluation. Although a great deal of research has emerged regarding the form of the problem and solution algorithms (integer programming, quadratic programming, and so on), it appears that not until the publication of Charnes and Cooper's comprehensive work did much effort focus on the form and significance of the objective function. In recent years the overriding importance of the singular functional has been the target of much criticism. Partly as the result of the usual programming emphasis on a unique objective, analysts have perceived problems as having only a single objective—or, if such was clearly not the case, then a single surrogate objective was developed. The usual objective function found in introductory texts deals with maximizing profit. One may reason, however, that a complex corporate organization has many objectives, including market penetration, public image, product diversity, level of sales, and, of course, long-term profitability.

Yuri Ijiri formulates numerous corporate planning and decision-making models as goal-programming models involving multiple objectives.[25] A. Charnes and A. C. Stedry, among others, find little evidence that profitability is the primary objective in planning; rather, it is only part of a set of objectives that includes growth, return on capital, and sales.[26]

The absence of the clear-cut profit motive in the public sector has led to the design of mathematical programs that can only be characterized as "constraint-sets in search of an objective." Charles Laidlaw inadvertently supports this characterization by stating: "An optimum combination of the two housing activity variables can be found with respect to the eleven constraints only by devising an objective function."[27]

P. Lieftinck et al. have formulated a linear program to assist in determining an optimal development of irrigation in West Pakistan.[28] Their model maximizes the net present worth of the total investment, subject to the resource availabilities. J. S. H. Kornbluth terms this "an almost insignificant statistic [since] the underlying objectives of the study were to suggest smooth development programs."[29]

Various linear programs have been used to treat the multiple-objective criterion. James Courtney et al. have employed goal programming to accommodate the locational preferences of college students.[30] Kamal Said presents a goal-programming framework as the basis for a model to assist in the evaluation of objectives and policies.[31] W. A. Wallace and D. Orne employ goal programming to provide an optimal development strategy in the case of new communities.[32] Sang Lee presents a computer code for solving the linear goal-programming problem when the objective function is of the preemptive ordered type.[33]

Laidlaw, while using a uni-objective linear programming formulation, treats additional considerations as satisficing constraints. The satisficing notion may be useful for many purposes, although, as the name implies, general optimality is lost. The policy-maker may state, for example, that he is willing to accept any optimal linear programming solution as long as, say, "the number of apartment units, x, does not exceed N."

Suppose that we minimize the property tax rate, subject to various structural constraints in the problem, and subject also to the constraint that apartment units be no greater than N. Assume the optimal solution is a tax rate of $100 and $x = N$. Curiosity, if nothing else, should lead us to investigate the case

min: t = tax rate

subject to: $x \leq N'$; where $N' \geq N$

Suppose the optimal solution to this problem is a tax rate t = $75, and $x = N'$. By further analyzing the problem with different values for N, it may turn out that the policy-maker's statement was not to be taken as a satisficing statement but actually as a multi-objective minimizing statement; that is

P_1 min: t = tax rate

P_2 min: x = number of apartment units

subject to the structural constraints

There may well be some implicit weighting scheme operating that reflects the policy-maker's decreasing concern for P_2 as x approaches N or is less than N. Although the disutility for apartments may drop rapidly within these bounds, the satisficing constraint hinders the analysis, in that the policy-maker is not given the opportunity to evaluate different points along the t-x frontier to find the one at which he wishes to operate. Goal programming, when formulated with preemptive objectives, leads to the same criticism.

In subsequent sections, four approaches to the multiple-objective community development problem are presented and evaluated: preemptive goal programming, relative-weighted goal programming, goal programming with nonlinear constraints, and multiple-objective programming with a quadratic form in the functional. As a general note, it must be stressed that these approaches yield solutions that are optimal only for the given municipality; and no consideration is given to global welfare maximization. This restriction, which is in keeping with the political realities inherent in the community development process, is discussed in the next section.

Externalities

A frequently noted problem in the application of evaluation methodologies such as cost-benefit analysis is the definition of the benefit stream and the beneficiaries. These difficulties have received wide attention in the literature, and have led some economists to become skeptical of the cost-benefit construct, especially when applied to evaluating public policy.[34]

The cost-revenue impacts concept, as a tool for evaluation, suffers from some of the same methodological shortcomings as cost-benefit. By practical necessity, the domain of analysis must be limited to a jurisdiction or constituency that in reality does not operate in isolation but is economically and socially intertwined with neighboring jurisdictions, the region, and the nation.

Cost-benefit analyses generally attempt to include any incident externalities. In one recent and ambitious undertaking, the flows of benefits and costs between city residents and suburbanites in the greater Washington, D. C., area were quantified and traced, with the objectives of the research being to determine whether a commuter tax on suburbanites working in the District of Columbia was, in fact, equitable.[35] Instead of the traditional methods for measuring costs of providing public services and delineating the direct beneficiaries, the authors propose a method that includes spillovers, and proceed to

NORMATIVE APPROACHES

estimate benefits received by citizens and jurisdictions that are not direct beneficiaries of public programs.

Well-known spillovers resulting from public expenditures in education, highways, and such have already been explored in the literature.[36] In addition, there has been discussion of income-redistribution effects resulting from public programs and projects.[37] The conceptual and methodological difficulties inherent in choosing optimal public policies are thus well documented.

Nonetheless, local policy decisions are made through the political process, in which the local chief executive is held accountable to his constituency only. The cost-revenue impacts analysis therefore is proposed as a method for plan evaluation with the complete recognition that decisions reached as a result of such an analysis do not represent a social optimum optimorum, but are merely best for the jurisdiction included in the domain of analysis.[38]

Indeed, if all local jurisdictions were to use such an evaluation as the basis for decision-making, the results would not be optimal because of the spillovers discussed above. And yet, to some extent, such analysis (applied intuitively) has been performed in many municipalities. In economic development circles, for example, it is a commonly told witticism that cities want industries that require costly investments in plant and equipment, have a high employment density, take little space, produce no smoke or odor, employ highly paid workers, and manufacture a product such that an entire month's production can be carried away in a station wagon. Such local suboptimization has already caused major industrial relocations that may not necessarily increase overall social welfare.

Thus, we are faced with the political reality that local jurisdictions will continue to evaluate decisions on the basis of local optimality considerations, while neglecting the spillover effects of their decisions onto neighboring municipalities.[39] It is quite useless, for example, to attempt to explain the possible dysfunctions (say, from a regional point of view) of a fiscal zoning policy to a local chief executive.

The cost-revenue impacts methodology is therefore proposed as a tool to assist in local plan evaluation. The limitations of this analysis, from the point of social welfare, are fully recognized. To the extent that localities cooperate in regional organizations, externalities will be internalized; and an analysis performed for an entire region may result in more optimal policies. In this respect, the current trend toward regionalism in planning is encouraging.

PREEMPTIVE GOAL PROGRAMMING

As a first approach to development of an optimization model of the community development problem, the CODIM construct was reformulated as a linear goal program for solution, using the code presented by Lee.[40] The goal programming problem can be stated as follows for the general case:

minimize: $Z = P_1(d_1^- + d_1^+) + \cdots + P_n(d_n^- + d_n^+)$

subject to:

(a) $\sum_{i=1}^{q} a_{ij} \cdot x_{ii} \leq B_j; \quad j = 1, \cdots, r$

(b) $c_k(x_1, \cdots, x_q) + d_k^- - d_k^+ = G_k; \quad k = 1, \cdots, n$ (GP)

(c) $x_i, d_k^+, d_k^- \geq 0$

and where the P_i of the objective function are premptively or non-Archimedean-ordered, such that

(d) $P_1 \ggg P_2 \ggg \cdots \ggg P_n$

Constraints such as (a) reflect the structural relations of the problem. These relationships are taken to be fixed over the period of analysis and, therefore, cannot be influenced by management. For example, if $a_{1,1}$ and $a_{2,1}$ represent the acres required per unit of housing for two housing types, and x_1, x_2 are the decision variables (number of units of the two housing types), then a constraint such as represented by (a) can be taken as an acreage limitation where B is the total available land.

Constraints such as (b) may be termed policy constraints in the sense that the G's are goals we wish to approach and the d^-, d^+ represent deviations. Take the constraint

$$cy + d^- - d^+ = g \qquad (1)$$

If $cy > g$, then $d^+ = cy - g$, and $d^- = 0$. Likewise, if $cy < g$, $d^- = g - cy$ and $d^+ = 0$. Therefore, d^+ measures deviations in excess of the stated goal. Because of the linear dependence of d^+ and d^-—cy cannot be both greater than and less than g—only one can appear in the basis at any given simplex iteration.[41] The constraint (1) above, therefore, implies

NORMATIVE APPROACHES

the additional condition $d^- \cdot d^+ = 0$, which, because of the independence properties of the basis, is guaranteed in linear programming.

Consider now the following objective function: min: $z = d^- + d^+$ subject to (1) and the usual nonnegativity requirements. This problem is identical to min: $|cy - g|$, where the vertical bars indicate absolute value.

Let us return to the original problem (GP). The solution is a sequential optimization process in which the P_1 term of the objective function is minimized first; then, constraining this portion of the objective to its minimum value, the P_2 portion is optimized, and so on. The method is as follows:

1. Set $j = 1$.
2. Minimize $Z_j = (d_j^- + d_j^+)$ subject to constraints (a), (b), (c). Let the minimum be Z_j^*, with $(d_j^- + d_j^+) = D_j^*$.
3. Add the constraint $Z_j^* = D_j^*$.
4. If all the goals have not been considered, set $j = j + 1$; otherwise, stop.

The concept of the preemptive ordered objective function implies that a goal of the highest priority must be met as well as possible, before any consideration is given to remaining goals. This eliminates the necessity of assigning relative weights to the goals and merely requires the policy-maker to express ordinal rankings that are strictly followed. Some authors have argued this feature to be an asset of the preemptive goal-programming formulation. However, preemptive ordering is not unlike devising satisficing constraints. In effect, $Z_j = D_j^*$ becomes a constraint when the next ordered goal, Z_{j+1}, is optimized. This brings us to a solution that is not optimal, in the sense that it may not be efficient and the policy-maker is not always given sufficient information to assist in making the proper trade-offs.

This problem was highlighted when the CODIM construct was formulated as a preemptive ordered goal-programming model. The highest-priority goal was taken to be one of meeting some desired tax rate. Subsequent goals involved population, density, retail sales, average family income, employment opportunity, low-income population, and elderly population. In the initial application, any reasonable tax-rate goal could be satisficed. Lower-priority goals would then be met as well as possible, subject to the minimum tax rate.

An objection to this formulation is the overriding importance placed on the first one or two goals, since once they are met, the problem becomes highly constrained (even when the order of the goals is changed). Thus, subsequent goals are not optimized but merely made feasible. Finally, determination of whether a particular solution is efficient can be accomplished only through trial and error.

Toward this end, consider that by parametrically varying the G's in problem (GP), any number of feasible goals can be found, given the additional constraint $Z = 0$. That is, there are numerous values for G_k ($k = 1, n$) in the set G, that can be simultaneously met. It can be shown that in the case of linear goals, this set of G is convex and that the vertices are efficient goals.[42] In searching for the efficient goals, the preemptive order is no longer important.

In view of the difficulties described, the problem was reformulated as a relative-weighted goal program for solution using the IBM MPS (Math Programming System) package. MPS affords greater versatility, in that it permits ranging, provides values of the dual variables, and is computationally more efficient than the code provided by Lee.

NOTES

1. Charles Lindblom, "The Science of Muddling Through," Public Administration Review 19 (Spring 1959), pp. 78-89.

2. See, for example, Alfred Marshall, Principles of Economics (8th ed.; London: Macmillan, 1920), III, Chs. 5-6.

3. For discussion of particular conditions under which additive independent utility functions exist, see Peter C. Fishburn, Utility Theory for Decision Making (New York: John Wiley, 1962); and "Methods of Estimating Additive Utilities," Management Science 13, no. 7 (March 1967): 435-53.

4. For a discussion of measurement and scales, see Russell Ackoff, The Scientific Method (New York: John Wiley, 1962).

5. See, for example, Martin Jones and Michael Flax, The Quality of Life in Metropolitan Washington, D.C. (Washington, D.C.: The Urban Institute, 1970).

6. Some research, based on the assumption of separable and additive utilities, has been done. See James R. Dyer, "Interactive Goal Programming," Management Science 19, no. 1 (September 1972): 62-70.

7. It is only necessary to minimize one variable subject to different values for the other variable. See William J. Baumol, Economic Theory and Operations Analysis (3rd ed.; Englewood Cliffs, N.J.: Prentice-Hall, 1972), p. 527.

8. Tjaling C. Koopmans, Activity Analysis of Production and Allocation, Cowles Commission Monograph no. 13 (New York: John Wiley, 1951), Ch. 3, pp. 33-97.

9. Ibid., p. 60.

10. A. Charnes and W. W. Cooper, Management Models and Industrial Applications of Linear Programming (New York: John Wiley, 1964), I, Ch. 9.

11. Ibid., p. 295.

12. See, for example, Arthur M. Geoffrion, "Proper Efficiency and the Theory of Vector Maximization," Journal of Mathematical Analysis and Applications 22 (1968): 618-30.

13. This term was first used by Kuhn and Tucker. See H. W. Kuhn and A. W. Tucker, Proceedings, Second Berkeley Symposium on Mathematical Statistics and Probability (Berkeley, Calif., 1950), pp. 481-92; and later redefined by Geoffrion, op. cit.

14. Geoffrion, op. cit., p. 621.

15. Charnes and Cooper, op. cit., pp. 295-96.

16. For example, Geoffrion, op. cit., p. 620.

17. Charnes and Cooper, op. cit., p. 306. A more systematic spiral method is presented on p. 308. For another systematic linear algorithm that uses the dual as a check for efficiency, see J. P. Evans and R. E. Steuer, "A Revised Simplex Method for Linear Multiple-Objective Programs," Journal of Mathematical Programming 5 (1973): 54-72. Further discussion of the linear case is in J. Phillip, "Algorithms for the Vector Maximum Problem," Mathematical Programming 2 (1972): 207-29; and B. Roy, "Problems and Methods with Multiple Objective Functions," ibid. 1 (1972): 239-66.

18. Geoffrion, op. cit., p. 621. There are other interesting anomalies in the nonlinear case that will be discussed in the following section.

19. Ibid.

20. A similarly interesting question, involving equal efficiency, is addressed in Charnes and Cooper, op. cit., p. 321.

21. Geoffrion, op. cit., p. 619.

22. Evans and Steuer, op. cit., p. 61.

23. Kornbluth gives some further discussion. J. S. H. Kornbluth, "A Survey of Goal Programming," Omega 1, no. 2 (1973): 193-205.

24. See, for example, Margaret Skutsch and J. L. Schofer, "Goals-Delphis for Urban Planning: Concepts in Their Design," Socio-Economic Planning Science 7 (1973): 305-13. Also see further discussion on goal setting in Chapter 4.

25. Yuri Ijiri, Management Goals and Accounting for Control (Chicago: Rand-McNally, 1965).

26. A. Charnes and A. C. Stedry, "Investigations into the Theory of Multiple-Budgeted Goals," in C. Bonini, R. Jaedicke, and H. Wagner, eds., Management Controls: New Directions in Basic Research (New York: McGraw-Hill, 1964).

27. Charles D. Laidlaw, Linear Programming for Urban Development Plan Evaluation (New York: Praeger, 1972), p. 31.

28. P. Lieftinck, A. R. Sadove, and T. Creyke, Water and Power Resources of West Pakistan, III (Baltimore: Johns Hopkins Press, 1969).

29. Kornbluth, op. cit., p. 197.

30. James Courtney, Theodore Klastorin, and Timothy Ruefli, "A Goal-Programming Approach to Urban-Suburban Location Preferences," Management Science 18, no. 6 (February 1972).

31. Kamal Said, "A Policy Selection/Goal-Formulation Model for Public Systems," Policy Sciences 55 (1974): 89-100.

32. W. A. Wallace and D. Orne, "Alternative Mathematical Programming Approaches to New Town Planning," in M. Whithed and R. M. Sarly, eds., Urban Simulation: Models for Policy Analysis (Leiden: A. W. Sijthoff, 1974).

33. Sang M. Lee, Goal Programming for Decision Analysis (Philadelphia: Auerbach, 1972), Ch. 6.

34. Robert Dorfman, ed., Measuring Benefits of Government Investments (Washington, D.C.: The Brookings Institution, 1965), p. 2; also see Samuel B. Chase, ed., Problems in Public Expenditure Analysis (Washington, D.C.: The Brookings Institution, 1968), pp. 219-21.

35. Kenneth Greene, Lillian Neenan, and Claudia Scott, Fiscal Interactions in a Metropolitan Area (Washington, D.C.: The Urban Institute, 1974).

36. See, for example, Burton A. Weisbrod, "Preventing High School Dropouts," in Dorfman, op. cit., esp. pp. 134-35; Herbert Mohring, "Urban Highway Investment," ibid., pp. 231-67; Wilbur R. Thompson, "Internal and External Factors in the Development of Urban Economics," in H. Perloff and L. Wingo, Jr., eds., Issues in Urban Economics (Baltimore: Johns Hopkins Press, 1968), pp. 43-62; N. Litchfield and J. Margolis, "Benefit-Cost Analysis as a Tool in Urban Government Decision-Making," in Howard Schaller, ed., Public Expenditure Decisions in the Urban Community (Baltimore: Johns Hopkins Press, 1963), pp. 118-46; Raymond Vernon, Metropolis 1985 (Cambridge, Mass.: Harvard University Press, 1960), Ch. 5, pp. 68-85.

37. See, for example, Burton A. Weisbrod, "Income Redistribution Effects and Benefit-Cost Analysis," in Chase, op. cit., pp. 177-222; Dick Netzer, Economics of the Property Tax (Washington, D.C.: The Brookings Institution, 1966), esp. Ch. 3.

38. Even within the jurisdiction, there are distinct client groups that are affected differently by any given project. See P. Schaenman and T. Muller, Measuring Impacts of Land Development (Washington, D.C.: The Urban Institute, 1974), p. 29.

39. Ibid., pp. 3, 26.

40. Lee, op. cit., pp. 126-57.

41. Charnes and Cooper, op. cit., p. 219.

42. Some techniques for finding G are given in Phillip, op. cit.; Roy, op. cit.; R. Benayoun et al., "Linear Programming with Multiple Objective Functions: Step Method," Mathematical Programming 1 (1972): 336-75.

CHAPTER 8

A LINEAR GOAL FORMULATION AND SOME INHERENT DIFFICULTIES

As discussed in Chapter 7, a preemptive ordered model is considered unsatisfactory for studying the community development problem. The construct was therefore reformulated as a goal program with relative (non-Archimedean) weights. This problem can be stated as follows:

$$\text{minimize: } Z = \sum_{k=1}^{n} P_k(d_k^- + d_k^+)$$

subject to: structural constraints

$$\sum_{i=1}^{q} a_{j,i} x_i \le B_j ; \qquad j = 1, r$$

policy constraints:

$$\sum_{i=1}^{q} g_{k,i} x_i + (d_k^- - d_k^+) = G_k ; \quad k = 1, n$$

$$x_i, d_k^-, d_k^+ \ge 0$$

The structural constraints fall into four areas, and are taken directly from the CODIM construct. First, there are physical constraints that express relationships dealing with land requirements, housing demand, and industrial acreage. Second, demographic constraints relate the characteristics of the population to the housing and include average family income, and age and income distributions. Job opportunity and retail consumption are treated by the economic

LINEAR GOAL FORMULATION

constraints. Finally, the fiscal constraints relate land development to the municipal and educational services required. The nature of the relationships and appropriate data sources were discussed in detail in Chapter 5.

Structural constraints represent those characteristics of the community that are unaffected by decisions or policies instituted by city management. They are, therefore, concerned with those characteristics that can be considered constant for the period being analyzed. The structural constraints thus represent "natural" (physical) relationships among variables. They are assumed to hold over the planning period and, further, are independent of policy decisions made by municipal management.

Policy constraints, on the other hand, are concerned with decision variables that can be affected and manipulated through management decisions. Thus, while the total available vacant land, for instance, and the density of various types of dwellings are related through structural constraints, the amount of development and the proportion of different dwelling types to be encouraged are clearly policy-oriented relationships.

Policy constraints take the form

$$aX + d^- - d^+ = B$$

where
 X is the decision variable
 d^- is the underachievement deviation from the goal level
 d^+ is the overachievement deviation from the goal level
 B is the desired goal level.

Both d^- and d^+ are minimized by the objective function, the result being that aX is made as close as possible to B. From the formulation, and by definition, it is clear that $d^- \cdot d^+ = 0$.

The model was run using the IBM MPS package. The program consists of 8 policy constraints and 36 structural constraints. As is discussed in the following section, results from this linear goal program are correct only when all goals have been met. Otherwise, the formulation is incorrect because of nonlinearities.

THE HIDDEN NONLINEARITY IN GOAL PROGRAMMING

The linear model presented suffers from a hidden nonlinearity. Once discovered, the case seems quite obvious. Nonetheless, the literature contains several examples where such nonlinearities occur and go unrecognized.[1]

In formulating policy constraints, we are often faced with a conceptual statement of the type "make X as close as possible to one-half of T." For example, the policy-maker may want "the number of apartment units with one bedroom (X) as close as possible to one-half of the total number of apartments (T)." This statement leads directly to the constraint

$$X - .5T + d^- - d^+ = 0 \qquad (a)$$

where the deviational variables (d^-, d^+) are to be minimized in the objective. The constraint seems appropriate, for as the deviationals become smaller, X moves close to "one-half of T." As was shown in an earlier section, where both deviationals are minimized by the objective, the constraint (a) is identical to the statement

$$\text{Min: } Z = |X - .5T| \qquad (A)$$

where the vertical bars indicate absolute value. Now consider problem (A) subject to the constraint:

$$X \leq .45\ T$$

As depicted by the diagram, the problem reduces to minimizing the vertical distance between the two lines, $X = .5T$ and $X = .45T$.

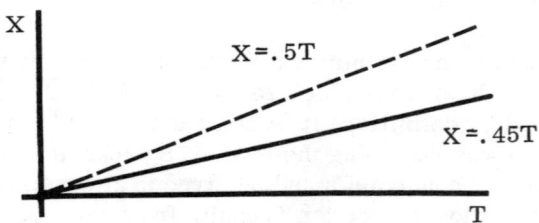

The policy-maker is indifferent anywhere along the constraint $X = .45T$, since that is as close as he can get to making "the number of one-bedroom apartments equal to one-half the total number of apartments." As can be seen from the diagram, the solution to the absolute-value minimization (A) is $X = T = 0$, implying that for optimality, there should be no apartments and no one-bedroom apartments!

The discrepancy arises, of course, because the policy-maker's constraint statement must be interpreted as

$$\text{Min } Z' = |X/T - .5| \neq \text{Min } |X - .5T|.$$

The absolute value on the left-hand side has the goal programming equivalent

$$X/T - .5 + d^- - d^+ = 0 \qquad \text{(b)}$$

where both deviationals are minimized in the objective. When multiplied through in the usual fashion, the constraint (b) yields the nonlinear terms Td^-, Td^+. Linearity is achieved only when the goal is precisely met (that is, $d^- = d^+ = 0$). J. S. H. Kornbluth suggests a method for solution in the case involving preemptive goals.[2]

When a constraint such as (a) (which measures absolute distance) is used with the intent to minimize a proportion (constraint b), the following statements are offered without proof:
1. If the constraints are such that the goal can be precisely met ($X = .5T$; $d^- = d^+ = 0$), the formulation (a) will permit the correct optimum to be found although there is an alternative optimum at $X = T = d^- = d^+ = 0$.
2. In the neighborhood of the goal, or whenever the deviational is very small compared with T, the solution is reliable (since, in effect, d^- and d^+ have been minimized).
3. If the constraints (or the objective) are such that a feasible solution does not come close to the goal, then the result is in no way optimal. Under this situation, at least one of the variables will be set to zero, or its lower bound.

These statements can be summarized as follows:
1. If the constraints are such that $\min |X/T - .5| < \min |X - .5T|$, then a proper solution can be reached.
2. If the problem is such that $\min |X/T - .5| > \min |X - .5T|$, it is the second value that will be minimized. This will usually result in $X = T = 0$, or the lowest bound.
3. If $\min |X/T - .5| = \min |X - .5T|$, then there exist at least two alternative optima.

An improper formulation of the type (a) (which actually represents a nonlinear problem) can be useful in the case of a satisficing model, since if the deviationals are minimized to zero, the nonlinear case becomes linear. However, all that can be said about a particular goal is that it has been achieved or not achieved. In the case of the former, the statement can be made with certainty. If the goal is not achieved, however, there is no guarantee that it could not have been met.

In a formulation of this type, the value of the deviational is actually the value Td. For cases where it seems that the solution lies near the desired goal, it is usually best to make an actual check of the ratio X/T, or calculate the value of d. In light of this discussion, some of the results of the linear goal-programming formulation are presented in the following section.

RESULTS OF THE LINEAR GOAL-PROGRAMMING MODEL

The linear formulation contains nonlinearities in the policy constraints that involve ratio goals, such as residential density, tax rate, and average family income. The results are presented below and will be compared with optimal solutions found by using a nonlinear model (Chapter 9). As will be shown, where goals are met or almost met, the linear formulation is reliable. In general, if the decision variables are set to zero or their lower bound in the optimal solution (such as $X = T = 0$), the formulation is suspect.

In this application, the goals were set as follows:

$(+)G_t^*$ = desired tax rate for municipal + school taxes = varied

$(+)G_d^*$ = desired residential density (units/acre) = 6

$(+)G_p^*$ = desired population goal = 20,000

$(-)G_s^*$ = desired retail sales volume ($) = 32,000,000

$(+)G_e^*$ = desired industrial employment level = 0

$(-)G_y^*$ = desired average family income ($) = 8,735

$(+)G_1^*$ = percent low-income population = 27.6

$(+)G_0^*$ = percent elderly households = 26

These initial values are no worse than the existing levels in the test city. In certain cases, the desired values represent a modest improvement over the present situation. The goals were minimized only on one side (only one of the deviationals was entered in the functional). The sign preceding the goal indicates the deviational that was minimized. Thus, for tax rate, only deviations above the goal (d^+) are entered in the objective function. This reflects the decision-maker's lack of concern regarding a tax rate that is below some desired value.

For the first run, G_t^* was set to $130/$1,000.* The optimal solution with all relative weights in the objective set of unity is

---

*In the formulation, school taxes and municipal taxes are handled by two separate constraints. The values used are $60 for the property tax and $70 for the school tax.

$U_1 = 122$; $U_2 = 93$; $U_3 = 288$; $U_4 = 117$ acres.

Next, the municipal tax rate goal was reduced to $55 and the desired school tax to $66.55, for a combined total of $121.50. All goals were met with the solution

$U_1 = 230$; $U_2 = 154$; $U_3 = 476$; $U_4 = 193$ acres.

The negative deviational associated with school tax shows that the actual rate is approximately 20 cents less than the goal, thus indicating that some further improvement is possible. Through trial and error,* the following run was obtained:

Property tax goal = $53/$1,000

School tax goal = $66/$1,000

$U_1 = 202$; $U_2 = 154$; $U_3 = 476$; $U_4 = 193$ acres.

Now all goals except the tax rates are met. The deviational associated with the school tax indicates that the actual value for that rate is approximately $0.35 above the goal, or $66.35. Also, the deviational associated with the property tax indicates that this goal has been exceeded by about $2.49, thus making the actual total tax rate $121.49, with no further improvement possible.

Although the tax rate cannot be reduced any further, additional improvement may be possible in the remaining objectives. By making additional runs, a complete set of efficient goals could be obtained. Such a procedure is cumbersome, and therefore a program that yields efficient solutions directly is presented in the next chapter. This formulation is nonlinear and, as we shall see, the solution obtained is identical to the solution given by the linear formulation, even though

---

*The tax rate goal cannot be set arbitrarily low in the hopes of minimizing taxation because of the hidden nonlinearity discussed earlier. The property tax rate can be expressed as e/T where e is the net municipal expenditure and T is the tax base. The policy constraint for taxation is $e - G_t \cdot T \pm d = 0$. If G_t is chosen such that, subject to the constraints, $\min |e/T - G_t| > \min |e - G_t \cdot T|$, then a proper optimal solution can be reached. However, if G_t is chosen such that $\min |e/T - G_t| > \min |e - G_t \cdot T|$, then, since e is a linear function of T, the right-hand absolute value will be minimized by setting e and T to zero, or their lowest constrained value. For example, in the initial application, a value of G_t that is below about $50 will cause the formulation to give "incorrect" results by setting $U_1 = U_2 = U_3 = U_4 = 0$.

the deviationals in the linear case are not zero. This demonstrates the fact that in the neighborhood of the goal, the "incorrect" linear formulation is reliable.

INTERPRETATION OF THE DUAL

Before presenting a nonlinear formulation for finding efficient solutions, the dual variable and its significance will be discussed. This discussion encompasses both the linear and the nonlinear case. As will be shown, the nonlinear dual variable is not easily derived. An alternative procedure for developing the information provided by this dual is, therefore, offered. This procedure employs the attainment-possibility frontier concept introduced in Chapter 7.

A distinct advantage of a linear formulation is the direct availability of the dual variable. In a linear problem, the value of the dual is given by the final simplex tableau, and computer L.P. codes generally provide this value as part of the output. In the nonlinear problem, the dual can be obtained by solving the Wolfe form of the dual.[3] M. L. Balinsky demonstrates a useful simplification of that form by using slack variables as an approximation of the first-order partials in the dual objective function.[4]

The nonlinear dual program has most of the properties of the linear dual. Some of the well-known relationships, however, must be amended in the nonlinear case.[5] For example, in a linear primal-dual pair of programs, there exists an optimal solution to one problem only if there exists an optimal solution to the other. This property does not always hold in the nonlinear case.

The dual variable is usually interpreted as the marginal improvement to the objective that can be achieved, given a unit increase in some resource (usually the right-hand side of a constraint). W. J. Baumol offers the definition that the dual variable (V_i) is normally equal to the marginal profit contribution of input i

$$V_i = \partial P / \partial C_i$$

where P is the profit function and C_i is the total capacity of input i.[6] Even in the linear case, discontinuities can occur that prevent such a precise marginal-value interpretation. These limitations have been thoroughly investigated by A. C. Williams.[7]

In the nonlinear case, V_i cannot always be interpreted as the marginal profit yield of the ith input, since the latter is not always defined.[8] However, it can be shown that V_i lies between corresponding right- and left-hand partials that exist and are finite. If, for a value

LINEAR GOAL FORMULATION

of C_i, the partial exists and is finite, then and only then is the precise marginal value interpretation applicable.[9]

In goal programming, the duals associated with policy constraints have limited value. Although Courtney et al. state that "a wealth of information is available . . . through the study of dual variables,"[10] the dual takes on only limited and predictable values and tells us little that the formulation itself does not reveal. Consider the following goal program:

$$\min: Z = d^+ + d^-$$

$$\text{subject to: } X + d^- - d^+ = K$$

$$bX \leq B$$

$$X, d^-, d^+ \geq 0$$

where X is the decision variable, K is the desired goal, and the d^-, d^+ are deviationals.

If the optimum solution is such that X is above the goal (such as $X > K$, $d^+ > 0$, $d^- = 0$), then the value of the dual variable is 1. That is, since there are no basic changes involved, for every unit increase in K, the objective will be improved (reduced) by 1. Likewise, if the optimal solution is such that X lies below K, then the value of the dual is -1, reflecting that for each unit increase in the right-hand side, the objective will be made worse (increased) by 1. If the goal is precisely met, the dual will lie between -1 and 1 (usually 0). Kamal Said lists the possible values of the dual, depending on which deviational is in the objective.[11] The authors' experience with the linear goal program confirms Said's findings.

While the policy-related duals are of limited value and offer little in the way of interpretive meaning, the duals associated with the structural constraints have the usual shadow price significance. In the results presented in the next section, the dual variable associated with the availability of industrial land, for example, has a consistent and useful interpretation. In the final run discussed, the value of this variable is $3.97 million. Recall that all goals are met except for the tax rate, which can be expressed as the following policy constraint:

$$e - G_t \cdot T + d^- - d^+ = 0$$

where e is net municipal expenditure, and where d^+ is included in the objective. The minimum value of the objective is $105.86 million total net expenditure.

Because of the hidden nonlinearity, a value for d^+ is actually the value of $d^+ \cdot T$. The optimum value of T (the tax base) is $42.5 million, making the tax rate deviation $d_t = d^+/T = \$2.49$, as discussed in the preceding section.

The value of the dual variable associated with the availability of industrial land (\$3.97 million) indicates that for each additional acre available, the tax rate can be reduced by $3.97/42.5 = \$0.093$.[*] In other words, the shadow price (in terms of taxes) associated with not allocating more land to industrial activity is approximately \$0.09 per acre. In Chapter 9 it is shown that when the problem is analyzed using the taxation-industrial land attainment-possibility frontier, the same result is given.

CONCLUSION

Several of the policy constraints in the linear formulation presented have hidden nonlinearities and, therefore, the model can only serve the role of a satisficing optimization. That is, it can be used to distinguish when the goal has been achieved and when it has not. As such, satisficing formulations of the type shown by Charles Laidlaw can be handled more effectively, without concerns for infeasibility when L.P. satisficing constraints cannot be met.[12]

Attempts at reformulating the linear model or using any one of a number of solution techniques failed. Consider the constraint

$$\frac{f_1(x) + C_1}{f_2(x) + C_2} + d^- - d^+ = 0 \qquad (1)$$

where f_1 and f_2 are linear functions of x_i, $i = 1, \cdots, 4$, C are known positive constants and d^+, d^- are the usual deviationals. The goal-programming formulation contains several policy constraints of this type. Set the denominator of the first term in (1) to u. Cross-multiplication yields the nonlinear term $u \cdot d^-$ and $u \cdot d^+$. By the method of Hadley, a nonlinear term of this type can be transformed into the separable term $y_1^2 - y_2^2$, with the addition of two more constraints.[13] A term such as $y_i^2 - y_j^2$ can be treated in standard linear programming through piecewise approximation.[14] This technique was not readily applicable in the problem, because several transformations and piecewise approximations would be necessary.

---

[*]The objective function, and hence the dual, is related to total net expenditure. In order to compute the shadow price on tax rate, the dual value must be divided by the tax base.

Harvey Wagner suggests the method of fractional programming when a ratio such as (1) is found in the objective.[15] The transformations involved are more complex and, because there are several fractions to deal with, may make the problem difficult to manage. A. Charnes and W. W. Cooper have shown that a problem involving a linear fractional objective can be solved by solving two related programs.[16] The difficulties associated with the method of Wagner apply. Therefore, given the nature of the problem and the constraints, a complete nonlinear formulation is more direct than attempts at linearization. A nonlinear model is presented in Chapter 9.

NOTES

1. For example, Sang M. Lee and Edward Clayton, "Goal-Programming Model for Academic Resource Allocation," Management Science 18, no. 8 (April 1972): 395-408; J. Forsyth, "Utilization of Goal Programming in Production and Capital Expenditure Planning," CORS Journal 7, no. 2 (July 1969): 136-40; R. Schroeder, "Resource Planning in University Management by Goal-Programming," Operations Research 22, no. 4 (July/August 1974): 700-09.

2. J. S. H. Kornbluth, "A Survey of Goal Programming," Omega 1, no. 2 (1973): 193-205.

3. Phillip Wolfe, "A Duality Theorem for Non-Linear Programming," Quarterly of Applied Mathematics 19 (1961): 239-44.

4. M. L. Balinsky and W. J. Baumol, "The Dual in Non-Linear Programming and Its Economic Interpretation," Review of Economic Studies 30 (July 1968): 237-56.

5. Ibid., pp. 240-41.

6. W. J. Baumol, Economic Theory and Operations Analysis (3rd ed.; Englewood Cliffs, N.J.: Prentice-Hall, 1972), pp. 112-13.

7. A. C. Williams, "Marginal Values in Linear Programming," Journal of the Society for Industrial and Applied Mathematics 11 (1963): 82-94.

8. Balinsky and Baumol, op. cit., pp. 242-43.

9. Ibid.

10. James Courtney et al., "A Goal-Programming Approach to Urban-Suburban Location Preferences," Management Science 18, no. 6 (February 1972): 265.

11. Kamal E. Said, "A Policy Selection/Goal-Formulation Model for Public Systems," Policy Sciences 55 (1974): 95.

12. Charles D. Laidlaw, Linear Programming for Urban Development Plan Evaluation (New York: Praeger, 1972), Ch. 4.

13. G. Hadley, Non-Linear and Dynamic Programming (Reading, Mass.: Addison-Wesley, 1964), p. 119.

14. See, for example, ibid., p. 105.

15. Harvey M. Wagner, Principles of Operations Research (Englewood Cliffs, N.J.: Prentice-Hall, 1969), p. 559.

16. A. Charnes and W. W. Cooper, "Programming with Linear Fractional Functionals," Naval Research Log Quarterly 9 (1962): 181-86.

CHAPTER 9

GOAL PROGRAMMING AND MULTIPLE-OBJECTIVE OPTIMIZATION: NONLINEAR FORMULATIONS

The linear optimization model discussed in Chapter 8 is not suitable for optimizing fractional objectives. In order to study the community development problem, it is essential that a capability exist for proper representation of such objectives. Numerous relationships occurring in the study of urban social phenomena involve criteria that are rates or ratios. Most demographic data, for example, are expressed in terms of proportions. Average family income, residential density, and age distribution of a population are expressed as a ratio of two other quantities. In industrial applications, considerations such as return on investment, margin on sales, market penetration, and possibly corporate growth are likewise expressed as fractional relationships.

Taken as ordinary linear constraints, the criteria above cause no special problems, since they can all be linearized directly. Thus, in a satisficing model, any of the above criteria can be constrained by an upper "good enough" bound and a lower "not too bad" restriction.

Taken as policy constraints, however, in which minimization of any deviation is desirable, such ratios can be handled only under certain circumstances. Where the criteria are to be taken as objectives, methods of fractional programming exist that enable transformations when both the numerator and the denominator are of a certain linear form. When several ratios are to be optimized, as in the case of a multiple-objective problem, the transformations become cumbersome.

Therefore, optimization of multiple criteria that reflect social, economic, or business applications will, more often than not, necessitate the use of nonlinear forms unless a satisfying model is acceptable. While there is often resistance on the part of the analyst (commercial computer codes do not abound), nonlinear programming does not involve particular difficulties in cases where the constraint set is convex and the functional is not unreasonable.

Two nonlinear formulations of the community development model were investigated. The first is simply a nonlinear extension of the goal-program presented at the beginning of Chapter 8. The form of the functional (such as to minimize the deviationals) is unchanged, but the nonlinear policy constraints are now properly expressed in fractional form. The second formulation has an objective of the form

$$\min: \sum a_i (f_i(x) - G_i)^2$$

where a_i are the weights or parameters, x is the decision variable, and G_i are the desired attainment levels or goals. As will be shown, this formulation, while losing the property of being able to distinguish between overachievement and underachievement of the goal, is more versatile, convenient, and computationally powerful, in that it possesses a definite known minimum.

METHODS OF NONLINEAR PROGRAMMING

Numerous methods of nonlinear programming exist.[1] Where the constraint set (in addition to the objective) is nonlinear, the method of gradient projection is well suited.[2] In this technique the search proceeds along the gradient (the vector of steepest descent) of the objective until that gradient is zero, so that optimality has been achieved. Where a projection along the gradient falls outside the constraint set, a projection back into the set is made.

W. L. Kephart and J. R. Copper propose some improvements in the gradient search by obtaining a history of the response surface.[3] This enhances the search by enabling the computer code to enlarge the step size where progress toward optimality on a smooth surface is too slow, or to reduce the step size where an optimum point may have been overstepped. Kenneth Cross incorporates additional capabilities into the gradient search routine to enable a consideration of both linear and nonlinear, equality and inequality, constraints.[4]

At this point it may be well to restate the two important theorems regarding efficient solutions, and to introduce the extensions necessary for the nonlinear case. A detailed discussion has been given in Chapter 7.

Consider the multiple objective problem

$$\min: f_1(x); f_2(x); \cdots; f_p(x)$$
subject to: x in the feasible set X   (P)

and the computationally related problem

$$\min: \sum_{i=1}^{p} a_i f_i(x) \tag{Pa}$$

subject to: x in the feasible set X
$a_i > 0 \quad (i = 1, \cdots, p)$

Theorem 1: Let a_i be fixed. If x^* is optimal in (Pa), then x^* is a properly efficient solution of (P).

Theorem 2: Let X be a convex set, and let the f_i be convex (concave) on X. Then x^* is properly efficient in (P) if and only if x^* is optimal in (Pa).*

From a computational viewpoint, therefore, finding efficient solutions to the multiple-objective problem is the equivalent of solving the problem (Pa) parametrically as the a_i take on different values, with $\Sigma a_i = C$. This procedure yields only efficient points (Theorem 1). If the objective function and the constraints are convex, then the procedure insures that all efficient points can potentially be found (Theorem 2).

In the two problem formulations that follow, convexity holds either in the functional (goal-programming form) or in the set (quadratic form), but not in both. In either case, the functional is well-behaved, possessing definite minima. A rigorous examination of the objective is given in Appendix B. The computer algorithm used proves to have no difficulty, even though nonconvexity exists.

A NONLINEAR GOAL-PROGRAMMING FORMULATION

In this application, the goal-program presented in Chapter 8 was reformulated to give proper consideration to nonlinear policy constraints such as the tax rate, average family income, and proportion of low-income families. The following variables were used:

x_1 = number of residential units of type 1 (4-bedroom, single family)
x_2 = number of residential units of type 2 (3-bedroom, single family)
x_3 = number of residential units of type 3 (apartments)
x_4 = number of acres devoted to industrial land use
x_5 = number of acres devoted to residential use = $f(x_1, x_2, x_3)$

---

*Thus, x^* can be efficient without being optimal. Recall that in the multiple objective problem max: x^2; max: $-x^3$, the point $x = 0$ is efficient but not optimal when the objective is summed with nonzero weights.

x_6 = total number of households = $g(x_1, x_2, x_3)$
x_7 = total residential income = $h(x_1, x_2, x_3)$
x_8 through x_{19} = deviational variables associated with the policy constraints.

The constraints take the form*

(a) Structural constraints

$$\sum_{i=1}^{4} b_{ji} x_i \le B_j ; \qquad j = 1, \cdots, 4$$

$$x_k - \sum_{i=1}^{4} b_{ki} x_i = 0 ; \qquad k = 5, 6, 7$$

(b) Policy constraints

$$\frac{\sum_{i=1}^{4} b_{n,i} x_i}{\sum_{i=1}^{4} c_{n,i} x_i} + x_m - x_{m+1} = G_n ; \qquad \begin{array}{l} m = 8, 10, 12, \cdots, 18 \\ n = 8, \cdots, 13 \\ b_n \ne c_n \end{array}$$

Several trial runs with this formulation revealed that it was incomplete. In Chapter 7 it was shown that the properties of the basis (in the simplex method) insure that a condition where both deviationals are positive is impossible. In the nonlinear case, these conditions do not hold and, hence, each policy constraint requires the additional restriction that the product of the deviationals be equal to zero. In the model above, this leads to the additional restrictions:

(c) Constraints on the deviationals

$$x_m \cdot x_{m+1} = 0 ; \qquad m = 8, 10, 12, \cdots, 18$$

If there were any doubts regarding nonconvexity of the set prior to the introduction of restrictions (c), there should be no question now. A constraint of this type introduces a pair of planes extending at right angles. This obviously is not convex.

---

*Three intermediate variables x_5, x_6, x_7 are computed. This simplifies manipulation of the computer program, since partial derivatives must be supplied by the user.

Where both deviationals appear in the functional (that is, both positive and negative deviations from the goal are to be minimized), the constraint set (c) is redundant. Since the deviationals are linearly dependent ($-d^- = d^+$), the minimum of their sum is achieved only if at least one deviational is set to zero.

The functional consists of the appropriate deviational (all goals are such that deviations on only one side are minimized) and the tax rate.

$$\min: Z = a_1 t + \sum_{p=8}^{13} a_p x_m ; \qquad m = 8, 10, 12, \cdots, 18$$

where t is the tax rate

$$\frac{f_1(x_i) + K_1}{f_2(x_i) + K_2} ; \qquad i = 1, 4$$

The fact that the tax rate is minimized, as opposed to being made as close as possible to some goal, is the only conceptual difference between this formulation and the linear model. This change was introduced because it was felt that the policy maker is always interested in minimizing taxation. In the linear program such a direct minimization is not possible.

The model has been run on an IBM 360/50. Total execution time is approximately 13 minutes, compared with less than one minute for the linear program. Exhibit 9.1 shows a sample of output where all weights are set to unity. The desired level of several goals is different from that of the formulation discussed in the previous chapter. The desired family income is increased to $9,633, and the percent of low income households goal is reduced to 15 percent. Both these changes reflect objectives more in line with regional statistics.

The solution in this case is different from the one obtained using the linear model. This is due largely to numerics in the objective function. In the linear formulation, a deviation in the tax goal is associated with a number on the order of magnitude of 10^6, since, in that formulation, $d = d \cdot T$. In the nonlinear case, the portion of the objective dealing with taxation is on the order of 10^2. The goal that conflicts most with taxation is employment. We have seen earlier that the shadow price of industrial acreage is approximately $.09/acre. Since there are 20 industrial employees per acre, the value of the associated dual is only $.09/20 = $.0045/job. Thus, it is clear that greater reduction in the objective can be achieved by meeting the employment goal, since the dual associated with employment is 1. (All objective function weights are set to unity.)

EXHIBIT 9.1

Output of the Goal-Programming Formulation

```
OPTIMAL VALUE OF THE VARIABLES - GOAL PROGRAMMING FORMULATION

PROPERTY TAX RATE              76.31
SCHOOL TAX RATE                68.33

MUNICIPAL FISCAL SUMMARY (MILLIONS OF $)
MUNICIPAL TAX BASE             29.561
SCHOOL TAX BASE                30.444
MUNICIPAL APPROPRIATIONS        3.780
SCHOOL APPROPRIATIONS           2.080
FULL VALUE OF TAXABLE PROPERTY 90.271

RESIDENTIAL DEVELOPMENT DETAILS
NUMBER OF TYPE 1 UNITS         52.237
NUMBER OF TYPE 2 UNITS         39.954
NUMBER OF TYPE 3 UNITS (APTS) 1703.143
ACRES OF RESIDENTIAL LAND      67.251
OVERALL RESIDENTIAL DENSITY    26.696

SOCIO-ECONOMIC CHARACTERISTICS
NUMBER OF HOUSEHOLDS         8355.334
TOTAL POPULATION            20000.000
PUBLIC SCHOOL PUPILS         2805.657
TOTAL INCOME OF HOUSEHOLDS     77.29($ MILL.)
AVERAGE INCOME OF HOUSEHOLDS 9250.426
RETAIL SALES      ($ MILL.)    33.998
ACRES INDUSTRIAL LAND          50.000
SQUARE FOOTAGE OF INDUSTRIAL 660000.000
EMPLOYMENT OPPORTUNITY-
    WHITE COLLAR    350.
    BLUE COLLAR     650.
    TOTAL          1000.

POPULATION DISTRIBUTION BY AGE OF HOUSEHOLD HEAD
          15-25    26-35    36-49    50-64    65+
TOTALS    727.    1999.    1617.    1917.    2095.
PERCENT   8.71    23.92    19.35    22.95    25.07

          DISTRIBUTION BY HOUSEHOLD INCOME
          $0-4,999 $5-9,999 $10-14,999 $15-19,999 $20,000+
TOTALS    2185.    2819.    2130.      751.       469.
PERCENT   26.15    33.74    25.49      8.98       5.61


          SUMMARY OF GOAL ACHIEVEMENT

GOAL              DESIRED VALUE      AMOUNT UNDER      AMOUNT OVER
TOTAL TAX RATE    144.641(MIN.)
POPULATION        20000.000              0.0               0.0
SALES ($MILLI)       34.000              0.002             0.0
AVG. INCOME        9633.000            382.574             0.0
% LOW INCOME         15.000              0.0              11.149
% OLDER HSHLDS       22.700              0.0               2.371
EMPLOYMENT         1000.000              0.0               0.0
```

The population goal of 20,000 persons is met, as is the goal for retail sales. The levels for average family income, percent low income, and percent older households are not met, although it should be noted that the achievement for average income exceeds the satisficing level of $8,735 used in the linear case. The value of the decision variables is $x_1 = 52$, $x_2 = 40$, $x_3 = 1,703$, $x_4 = 50$.

Although it is not readily apparent, this solution is efficient. A further reduction in taxes would be possible by increasing the industrial employment level (for instance, increase x_4), or by decreasing population. A decrease in population is desirable, but can be accomplished only at the expense of reducing retail sales and worsening the other desired population profiles.

Disadvantages of the Nonlinear Goal Program

The computer code employed is highly efficient and can deal with linear and nonlinear constraints, even where nonconvexity exists in the set or the objective. As a decision-making tool, however, the nonlinear form of the goal programming model does not possess desirable characteristics. In general, it has the following drawbacks.

Computational Efficiency

With 19 constraints (6 policy restrictions) and 19 variables (12 deviationals), the code requires 13 minutes for execution. For every new policy consideration, at least two additional equality restrictions and two additional variables are needed.

The computer code, although capable of handling equalities, has difficulty with constraints of the type $x_i \cdot x_j = 0$. For example, if another policy consideration is added to the formulation presented, execution time increases nearly 50 percent. Finding efficient points requires parameterization of the weights in the objective. Given the execution time involved, this formulation does not readily permit even a limited search for different efficient solutions.

Feasible Starting Values

As a tool for decision-making and evaluation, the model should be flexible enough to easily accept changes in desired levels for goals or in the constants. The nonlinear code uses a feasible set of starting values as initial input. Because the policy constraints are equalities, any changes in the G's (the desired goals) requires new starting values. The algorithm readily overcomes infeasibilities when the constraints are linear by projecting back into the feasible set. Infeasible starting values are not overcome when the constraints are nonlinear.

Efficient Solutions

The nonlinear goal program could be used to develop efficient solutions through methods discussed in Chapter 7. Such an approach, which involves finding a set of efficient goals, would be cumbersome.

By reformulating the model, it was possible to overcome the computational and technical difficulties described above. In the reformulation, policy constraints are eliminated from the set and put directly in the objective.

In Chapter 8, it was shown that the policy constraint

$$X + d^- - d^+ = G$$

is the equivalent of

$$\min: |X - G| = \min: \{(X - G)^2\}^{\frac{1}{2}}$$

if both d^+ and d^- are included in the functional. It is, therefore, possible to eliminate all policy constraints and optimize goal achievement directly in the objective. The advantages are that the formulation is enhanced through the elimination of p policy constraints, p additional restrictions on the deviationals, and 2p variables.

The only drawback to this formulation is that overachievement cannot be differentiated from underachievement in the objective. As has been discussed, the goal-programming formulation is a satisficing model. The formulation presented next improves on this while enabling the objective to be formulated so as to reflect greatly reduced concern, on the part of the policy maker, for a goal that is within some bound of the objective.

A NONLINEAR MULTIPLE-OBJECTIVE OPTIMIZATION

The Model

A formulation of the community development problem that is useful for finding efficient solutions through a parametric variation of the weights is obtained when all policy constraints are removed from the set and placed in the objective. The goal program presented earlier was revised in this manner, yielding the problem

NONLINEAR GOAL FORMULATIONS

$$\text{min:} \quad \sum_{j=1}^{p} a_j \{f_j(X) - G_j\}^2$$

where the G_j are desired levels of attainment for the various policies and the a_j are parameter weights,

subject to:

$$x_1 \quad\quad\quad\quad\quad\quad - b_1 \cdot x_4 \geq 0 \quad\quad (a)$$

$$\quad\quad x_2 \quad\quad\quad\quad\quad - b_2 \cdot x_4 \geq 0 \quad\quad (b)$$

$$\quad\quad\quad\quad x_3 \quad\quad - b_3 \cdot x_4 \geq 0 \quad\quad (c)$$

$$c_1 \cdot x_1 + c_2 \cdot x_2 + c_3 \cdot x_3 \quad\quad \leq B_R \quad\quad (d)$$

$$x_4 \leq B_I \quad\quad (e)$$

The first three constraints relate the amount of land devoted to industrial use (x_4) to the resulting housing demand, as discussed in Chapter 5. The parameters b_1, b_2, and b_3 are equivalent to FAM(I), I = 1, 2, 3.

Constraint (d) defines the total availability of residential land (B_R). The parameters c_1, c_2, and c_3 have the dimension acres/unit, and are the inverse of DENS(I), I = 1, 2, 3 (also discussed in Chapter 5). x_1, x_2, and x_3 are the equivalent of U(I). The constraint (e) defines the total availability of industrial land.

The specific components of the objective, f_j, $j = 1, \cdots, 7$, are discussed below and related to the notation of Chapter 5. The general form of each objective is given in Appendix B.

f_1 is the total property tax rate, which can be expressed as $f_1 = \frac{\text{expenditures - revenues}}{\text{total taxbase}}$. The total tax base is a linear function of the variables that can be written as

$$T_0 + \sum_{i=1}^{4} T_i \cdot x_i$$

where T_0 is the existing tax base and the T_i are equalization rates.

Both municipal expenditures and school expenditures can be related directly to the four variables. Chapter 5 developed an expression for municipal expenditure in terms of total population. By using the population per unit, PPUNIT(I), I = 1, 2, 3, expenditures can be expressed in terms of x_1, x_2, and x_3. Likewise, by using the pupil loading per household, PUPH(I), I = 1, 2, 3, education expenditure can be expressed in terms of x_1, x_2, and x_3. Municipal and education revenues are linear functions of population and total value of real property, and therefore also can be written directly in terms of the decision variables.

f_2 is the average family income, expressed as

$$\frac{\text{total income of households}}{\text{number of households}}.$$

The total income is computed from $Y_0 + \Sigma_{i=1}^{3} Y_i \cdot x_i$, where Y_i is the average income for household type i and Y_0 is the current income of residents projected to the horizon year. The total number of households is taken as $N_0 + \Sigma_{i=1}^{3} x_i$, where N_0 is the current number of households projected to the horizon.

f_3 is the percent of low-income families, written as

$$\frac{\text{number of low-income households}}{\text{total number of households}}$$

where the numerator is computed through $F_0 + \Sigma_{i=1}^{3} F_{ij} \cdot x_i$ for income group $j = 1$. F_{ij} is the equivalent of INCDIS(I, J) discussed in Chapter 5. F_0 is the current number of low-income households projected to the horizon.

f_4 is the percent of elderly households, taken as

$$\frac{\text{number of elderly households}}{\text{total number of households}}.$$

The numerator is computed through $D_0 + \Sigma_{i=1}^{3} D_{ij} \cdot x_i$ for age group $j = 5$. D_{ij} is the age distribution, equivalent to AGEDIS(I, J) discussed in Chapter 5.

f_5 is the total population, taken directly as $P_0 + \Sigma_{i=1}^{3} P_i \cdot x_i$, where P_i is the population per household for dwelling type i and P_0 is the existing population projected to the horizon year.

f_6 is total retail sales, expressed as $S_0 + \Sigma_{i=1}^{3} Y_i \cdot S_i \cdot x_i$, where S_i is the fraction of household income that families in housing type i will spend locally and S_0 is externally generated retail activity.

f_7 is the number of jobs created through industrial development and is expressed as $v \cdot x_4$, where v is the number of jobs per acre.

The numerator in f_1 is a nonlinear function of the variables. All other numerators and denominators are linear. f_5, f_6, and f_7 are also linear functions of the variables.

The objectives can thus be formulated as minimization (or maximization) criteria by setting the G_j to some arbitrary, unachievable value. The quadratic form of the objective seems more desirable than the linear form usually associated with goal programming. In the quadratic form, larger deviations are given greater consideration in the objectives than are small variations from the desired level.[5] It is also advantageous to maintain a formulation of the type min: $(X - G)^2$, since such a function, regardless of whether convexity holds, has a known minimum whose location lies inside or outside the feasible set, depending on the value of G. (Appendix B gives further discussion of the quadratic form of the functional and proposes a direct method for finding the set of all efficient points under certain conditions.)

A Note on Parameter Weights

The a_j parameters associated with the objective have been termed "relative weights" by several authors (see Chapter 7). The nomenclature is misleading, since it implies that if one objective (say f_1) is weighted by 7, and a second objective (say f_2) is weighted by 2, then f_1 is more heavily weighted than f_2 and will, hence, be given greater consideration in the objective, and f_1 will be given 3.5 times as much consideration as f_2.

Neither of the statements is true. The purpose of the parameters is to contort the functional, so that different optimal (efficient) solutions can be found. This procedure yields only efficient points.[*] However, the effect that the weighting has on the objective is a function of the numerics involved and of the degree of convexity. Consider the problem

min: $a_1 x_1 + a_2 x_2^4$

subject to: $\sum c_i x_i \geq B$

Even a relatively small value for a_2 (as compared with a_1) will tend to satisfy the objective associated with x_2, before any improvement at all is attempted on x_1. This is because of the large marginal improvements that are made in the objective when x_2 is reduced, compared with the smaller marginal improvement that is obtained by

---

[*] Where convexity does not hold for the set and the objective, there may be nonoptimal points that are efficient. See theorems 1 and 2, at the beginning of the chapter.

reducing x_1. The issue is further compounded when x_1 and x_2 are of different orders of magnitude.

For instance, if x_1 is on the order of 10^0, and x_2 on the order of 10^2, it may be that virtually any combination of weights ($a_i > 0$, $\Sigma a_i = C$) yields the same result. Thus, there may exist an a_2' such that for any value, $a_2 > a_2'$ (regardless of the value of a_1), the second part of the objective will not show any further improvement. This implies that only one efficient point can be found for all $a_2 > a_2'$.[6]

Since the objective in the above problem is convex, it is theoretically possible to find all efficient solutions. These points would be found with $a_2 < a_2'$. In the quadratic form of the community development model, variation of parameter weights does, at times, result in unchanged solutions. Also, various portions of the objective can be made more sensitive to the parameterization by scaling.

Setting Goal Levels and Scaling the Functional

Some objectives, such as tax rate or (the negative of) retail sales, are clearly of the minimization type ($G = 0$). This statement does not imply that the utility of the objective is linear. For example, once sales volume reaches a certain level, the policy-maker is less concerned with any further increases. Other objectives could be of the goal type where deviations both above and below a particular level are undesirable. Population could be taken as such an objective. The policy-maker may be interested in a city that is "just right"—not too small, and yet not too large. In defining this level quantitatively, the policy-maker includes such considerations as the city's image, capacity for municipal services, and a desire for open space.

In the objective function, the G's must be set to reflect the nature of the goal. Once that is accomplished, numerical modifications can be made to reflect conditions of decreasing concern that may exist whenever the value of the objective is within some specified bound of the desired level.

Cases 1-7 (see output, Appendix C) show the results of optimization runs where all a_i weights except one are zero. The purpose of these runs is to find the best attainment possible for each objective, taken by itself, and subject only to the four structural constraints. Thus, we find that the minimum representation of low-income families in the population is 21.5 percent (case 5). The G for this objective has been set according to prevailing regional data. For convenience, the G could now be raised from 15 percent to 21.5 percent, so that when the minimum is attained, the "Deviation" column in the output will show a zero.

NONLINEAR GOAL FORMULATIONS

Now numeric changes can be made in the functional. These are, in a sense, similar to bounding the desired level with an upper and lower satisficing constraint. Suppose the G associated with low-income families (G_3) is set to 23 percent in the formulation

$$\min: a_3\{(f_3(x) - G_3)/1.5\}^2 + \{a_i f_i(x) - G_i\}^2 ; \quad i \neq 3$$

where the f_i are the remaining objectives. Assume that all objectives are of an equal order of magnitude. As f_3 approaches within 1.5 percentage points of the desired level (23 percent), from either the lower side or the upper side, the part of the functional associated with f_3 becomes small very rapidly. Thus, as we reduce below 24.5 percent (from the upper side), the value inside the brackets of the first term in the functional above is less than 1. Since this value is, in turn, squared, it can be seen that the objective f_3 receives little consideration within the region 21.5 percent to 24.5 percent.

This technique, therefore, is a means of devising a bounded or satisficing objective, which is an improvement over a bounding constraint, since even within the bound, further minimization takes place, albeit with reduced emphasis. The interpretation given to satisficing, then, is that even within the satisficing limits, the decision-maker would still like to see improvement (rather than merely having the value "knock around" within a pair of hard constraints), although the utility increases associated with further improvement are now taken to be at a much lower rate.

The numerics can be changed, depending on the specific result desired. In the case above, for example, the result is not only a bounding of the desired level but also a reduced concern with any value of the objective below 23.0 percent. This is because the lowest possible value of the objective f_3 is 21.5 percent. By varying the G and the bound, a number of different results can be achieved. In the case of the population objective (f_5), a bounding value of 1,000 was chosen after a certain amount of trial and error.

The resulting function combines objectives that are to the minimized (such as taxation), objectives that are only to be satisfied (such as family income), and objectives that are to be satisficed within a region (such as population). Thus, the total objective function may be characterized as a satisficing-optimization model.

Advantages of the Quadratic Formulation

The model has been shown to be computationally efficient. On the average, 25-30 cases can be run in 10 minutes, using the gradient search code discussed earlier. The number of constraints and variables (both four) has been greatly reduced. All manipulation, sensitivity analysis, and other parameterization is accomplished in a straightforward manner in the objective, so that the program itself, including the starting basis and partial derivative, does not have to be altered.

As a tool for finding efficient solutions to the nonlinear multiple-objective problem, the quadratic formulation is versatile, useful, and computationally powerful.

APPLICATION I: BETTER THAN BEST?

In Chapter 7, four cases were described as possible outcomes of the process in which users interact with CODIM in an effort to find suitable development strategies. The first possible outcome is one in which the policy-makers find a strategy they consider best. As defined earlier, such a strategy meets all the desired objectives, such as population size, level of taxation, and employment, and also is desirable in terms of factors not considered by CODIM.

Exhibit 9.1 shows such a policy as it was formulated by users of CODIM. The essential characteristics are shown below.

Objective	Level
Taxation	$142.86
Population	19,024
Retail sales (millions)	$32.454
Average family income	$8,991
Percent low-income families	27.6
Percent elderly households	25.7
Industrial employment (jobs)	1,000

The solution yielding the above is

$$X_1 = 152; \quad X_2 = 439; \quad X_3 = 198; \quad X_4 = 40$$

As argued in Chapter 7, an optimal-desirable policy is efficient only if one takes the narrow perspective that there are no improvements that the policy-maker wants, and that no reduction or increase in any objective (without changing the others) would make him feel that he is any better off. If a broader view of efficiency is taken, then, for example, a solution that meets all the criteria (as shown in Exhibit 9.2), yet yields a lower tax rate, must be considered an improvement.

NONLINEAR GOAL FORMULATIONS

Using the output from CODIM (the level of the objectives) as the desired goals (G), several runs were made with the quadratic form of the optimization to see whether any improvement could be made. In the first run, an attempt was made to reduce taxation from its level of $142.86 while keeping all the other objectives fixed. The results of this run were

Taxation: $142.91
Other objectives: unchanged
Solution: $X_1 = 265$; $X_2 = 40$; $X_3 = 711$; $X_4 = 50$

In this case, with all other objectives fixed, no improvement in the tax rate is possible.* In general, it has been found that the six remaining objectives constrain the problem sufficiently so that little variation takes place in the tax rate. This is because each objective acts as a constraint such that when it is satisfied, solutions are limited to a hyperplane along which the tax rate cannot vary much. Thus, for the most part, it seems the solutions emerging from the CODIM simulation are efficient with respect to tax rate.

In a second run an attempt was made to reduce population (under the assumption that population may be a negative good) while keeping all other objectives constant. The results show the population can be reduced only at the expense of increased taxes. A new solution is obtained with

Taxation: $143.70
Population: 18,859
Other objectives: unchanged

Now let us determine whether an improvement in another objective—for example, average family income—can be made "for free." Exhibit 9.3 shows the results of a third run in which the family income goal is increased. The value for each objective is found under "Optimal Value of the Variables." For example, the property tax is $76.02, the population (under "Socio-Economic Characteristics") is 18,859, and the percent low income is 27.44 (as read in the first category under "Distribution by Household Income"). As shown, average family income is increased to $9,056 (from a value of $8,991 in the CODIM results) without affecting any other objective.

---

*Note that the tax rate in the optimization is, in fact, $.05 higher than in the simulation. This small difference is attributed to computational variations.

EXHIBIT 9.2

Sample Output of the Interactive Model

```
DEV. CHOICE? (1=RES; 4=IND; 9=BOTH) ?9

INPUT NO. OF INDUSTRIAL ACRES(USE DECIMAL)?50.

RESULTS OF INDUSTRIAL DEVELOPMENT
JOBS CREATED        350 NON-PROD.    650 PROD.      0
HOUSING DEMAND       52 HIGH          39MOD.     123APT

SQ. FT. OF INDUSTRIAL SPACE-  660000.


INPUT NO. HIGH, MOD, & APTS?100,400,75

PRINT RESIDENTIAL DEV. DETAILS? (YES-NO;1-0)?1



                        RESIDENTIAL ZONE TYPE
                        HIGH          MODERATE         APTS.
NO. UNITS                152            439             198
ACRES USED                61.           135.              4.
TOTAL ACRES              100.           300.             16.
FULL VALUE ($MIL.)         5.32          13.17            1.58
UNITS/ACRES (OVERALL)      1.52           1.46           12.37



PRINT INCOME DISTRIBUTION? (YES-NO; 1-0)?1

CAT.      NO.FAM.       %
$0-5      2016.        27.6
 -10      2525.        34.5
 -15      1813.        24.8
 -20       554.         7.6
 20+       400.         5.5

TOT. INCOME ($M) -  65.707
NO. OF FAM. -  7308.
AVG. FAM. INC.-   8991.
```

```
PRINT SOCIO-ECO. DATA? (YES-NO;1-0)?1

SOCIO-ECO. CHARACTERISTICS
                         DWELLING TYPE
                    HIGH     MODERATE    APTS      'OLD'
NO. OF HOUSEHLDS     144       426        178      6560
POPULATION           578.     1490.       356.    16600.
HOUSEHOLD INCOME   17661.    13153.     11994.     8453.

NEW POPULATION       2424.
TOTAL POPULATION    19024.
PUB. SCHOOL PUPILS   2972
TOT. H'SHOLD INCOME  65.707($ MIL.)
AVG. H'SHOLD INCOME  8991.
RETAIL SALES($MIL.)  32.454

PRINT AGE DISTRIBUTION? (YES-NO;1-0)?1

AGE OF HOUSEHOLD HEAD
   15-25    26-35    36-49    50-64    65+
   459.     1737.    1526.    1750.   1877.
    6.3      23.8     20.9     23.9    25.7    (PERCENT)


 MUNICIPAL FISCAL DATA($ MIL.)
NEW TAXBASE    -    9.708
TOT. TAXBASE   -   30.475
SCHOOL TAXBASE-    31.359
FULL VALUE         93.693
STAUTOTRY DEBT LIMIT -   6.559

PROP. TAX RATE-    $74.01
SCHOOL TAX RATE    $68.85

1970 EQUIV. APPROP-     2.993
MUN. APPROPRIATION-     3.649
FIXED REVENUES     -    1.393
SALES TAX REDIST.  -    0.752

SCHOOL APPROP.     -    5.072
STATE AID RATE(ED.)     57.430%
LOCAL SHARE        -    2.159

MUN. APPROP./CAPITA $155.36
STATE AID(MUN.)    -    0.641
NO. OF PUPILS      -    2972
```

EXHIBIT 9.3

Sample Output of the Nonlinear Formulation

OPTIMAL VALUE OF THE VARIABLES

PROPERTY TAX RATE	76.02
SCHOOL TAX RATE	67.67

MUNICIPAL FISCAL SUMMARY (MILLIONS OF $)

MUNICIPAL TAX BASE	28.747
SCHOOL TAX BASE	29.630
MUNICIPAL APPROPRIATIONS	3.623
SCHOOL APPROPRIATIONS	2.005
FULL VALUE OF TAXABLE PROPERTY	87.013

RESIDENTIAL DEVELOPMENT DETAILS

NUMBER OF TYPE 1 UNITS	151.619
NUMBER OF TYPE 2 UNITS	39.989
NUMBER OF TYPE 3 UNITS (APTS)	859.573
ACRES OF RESIDENTIAL LAND	90.143
OVERALL RESIDENTIAL DENSITY	11.661

SOCIO - ECONOMIC CHARACTERISTICS

NUMBER OF HOUSEHOLDS	7611.181
TOTAL POPULATION	18859.346
PUBLIC SCHOOL PUPILS	2769.691
TOTAL INCOME OF HOUSEHOLDS	68.934
AVERAGE INCOME OF HOUSEHOLDS	9056.914
RETAIL SALES	32.410

RESULT OF INDUSTRIAL DEVELOPMENT

ACRES INDUSTRIAL LAND		50.045
EMPLOYMENT OPPORTUNITY-		
WHITE COLLAR	350.	
BLUE COLLAR	651.	
TOTAL	1001.	
SQUARE FOOTAGE OF INDUSTRIAL		660587.990

POPULATION DISTRIBUTION BY AGE OF HOUSEHOLD HEAD

	15-25	26-35	36-49	50-64	65+
TOTALS	543.	1727.	1550.	1819.	1972.
PERCENT	7.14	22.68	20.37	23.90	25.91

DISTRIBUTION BY HOUSEHOLD INCOME

	$0-4,999	$5-9,999	$10-14,999	$15-19,999	$20,000+
TOTALS	2088.	2600.	1885.	606.	427.
PERCENT	27.44	34.16	24.81	7.96	5.61

SUMMARY OF GOAL ACHIEVEMENT

GOAL	DESIRED VALUE	DEVIATION
POPULATION	19024.00000	164.65363
SALES ($ MIL)	32.45400	0.04407
AVG. INCOME	9126.99997	70.08615
% LOW INCOME	27.59999	0.16329
% OLDER HSHLDS	25.70000	0.21042
EMPLOYMENT	10000.00000	0.89089

NONLINEAR GOAL FORMULATIONS

This section has described how the nonlinear optimization can be used to improve initial solutions found by using CODIM. Where use of the simulation does not result in an acceptable solution, it may be necessary for the user to make trade-offs among competing goals in order to best satisfy all the objectives. The next section describes how the quadratic formulation assists in this process.

APPLICATION II: MAKING TRADE-OFFS ALONG THE ATTAINMENT-POSSIBILITY FRONTIER

Several outcomes of the interactive procedure involve situations in which optimality is not reached and the user is not able to make the necessary trade-offs to satisfy the objectives as well as possible. CODIM does not assist in answering such specific questions as "If industrial land use is decreased by 10 acres, what is the minimum increase in taxes that must take place?" In a linear optimization, such information is available from the duals, to the extent discussed in Chapter 8. In the nonlinear case, the dual is not directly available.

In Chapter 7 the concept of an attainment-possibility frontier (APF) was introduced. This curve depicts the optimum level for one objective, given any level in a second objective. The points along the frontier, in general, will depict the locus of efficient combinations. In plotting values to obtain such a frontier, it is assumed that utility (or goodness) increases or decreases monotonically as the value of the objective is varied over its range. As is shown in this section, the APF contains information similar to that given by the dual. It is, therefore, proposed as a graphic aid to assist the decision-maker in deciding on necessary trade-offs.

Constructing the APF

Figure 9.1 is a plot of the minimum total tax rate versus population. The plot was obtained from a series of runs with the following form:

min: $a_1\{f_1(X) - C_1\}^2 + a_5\{f_5(X) - C_5\}^2$

subject to: the structural constraints

where
$f_1(X)$ is the total tax rate; $C_1 = 0$;
$f_5(X)$ is the total population

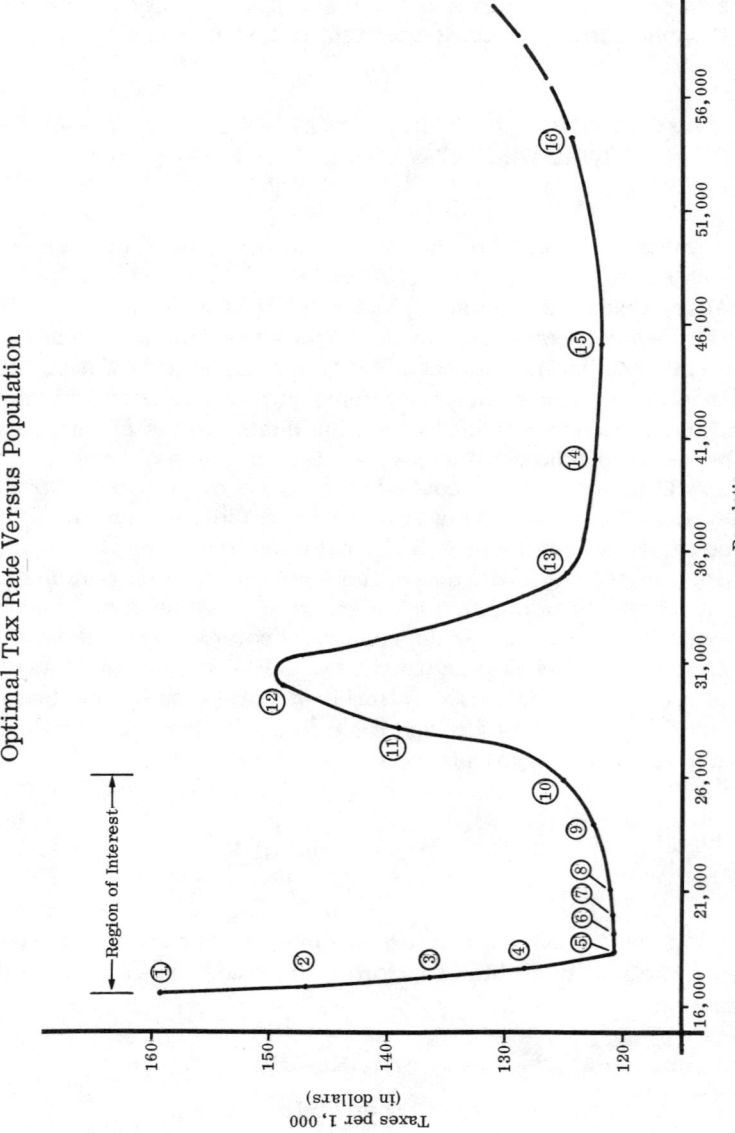

FIGURE 9.1

Optimal Tax Rate Versus Population

NONLINEAR GOAL FORMULATIONS

and C_5, the desired population level, is varied. The result, when $(f_5 - C_5) = 0$, is that taxation has been minimized subject to the population being constrained to the value C_5.

As population increases from 16,600, the optimal tax rate declines rapidly, reaching its lowest value at a population of 18,748 persons. This decline is caused by an underutilization of municipal infrastructure in the test city. Beyond 18,748, the optimal tax rate increases, reflecting a more intensive use of municipal plant. At a population of approximately 30,000 persons, the tax rate begins to fall off again. Capital improvements are more fully utilized, thus reducing the level of taxation until another low is reached at 45,000 persons.

The curve plotted in Figure 9.1 is representative of a typical short-run average-cost curve. The region of interest for the city being studied lies between 16,600 and 28,000 persons, but let us continue with the full range of structurally feasible cases.

Assume that population is a negative good. Such an assumption is reasonable, since population is another measure of density. It can, therefore, be taken that a larger number of persons is less desirable in the city. Taxation, likewise, is a negative good. If plotted along a preference scale, a higher level of taxation implies a lower utility. For convenience, both measures can be converted to a preference index by subtracting the value of the measure from the maximum it can achieve. Thus, if taxation is maximized, subject only to the structural constraints, a value of $159.80 is obtained. Similarly, the highest value for population is 54,039 people.

The resulting index for taxation can be plotted against the index for population, thereby yielding a taxation-population APF (Figure 9.2). Numbers along the frontier relate to corresponding points in Figure 9.1. The domain of interest lies between points 1 and 11. The usual conditions that result in a smooth production possibility frontier (such as a linear-homogeneous production function) do not exist here and, hence, the curve is not well shaped. Nodes such as 12 are caused when the production function has a maximum.

Interpretation

Points on the segment between 1 and 5 are K-efficient (see Chapter 7). Along this portion it is not possible to improve one objective, say taxation, without reducing the second objective. Points on the segment between 12 and 15 are locally efficient.[*] Along this

---

[*] A point x' is locally efficient if it is properly efficient with some (open convex) neighborhood of x'.

FIGURE 9.2

Taxation-Population APF

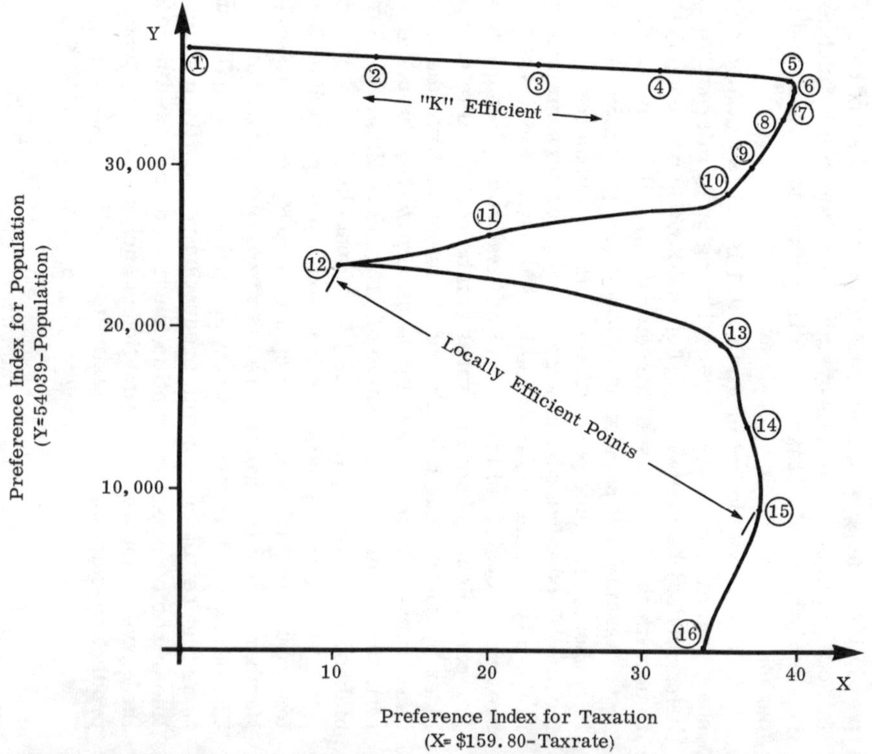

Preference Index for Taxation
(X= $159.80−Taxrate)

Preference Index for Population
(Y=54039−Population)

segment it is also possible to improve one objective only at the expense of the other; but if we proceed past the node, points such as 5 are reached, at which both objectives are better than between 12 and 15.

Both axes retain their original units, dollars in the case of taxation and number of persons in the case of population. The APF states the relationship between these two objectives quantitatively. If we are at point 8, for example, population can be improved by 2,000 and the tax rate by nearly $1.00 by moving to point 5. From there the taxation index drops rapidly for small marginal gains in the population index. The policy-maker can evaluate moves from one point to another along the APF, in light of his notions regarding the utilities involved. Because these utilities vary, the policy-maker may find that he is better off by giving up a certain amount in one objective in order to improve another.

Another factor that strongly affects taxation is employment. The level of industrial employment directly sets the acres of industrial land use, which plays a strong role in determing the tax rate. A taxation-industrial land APF can assist in making choices between these two competing goals. Figure 9.3 shows the APF for taxation versus industrial acreage, where the latter is taken as a negative good to be minimized. The segment TT' consists of properly efficient points. When the index for industrial land is at 193 (zero acres developed), then taxation can be improved from 0 to 11 "for free."

Determining the Shadow Price

The overall slope of the segment TT' indicates that on the average, industrial acreage can be improved (reduced) at a per-acre cost of approximately $.15 in the tax objective. However, the curve is not quite linear; and in the neighborhood of the abscissa, the slope indicates an increase of nearly $.10 in taxation for every acre improvement. It is by now apparent that the slope of TT' is the inverse of the dual variable associated with industrial acreage when taxation is the only objective in the functional. Chapter 8 discussed this variable and gave its value as approximately $.09 when the maximum amount (193 acres) of industrial land is allocated. For cases where X_4 (industrial acreage) is less than 193, the L.P. solution shows the dual equal to zero.[*] Thus,

---

[*] The structural constraint is $X_4 \leq 193$. Therefore, when the optimal solution has acreage allotted ($\bar{X}_4$) less than total available (193), the dual is zero, since availability of additional acreage will not alter the functional.

FIGURE 9.3

Taxation–Industrial Acreage APF

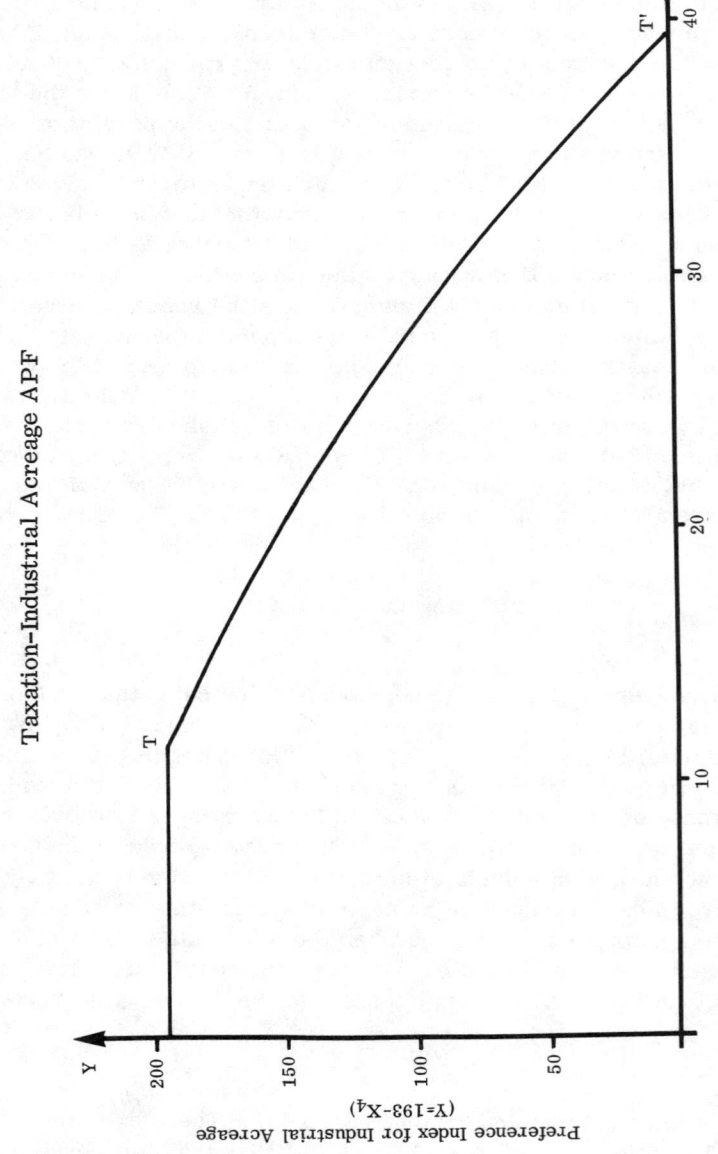

NONLINEAR GOAL FORMULATIONS   211

unless X_4 is at its upper bound, the dual does not yield the information contained in the APF.

APF's can be used to graphically display gains and losses from trade-offs between two competing objectives. All points on the frontier are efficient and the choice of where to operate is dependent only on the user's preference. APF's can, therefore, be of help to the decision-maker in his search for optimal and desirable policies.

APPLICATION III: A SET OF EFFICIENT SOLUTIONS TO THE COMMUNITY DEVELOPMENT PROBLEM

A set of efficient solutions, for example, as shown by TT' in Figure 9.3, gives the policy maker a locus of points along which he should operate, and shows what sacrifices need to be made in order to move from one efficient point to another. If the associated utilities are also known, then the entire segment of points along TT' can be reduced to a unique "constrained bliss" optimum. This point lies at the tangency of the possibility frontier and the n-dimensional utility surface (welfare function). This surface, however, is not known and, because of the nonadditive nature of utility, may be impossible to construct a priori, even if individual preference functions for the various objectives were known. Furthermore, research indicates that it may be theoretically impossible to derive any transitive social choices through the democratic process.

In his role as policy-maker, the municipal executive reflects the social choice of the electorate through their revealed preferences.[7] Thus, while the welfare function is not known on an a priori basis, the policy-maker can evaluate a pair of efficient points and determine which one is preferred.

The role of analysis in the problem, therefore, reduces to providing efficient solutions and, where possible, to assisting in their evaluation through such tools as the APF. Use of the two-dimensional APF has already been discussed. In this section efficient solutions to the community development problem, found with the quadratic model, are presented.

The quadratic form of the nonlinear optimization is well suited for this application. The computer routine is geared to generating numerous efficient solutions in each run. Nearly 100 cases were designed for analysis, with each case representing different values of the parameters. As discussed earlier in the chapter, every parameterization does not necessarily lead to a different result and we are, therefore, left with approximately 50 different solutions.

After an initial run of the cases, goal levels were altered and the cases rerun. Finally, several runs were made to investigate the sensitivity to changes in coefficients. Appendix C contains sample output.

Results

The parameter weights for the runs are taken so that $\Sigma a_i = 10$. These weighting factors are shown in the output, under "Summary of Goal Attainment." Also available from the output is the G or desired value for each objective. The deviation is the absolute difference between the desired value for the goal and its actual level in the solution. The actual value for all goals can be found in the body of the output. For example, population is presented under "Socio-Economic Characteristics."

Cases 1 through 7 were run with one weight $a_i = 10$, and all other weights, $a_j = 0$; $j \neq 1$. The solution to these cases represents the optimal attainment when only one objective is optimized. For example, case 1 shows the minimum taxation level to be $120.64, with

$$X_1 = 202; \quad X_2 = 154; \quad X_3 = 476; \quad X_4 = 193^*$$

where

X_1 is the number of four-bedroom single-family units
X_2 is the number of three-bedroom single-family units
X_3 is the number of apartment units
X_4 is the number of acres devoted to industrial use.

Industrial land use tends to contribute strongly to reduced taxation; and the minimum for this objective can, in fact, be achieved only when X_4 is at its upper bound of 193 acres. The associated values for the other three variables reflect the minimum housing that must be built as a result of the structural requirement relating housing demand to industrial activity.

The set of parameters that yields this solution is $a_i = 10$, $a_j = 0$; $j = 2, \cdots, 7$. This set is not unique, and other weightings will give the same results. Cases that are similar have, therefore, been omitted from Appendix C.

---

*Note that this case yields the same result as the L.P. model presented in Chapter 8.

NONLINEAR GOAL FORMULATIONS

Case 2 shows that a population objective of 20,000 is attainable with the solution

$$X_1 = 331; \quad X_2 = 307; \quad X_3 = 610; \quad X_4 = 50$$

When population is the only objective, the functional appears to be very flat, and any number of solutions will satisfy the goal.

Cases 4, 5, and 6 deal with average family income, percent of low-income families, and percent of elderly households. A family income of less than $5,000 is taken as low, while elderly households are classified as those whose head is over 65 years of age. In general, by inspecting the various cases presented, it will be noted that the three objectives are strongly related to each other as well as to retail sales. This will be treated again in greater detail. In case 5, the reader will note that the proportion of low-income families is minimized with the housing mix

$$X_1 = 0; \quad X_2 = 125; \quad X_3 = 3,500$$

The current (1970) proportion of low-income households in the test city is considerably higher than the 21.5 percent achieved by the optimal solution, so that this objective is approached from the upper side. The income distribution for in-migrants is higher than the income distribution for existing city residents, so that, in general, the proportion of low-income families declines as the population grows. Occupants of four-bedroom single-family housing have the highest income distribution. Yet the optimal solution includes no four-bedroom dwellings, only smaller, single-family units and apartments (which are at their upper bound).

The reason is as follows: Four-bedroom units are built at a lower density than other single-family housing and, of course, apartments. With available residential land (416 acres) a maximum of 1,040 four-bedroom, single-family dwellings and 1,352 three-bedroom units can be accommodated. The structural limitation on apartments is 20,800, but a somewhat arbitrary upper bound of 3,500 has been applied. Although the income of apartment families is not as high as the income of households in single-family units, it is still higher than the income of present residents. Thus, because of density considerations, apartment dwellers, through sheer numbers, result in the maximum improvement to the city's income distribution.

Similar interactions take place in case 102. The solution is

$$X_1 = 202; \quad X_2 = 154; \quad X_3 = 1,419; \quad X_4 = 193$$

The values for X_1 and X_2 will be recognized as the minimum necessary to satisfy the constraint requirements for housing demand arising from industrial activity. Such a solution, involving only X_1, X_2, and X_4, will satisfy the minimum taxation portion of the objective, but fail to meet the goals for retail sales and age and income distributions. In order to meet those objectives, apartments enter the solution well in excess of the minimum necessary (476) to meet structural requirements. In this case, apartment units contribute toward fulfilling the socioeconomic goals with the minimum detriment to taxation.

Earlier it was indicated that average family income, percent of low-income families, and proportion of elderly families are related. For illustration, refer to Cases 118 and 119. The pertinent results are summarized below:

		Family Income	Percent Low Income	Percent Elderly
Case 118	Deviation	$391(−)	11.3 (+)	1.9 (+)
	weight	3.0	1.0	2.0
Case 119	Deviation	$296(−)	10.7 (+)	1.3 (+)
	weight	0.1	0.1	6.5

The signs in parentheses indicate overachievement (+) or underachievement (−) of the particular goal. Note that although the parameter values associated with family income and low income are smaller in Case 119, the deviation from the desired level is smaller. Note also that the objective for percent elderly is given a higher weight in Case 119 (6.5) than in Case 118 (2.0). It therefore appears that the increased emphasis on the elderly population goal reduces not only the deviation in that objective but leads to improvement in the other two objectives as well. Case 120 shows still further improvement when the parameter value of 6.5 is shifted to the low-income goal. These two cases demonstrate the strong interaction among the three objectives.

Another interaction among objectives is shown by Cases 312 and 313.

		Family Income	Retail Sales
Case 312	Deviation	$1,081 (−)	$2.4 million (−)
	weight	1.0	3.0
Case 313	Deviation	$1,092 (−)	$2.5 million (−)
	weight	3.0	1.0

NONLINEAR GOAL FORMULATIONS

In Case 313, the weighting for family income has been increased, yet the deviation is larger than in Case 312. This indicates that average family income and retail sales are closely related and, more significantly, that a given weight on the sales objective is more effective in minimizing the deviation of both.

Sensitivity to Changing Goals

In order to assist in the policy-making process, the effect of altering goal levels must be assessed. In this section, the results of Cases 201-340 are discussed. These cases use the same weights as corresponding Cases 1-140. The difference is that several desired levels have been changed. The desired level for population is reduced from 20,000 in the first set of cases to 18,000 in the second. Average family income is raised to $10,000, and desired employment is reduced to 50 (the equivalent of 2.5 acres of industrial land use). Cases 201-07 present the results when only one of the objectives has a weight greater than zero.

As a general result, it is found that the efficient solutions in Cases 208-340 carry a higher tax rate than in Cases 8-140. This is explained by the reduction in desired employment, which results in a lower number of industrial acres and drives up the tax rate. Comparing the runs on a case-by-case basis (for instance, Case 311 compared with Case 111) indicates that the low-income and elderly household goals are better met in the first set of runs. The reduction in desired population to 18,000 makes attainment of these socioeconomic objectives more difficult. Because of the interrelationship among objectives, the retail sales situation also worsens.

Under the first set of objectives (for example, Case 111), sales are only $376,000 short of the $34 million goal. In the second set of runs (for example, Case 311), the deviation is $2.7 million. This difference, along with the fact that average family income is lower in the second set of runs, can likewise be attributed to the lower population goal. A reduced population has two effects on these objectives. First, a smaller population implies a smaller aggregate residential income, which hampers retail activity. Second, the aggregate income is smaller, not only because of a smaller population but also because the population includes fewer in-migrants who have higher income profiles.

Sensitivity to Changing Coefficients

As a tool for policy evaluation and planning, the optimization model must be capable of dealing with uncertainty in the environment. One of the advantages of the quadratic formulation, compared with a nonlinear goal-programming formulation, is the ease with which coefficients can be altered. The decision variables, and hence the policy constraints, are assumed to be controllable by municipal management. In any decision-making process, however, factors exist that cannot be controlled by the policy-maker. Such factors need not be excluded from consideration.

One variable that has considerable impact on the municipal fiscal picture is nonproperty tax ("fixed") revenue. State aid and other intergovernmental transfers are, without question, subject to economic uncertainties. More significantly, they are subject to uncertainty regarding the policies and political forces that determine these revenues. A legislative revision of the state's aid formula, for example, could drastically alter the funds received by a municipality.

Assessing the variability of politically related factors is difficult. First, the probability of any change occurring must be evaluated. Second, given that a change will occur, it is necessary to ascertain the nature of the change. The two factors combined could then lead to an assessment of the reliability of such variables as nonproperty tax revenues.

Uncertainty can be considered in a more direct fashion through the strategy of contingency planning. This concept was introduced in Chapter 4, using a military case as an example. Given this approach, coefficients in the model can be altered to yield results for the worst possible and best possible contingencies. Cases 501-604 and 701-840 show how such planning can be undertaken using the quadratic formulation.

In Cases 501-640, it was assumed that the revenues received by the city through governmental transfers would increase by 25 percent. That is, the various formulas governing state aid and county redistribution of ad valorem taxes would change so as to result in a 25 percent increase in funds to the city. In Cases 701-840, a reduction of 25 percent was assumed.

In general, these changes did not affect the optimal solutions. For example, Case 501 yields the solution

$$X_1 = 202; \quad X_2 = 154; \quad X_3 = 476; \quad X_4 = 193$$

which is identical to the results of the previous corresponding cases, 1 and 201, the only difference being the value of the functional. The sensitivity of the level of taxation to a 25 percent increase in the fixed revenues is about $8.00 (from a base value of $120.64). A case-by-case comparison of these runs with Cases 1-140 indicates that the solutions are virtually identical in every case. The solutions for Cases 701-840 are also very similar. This finding has important policy implications.

As is shown by the results, a given efficient solution remains optimal, even if fixed revenue varies by 25 percent. Although the level of taxation worsens when aid is reduced, the solution still represents the best that can be achieved. Thus, uncertainty about state aid and other nonproperty taxes (within the limits ±25 percent) need not be included in the decision-making process, since optimality is not affected.

CONCLUSION

Many urban and social-related objectives are not linear. In particular, there are frequent examples of goals that are ratios of two variables. Transformation of the variables may be inapplicable or cumbersome, and a nonlinear model is required. Certain exceptions arise when linear satisficing constraints can be substituted for an optimization of nonlinear objectives.

Two nonlinear forms were examined in this chapter. The first is a direct extension of the linear goal program. Such a formulation is applicable, but has the disadvantage of requiring additional constraint to limit each pair of deviationals, and an extra pair of variables (deviationals) for each policy consideration. Because the formulation consists almost entirely of equality constraints, changes in goal levels are not easily carried out, since a new starting basis is required. Also, equality constraints have a strong adverse effect on the computational efficiency of nonlinear algorithms.

The model can be simplified by eliminating policy constraints and deviational variables, and optimizing the multiple objectives directly in the function. This quadratic form of the model is computationally efficient and, hence, useful for policy analysis and decision-making, since finding solutions to the vector optimization problem involves a parametric variation of the weights. The quadratic form does not directly permit a distinction between underachievement and overachievement of goals. However, goals can be classified into certain types, and the objective designed so as to achieve the desired result. The quadratic form is also useful in sensitivity analysis, where coefficients are to be altered.

In linear programming, the dual associated with structural variables may yield useful information. In goal programming or any multiple-objective programming, the appropriate dual variable may not be meaningful. The APF can assist the policy maker when trade-offs among competing objectives must be made. Under certain circumstances, the APF is identical to the dual. It can provide useful information even where the dual is not meaningful or has a value of zero.

The efficient solutions of the nonlinear optimization are presented to the policy-maker, who evaluates the results and chooses desirable operating points. In reflecting the revealed preferences of his constituency, the decision-maker chooses, from among efficient alternatives, the point that maximizes the social desires of the community.

The reader may note that the efficient solutions presented are all boundary solutions. This is due to the nature of the quadratic formulation, and is helpful in developing an analytic description of the solution space. Appendix B discusses the characteristics of the quadratic form of the functional and proposes a straightforward method for finding all efficient points without the use of an optimization program.

NOTES

1. See, for example, G. Hadley, <u>Non-Linear and Dynamic Programming</u> (Reading, Mass.: Addison-Wesley, 1964).
2. Ibid., Ch. 9.
3. W. L. Kephart and J. R. Copper, <u>Some Improvements in the Gradient Search Method of Optimization</u> (Oak Ridge, Tenn.: Union Carbide Corporation, Nuclear Division, Computing Technology Center, 1965).
4. Kenneth E. Cross, <u>A Gradient Projection Method for Constrained Optimization</u> (Oak Ridge, Tenn.: Union Carbide Corporation, Nuclear Division, Computing Technology Center, 1968). The authors wish to extend special thanks to Mr. Cross for his personal assistance during the initial stages of problem development, and for suggesting some useful computational modifications.
5. For a discussion of the various distance metrics and their significance in goal programming, see A. Charnes and W. W. Cooper, <u>Management Models and Industrial Applications of Linear Programming</u>, I (New York: John Wiley, 1964), pp. 156-57.
6. See ibid., pp. 303-05, for further discussion.
7. Originally suggested by Paul A. Samuelson. For a straightforward treatment, see W. J. Baumol, <u>Economic Theory and Operations Analysis</u> (3rd ed.; Englewood Cliffs, N. J.: Prentice-Hall, 1972), pp. 221-26.

CHAPTER 10
SUMMARY, CONCLUSIONS, AND SUGGESTIONS FOR FURTHER STUDY

The purpose of this research has been the development of policy-evaluation tools to assist in community development planning. The first several chapters have shown the need for effective analytic procedures that will assist the policy-making process of the smaller municipality. As indicated, fiscal, economic, and social factors are important "bottom line" considerations that municipal chief executives must ultimately deal with in evaluating alternative development strategies. The descriptive construct presented in Chapter 5 allows for rapid evaluation of alternative development strategies using a consistent framework for analysis. As noted, however, this construct cannot deal with goals explicitly. The model was therefore reformulated as a normative schema to permit the optimization of mutually unattainable community development goals. The next section summarizes the significant findings of this research.

SUMMARY

Prior to the American Revolution, there were some excellent examples of town planning in colonial America. This tradition was not carried on after the formation of the United States. The lack of definitive municipal authority with regard to land-use control and planning was the principal reason for the early decline of the colonial planning tradition. Speculation, a weak federation of governments, and the culturally imbedded concepts of land ownership and rugged individualism are secondary, but nonetheless significant, reasons.

These factors combined to place pressures on land that resulted in blighted and "pestilential" urban forms of the industrial city of the late nineteenth century. It was during this era of reform and romanticism that modern planning developed. The profession rapidly expanded from its early responsibilities of urban beautification through the construction of civic edifices to undertake more comprehensive planning, including transportation, parks and recreation, and housing. While maintaining the original consultant-client relationship, planners produced comprehensive plans for cities throughout the United States. For the most part, these plans differed little in style or content, and required only the adoption of a municipal zoning ordinance for implementation.

A significant defect of the master plan is its assumption that certain kinds of urban forms are best; and for the most part, these plans are based on axioms developed early in this century. Such concepts as open space, greenery, and the separation of different land uses are the result of the concern of urban reformers of the late 1800s for elimination of urban blight. Thus, although planning is a problem-solving process that can employ the scientific method, it differs from other problem-solving situations in the important respect that the objectives are by no means clear. Yet the master plans of the last fifty years have been prepared under the assumption that community objectives regarding land use are clear and, further, are understood by the planner. Thus, the need exists to deal with policy formulation as an explicit first step in the planning process.

Chapter 5 presents a construct for evaluating alternative land development strategies. This construct is based on the cost-revenue impacts analysis, which is expanded to include socioeconomic and demographic considerations. The tool presented is practical, is directly implementable with available data, and presents decision-making information to the municipal chief executive. Although previous examples of large-scale urban simulation exist, these have not proved successful "when it came time to deliver the goods."[1] The construct presented in Chapter 5, on the other hand, has had two practical applications. One of these was discussed in Chapter 6; the other will be discussed in a subsequent section.

The impacts analysis methodology can be used in two ways. First, it enables municipal officials to react to specific land development proposals by evaluating their fiscal, socioeconomic, and demographic impacts. Second, since the tool permits a rapid evaluation without the burden of manual calculations, numerous hypothetical strategies can be evaluated. In this way, the user "muddles through" until finding a strategy that best meets his objectives. In order to facilitate a direct treatment of goals and objectives, the descriptive construct was reformulated as a prescriptive multiple-objective

SUMMARY

model. Several linear formulations are discussed and evaluated. It is shown that the linear formulation of the goal-programming problem suffers from inherent nonlinearities unless all goals are met. While this model is incorrect, it may prove useful with judicious interpretation of the results.

Two nonlinear applications are presented. The first model is found to be computationally cumbersome. The second formulation, involving a quadratic form of the functional, is well-suited for finding efficient solutions to the vector optimization problem. In addition, several interesting properties of the quadratic form allow a direct method for finding efficient points without use of an optimization procedure.

In subsequent sections, an application of the descriptive model to community participation is discussed. Finally, suggestions for further research are given.

EXTENSIONS TO COMMUNITY PARTICIPATION

In November 1974, the authors had an opportunity to test the usefulness of the CODIM construct as an aid to decision-making in a community participatory setting. The work described was carried out in Dunbar, Pennsylvania, with the assistance of personnel from the Institute on Man and Science.*

Dunbar is a rural borough located in the mountains of southwestern Pennsylvania. Its population declined slightly between 1960 and 1970, at which time it numbered 1,500 persons. Nearly half of the adult population has not completed high school, and only 2 percent have a college degree. Dunbar suffers the common symptoms of rural decay—low family income, loss of economic base, and dilapidated housing.

As a unique experiment in rural revitalization, the Institute on Man and Science located personnel in Dunbar to assist the community in redevelopment. Several citizen task forces were established to set priorities and objectives for development. Their fields of interest included housing, the economy, and recreation. The groups met on a regular basis to discuss development potential, and the Institute staff prepared analyses for group evaluation. It was thus recognized that the CODIM construct could assist the task forces because it had the capability of quick response to "what if" questions. On the basis of

---

*The Institute's main campus is located in Rensselaerville, N.Y. The authors would like to acknowledge the direct assistance of R. Cohen, Assistant Director, Dunbar Project.

data collected during a two-day site visit, the computer code was modified for Dunbar. Then, using a remote terminal at the meeting facility, it was possible to provide the task forces with evaluations rapidly, while the meetings were in progress. N. Johnson and E. War have called for such techniques of presenting and utilizing information at community meetings to create support and participation and to help citizens ". . . avoid unintended and unwanted consequences."[2]

Description of the Citizen Task Forces

Two task forces were presented with the concept of using an automated tool to assist in calculating impacts of development: the housing task force, which focused on long-range residential planning, and the local economy task force, which was charged with planning for commercial and industrial revitalization. The constructs employed in the model were explained to the members. In addition, in order to minimize the novelty of the interactive technology, members were invited to use "canned" software routines such as tic-tac-toe and blackjack ("twenty-one") in order to become acquainted with the terminal and the concept of being connected to a distant computer facility.

The housing task force was the first of the long-range planning teams to be established, and had been meeting for several weeks prior to introduction of the computer model. The group's approach to housing choices involved consideration of the age-income distribution of the population that might be drawn into Dunbar and the local impacts of alternative housing developments. The composition of the housing task force, ranging from seven to twelve residents at any meeting, was almost exclusively male. Among the men, four had substantial experience in dealing with the local housing problem—two were large property owners (one was commonly identified as the owner of much of the borough's slum property), another was a building contractor, and the fourth had been the borough's building inspector. The other members, all homeowners, were motivated by concern about the housing problem and general civic pride. None of the members had a college education and none held public office.

The local economy task force had not met prior to the introduction of the computer model. The group was composed entirely of small businessmen, storeowners, and self-employed craftsmen, all but one of whom were male. Like the housing task force, almost all were in the age groups between the early thirties and mid-fifties.

SUMMARY

Implementation and Results

It had been decided at the outset that the progress of the task forces would have priority over the implementation of the computer model. Thus, the model would not be forced on the groups, or "sold" to them. The housing task force had already generated options and made its initial decisions for future housing development, based on its perceptions of open space availability and suitability. The computer model was first introduced as a means for the group to make decisions of magnitude—how much of what kind of housing. The task force viewed the computer output as representing the following: (1) the hard evidence the task force could use to justify its choices; (2) useful information to present to governmental agencies when applying for grants; and (3) a weapon that put the citizen on an equal footing with the Borough Council by providing powerful information.

The notion of the model as an aid in decision-making was slow in coming. However, when the pressure of a borough-wide meeting required the group to formalize recommendations, the task force requested that the model be used to assist in choosing among garden, row, and efficiency units. After a discussion of the results, the hard evidence on the output was tempered by a more emotionally based decision criterion—how would people feel about a particular development package? Explicitly, the participants voiced concerns such as "Are the people of Dunbar ready for three clusters, or will two be as much as they can handle?" "Will cluster developments or rehabilitated apartment buildings make us feel better, prouder of our community?"

Thus, the interactive process helped the group focus initially, and answered the quantitative questions regarding taxation, demographics, and so on. In the final discussion, however, the group relied on unquantifiable value judgments to reach a consensus.

The local economy task force was presented with the concept of the computer model at its first meeting. A verbal description of how the model might be used evoked little response. Despite the presence of two housing task force members, the group didn't seem prepared to accept the possibility of a computer terminal in Dunbar, or that a computer model could assist. A second description of the model was accompanied by three sample printouts, based on housing task force options, ranging from no growth to relatively high residential development. After discussing the output, the group accepted the model as a potentially useful tool. However, what interested this task force most (and this was directly related to the group's exposure to the sample printouts) was the realization of the interrelation between housing and economy. By comparing the three printouts, participants could see that different residential packages generated different retail sales patterns, a factor of Dunbar's economy that directly concerned the group. The group also recognized that the model might be used to postulate changes in economic structure and to evaluate the requirements for housing. The participants' excitement with these ideas provoked them to ask for a joint meeting of the local economy task force and the housing task force.

At that meeting, the local economy group came to the decision that housing development could stimulate the economy (as opposed to housing being shaped by economic development). Thus, rather than planning housing development in accordance with the requirements of the industrial and/or commercial expansion planned, the joint group felt that the economy should be left to respond to the types and size of housing development. Instead of investigating alternative scenarios based on different economic strategies, the local economy task force joined the housing task force in evaluating various residential alternatives.

The community participatory process was thus enhanced, directed and focused with the use of an interactive tool that rapidly calculates the impacts of community development. Use of media technology, such as the Advent system for projecting computer output from a CRP onto a large screen, might serve to further improve and streamline the presentation of information at community meetings.

SUGGESTIONS FOR FURTHER STUDY

Conceptual and Technical Suggestions

The impacts analysis methodology is still in its infancy. Phillip Schaenman and Thomas Muller present an evaluation of the current state of the art, and make recommendations.[3] The authors suggest, for example, that municipalities institute "post" studies to determine the accuracy of the initial calculations. It is doubtful that local officials will be willing to expend public funds for such purposes. Such validations will therefore have to be supported with private or national research funding.

Philip Schaenman and Thomas Muller present 48 measures for evaluating the impact of land development, not all of which are quantifiable.[4] Previous works have also proposed indicators of urban quality.[5] These lists are by no means exhaustive; and any practitioner can devise still additional criteria, perhaps ad infinitum. However, we must pose the following questions:

SUMMARY

- Are the criteria measurable along some scale?
- Do the criteria help the local policy maker and the community?
- Do the criteria improve our ability to evaluate alternatives?
- Do the criteria improve our understanding of the impacts?

One criterion that has been omitted from previous lists and that may be useful is the projected tax rate expressed in terms of the residents' ability to pay. Such a criterion is clearly measurable and, from a social welfare point of view, perhaps more desirable than merely stating the tax rate absolutely. Yet does this measure help the local chief executive? He is responsible to the constituents and has a very simple, but nonetheless important, barometer of his success: whether he is reelected.

Over the long term, a development policy that results in higher taxes, but a lower burden when expressed in terms of ability to pay, may be more beneficial to a given community than a policy that directly reduces taxation. Yet, given political realities (which force the policy maker to maximize return over the short term) and the media, it is suspected that a policy-maker will be unwilling to promote a strategy that results in higher taxes, regardless of any more esoteric considerations.

Thus, the measure proposed is quantifiable, is easily computed, and improves our understanding of the impacts of a given development strategy. But such a measure would more than likely be disregarded by the decision-maker. In short, while this measure improves our ability to compare alternatives, it does not improve politics. Garry Brewer has criticized urban-simulation efforts that practice "throwaway politics."[6]

Whether used in a descriptive construct or normative model, impacts analysis as a decision-aiding tool relies on user evaluation. It is the purpose of the tools developed in this research to assist in such evaluations by highlighting relationships and focusing issues. The cognitive capabilities of any user are limited. Toward this end, presentation techniques such as the attainment-possibility frontiers can assist. The important point to consider when the inclusion of new measures is contemplated is whether the new criteria will improve understanding, or stretch the user's cognitive capability to the point where he cannot intelligently deal with the information presented. This, of course, is a fundamental concept in the design of any management information system.

The measures employed in the CODIM construct were found to be directly useful in the two applications discussed: Cohoes, New York, and Dunbar, Pennsylvania. The following section proposes some criteria for evaluating the CODIM construct as a decision-aiding tool.

Usefulness of the Constructs as Decision Tools

In the Dunbar application, it was found that the community participation process was enhanced with the use of the CODIM construct. As noted earlier, multimedia technology can further serve to improve the presentation of information in the course of community meetings. In this section, some criteria are proposed that could be used in conjunction with a controlled experiment to further evaluate the interactive process.

Three overall tests are proposed as surrogates for measuring the elusive criteria: Do the tools developed in this research improve the quality of planning decisions? The impact of the constructions on each of the three criteria can be evaluated by selecting experimental groups (who have used the model) as well as control groups. The groups can further be divided into professional planners, community participants, and elected officials. The three tests for usefulness are

T_1: Impact on the user's awareness of the urban system
T_2: Impact on the planning process
T_3: Impact on analysis for planning.

The first test is designed to measure whether use of the tools presented in this research improves the user's ability to discern the relationship of the indicators to various development mixes, and how the system responds to changing input. This can be determined through testing experimental and control groups using the following as a sample of questions:

- I understand the effect of industrial development on the tax rate.
- I understand the effect of different types of residential development on the age distribution of the city.
- Development of high-cost single-family homes pays for itself in terms of school costs.
- In order to keep taxes low, I would recommend a development mix that results in the lowest municipal expenditures.
- Industrial development affects the city's population as follows:
  no effect
  population increase
  population decrease.
- Industrial development is good for taxes because it does not place any added burden on the school system, yet increases the tax base (true-false).
- Any increase in city size (from what it is now) would raise taxes, since extra services would have to be provided (true-false).

The second criterion, T_2, tests the impact of the evaluation tools on the planning process as viewed by the user. The following are offered as a sample of questions that can be further developed into evaluation criteria:
- The planning process is similar to the decision-making process (true-false).
- I know which alternative or mix of alternatives is best.
- I think planning involves the process of locating structures on land.
- Laymen are not aware of the implications of a certain plan and hence cannot contribute to planning.
- Overall planning is best done by the community, since citizens are most aware of their needs.
- Given appropriate data, I can evaluate different types of development and decide which I like best.
- I have a set of goals in mind that I feel should be met through planning.

T_3, the impact on analysis, measures the usefulness of the constructs in improving the analysis of alternatives and their consequences. The following sample criteria, in the form of questions, can test this impact:
- The output helps my analysis.
- The input is too constrained.
- I can find a logical search path (that is, I understand the cost-benefit function).
- I have a priority set for the goals and can try to meet them accordingly.
- Not enough output or irrelevant output.
- Important goals are not considered (I get no indicators for them).
- Too abstract, simple, and trivial exercise.
- Can't digest output easily.
- Can't interpret or relate to output (nothing to compare with, no "feel" for the numbers).
- I have a priority set for the goals, but output does not help in trying to meet them.
- Not interested in the goals used in the model (output does not meet my needs).
- Results are confusing; too much information to look at and comprehend.

Municipal Costs and Revenues

Further empirical work detailing the impacts of development on municipal costs and revenues would serve to improve precision. The groundwork for such analysis has already been laid.[7] George Sternlieb has given the results of surveys that provide useful socioeconomic and demographic data related to community type.[8] Similar survey work on municipal expenditure, as a function of community type (older declining city, rural township, suburb), could be undertaken and would serve to enhance our understanding of factors that influence the level of municipal expenditure as a community develops.

Efficient Solutions and Goal Priorities

In Chapter 7 a preemptive ordered goal program was described as leading only to satisficing. However, the community may be able to rank its preferences ordinally for competing objectives. The results of a relative-ordered search for efficient solutions (such as parameterization) could be sorted and the information presented in a manner that combines the concepts of relative and preemptive ordering.

This would be accomplished through the following steps.
- Take the highest priority goal.
- Sort the efficient solutions and rank from best to worst.
- Show the relative standing of the remaining goals (rank the remaining goals, given the sorting accomplished in the first step).
- Take the next priority goal; repeat the second and third steps for all goals.

The procedure is illustrated below. Assume 10 solutions are found and there are three goals. On the first iteration, the ranking of all goals is presented based on the sort performed for G_1.

Ranked Solutions

G_1	(10)	(9)	(8)	(7)	(6)	(5)	(4)	(3)	(2)	(1)
G_2	(5)	(1)	(3)	.	.	.	.	.	.	(7)
G_3	(2)	(7)	(10)	.	.	.	.	.	.	(4)

The diagram shows the results, with the solutions ranked from best (10) to worst for G_1. When G_1 attains its best level (10), G_2

SUMMARY   229

attains a relative (ordinal) level of 5. That is to say, there are five
solutions for which G_2 is better, and four for which it is worse. Thus,
if the policy-maker wants the highest attainment for G_1, he must
accept a fair attainment for G_2 and a rather poor attainment for G_3.
He might therefore be interested in the results if the goals are ranked
on the basis of G_2.

On the second iteration, the goals are presented based on the
sort performed for G_2:

Ranked Solutions

G_2	(10)	(9)	(8)	(7)	(6)	(5)	(4)	(3)	(2)	(1)
G_1	(3)	(6)	(7)	(1)	.	.	.	.	.	(9)
G_3	(8)	(2)	(6)	(4)	.	.	.	.	.	(7)

Now the table shows that the best attainment of G_2 also yields a good
attainment for G_3. By sacrificing somewhat in the attainment of G_2
(such as moving from 10 to 9), the relative standing of G_1 greatly
improves (from 3 to 6), but G_3 is reduced in its ordinal ranking.

On the final iteration, a sort would be performed for G_3. Using
this technique, the user can see how various priority goals fare for
any ranking of another goal (accomplished by reading down the columns).
Such presentation of results may help policy-makers evaluate the results
in a more orderly manner. By normalizing the solutions, a cardinal
ranking could be presented that will assist in making trade-offs.

NOTES

1. Garry D. Brewer, What's the Purpose? What's the Use?
(Santa Monica, Calif.: RAND Corp., 1973), p. 9.
2. N. Johnson and E. Ward, "Citizen Information Systems:
Using Technology to Extend the Dialogue Between Citizens and Their
Government," Management Science 19, no. 4 (December 1972).
3. Phillip Schaenman and Thomas Muller, Measuring Impacts
of Land Development (Washington, D.C.: The Urban Institute, 1974),
pp. 2-3, 5-6.
4. Ibid., pp. 10-11.
5. Raymond Bauer, ed., Social Indicators (Cambridge, Mass.:
MIT Press, 1966); Martin Jones and Michael Flax, The Quality of Life
in Metropolitan Washington, D.C. (Washington, D.C.: The Urban
Institute, 1970).

6. Brewer, op. cit., p. 14.
7. For example, County and Municipal Study Commission, Housing and Suburbs (Trenton, N.J.: the Commission, 1974).
8. George Sternlieb, Housing Development and Municipal Costs (New Brunswick, N.J.: Center for Urban Policy Research, Rutgers University, 1973).

APPENDIX A:
NOTES ON CONSUMER BEHAVIOR AND SOCIAL WELFARE THEORY

CONSUMER BEHAVIOR, SOCIAL WELFARE, AND
THE IMPOSSIBILITY THEOREM

Concepts such as indifference curves, utility, and budget constraints, normally applied to the analysis of individual consumer behavior, can be extended to assist in social policy formulation. In the analysis of consumer behavior, it is assumed that the individual is economically rational, and can rank his preferences ordinally. That is, he wishes to maximize his utility and is aware of the utility derived through the consumption of various goods.

In Figure A.1, curves such as I, II, and III show the consumer's indifference among bundles in which goods X and Y are represented in varying proportions. Thus, the consumer feels just as well off with a mix of X and Y represented by point a, as with a bundle represented by point b. The utility at any given point along a curve such as I, II, or III, therefore, is constant ($dU = 0$). Also represented by the diagram is the assumption that the consumer prefers to be on the highest indifference curve possible, or that he prefers any point on curve III to any point on curve II. By the theorem of transitivity, if curve III is preferred to a curve such as II, and II is preferred to a curve such as I, then III is also preferred to I.

The line BB' represents the only constraint on the problem. In the analysis of consumer behavior, this line is the budget function and has a slope that indicates the (negative of the) relative prices of the two goods involved. At any point along the line BB', the consumer expends his entire budget. It is, therefore, clear that there is no reason for the consumer to operate anywhere below the line BB', since at such a point (for example, point R), the consumer can increase his utility by consuming more of good X or good Y, or both. In other words, he can increase the consumption of at least one good without reducing the consumption of the other. Once he is on the line BB', however, the consumer can increase the consumption of one good only at the expense of the other. The budget constraint BB', therefore, forms the locus of all Pareto-optimal (efficient) points.

The problem now is to determine whether there is a unique optimum point along the Pareto locus at which the consumer should operate. Classical economics shows the point to be at the tangency of

FIGURE A.1

The Consumer's Problem

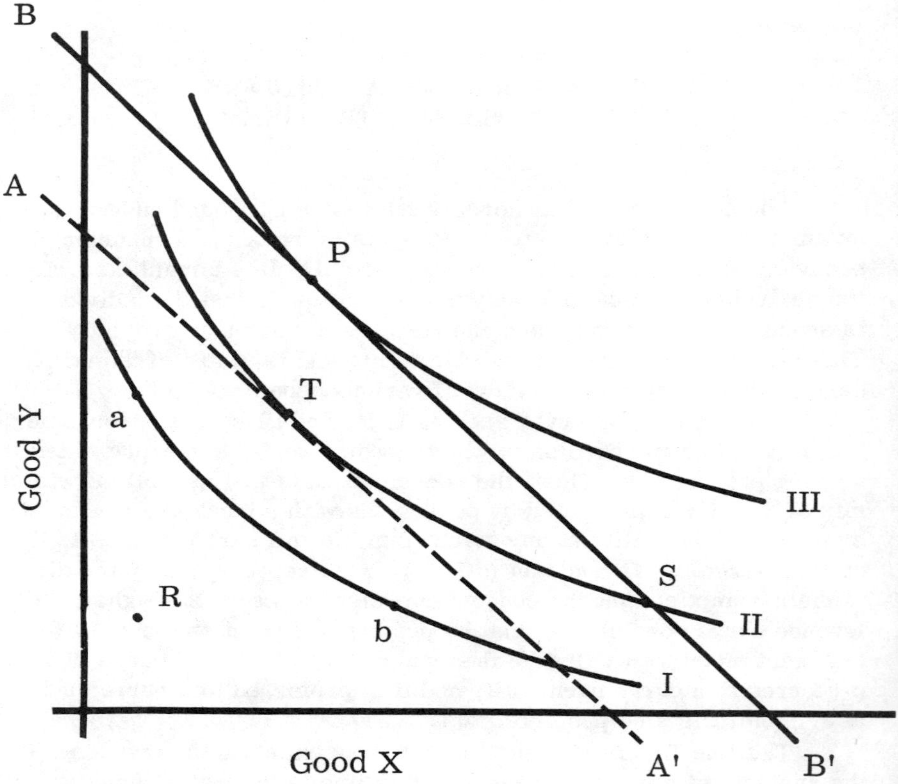

an indifference curve such as III and the budget line BB'. At this point, the marginal rate of substitution of one product for the other is equal to the slope of the budget line.[1]

An intuitive proof of the theorem that equilibrium lies at the tangency of an indifference curve such as III and the budget line is as follows: Suppose the consumer were operating at the intersection of the budget line BB' and some indifference curve such as II (point S). Without changing his total budget, the consumer could "slide" along the budget function to point P. Since under the original assumptions of ordinal ranking, any point on III is preferred to any point on II, P is preferable to S (P > S).

APPENDIX A

If the consumer is originally at S, then he could also move to any other point on II without affecting his total utility (constant utility along an indifference curve). Suppose he moves to a point such as T, which is tangent to the imaginary budget line AA'. In terms of utility, T = S, but it is clear that T < P. Therefore, from a point such as T, the consumer will want to increase his consumption of either X or Y, or both, until he is constrained by his real budget line. In more precise terms, he will move from point T to similar points on higher indifference curves until the stable point P is achieved.

Thus, if the consumer's indifference function is known, a unique stable equilibrium can be found. Without knowing the shape of the indifference (or welfare) function, the best solution available is that he operate somewhere on the Pareto curve or budget line. Operating anywhere below that line will lead to a needless sacrifice of utility. Operating anywhere above the Pareto line is impossible, since the total available budget is exceeded. The next section discusses various criteria for maximizing social welfare where the shape of the utility curve is usually unknown.

SOCIAL WELFARE

The budget line of the previous section has several counterparts, each of which is also the locus of efficient points. Consider, for example, the case of a farm that produces tomatoes and peas, which require two inputs, land and labor, that are available in fixed quantities. Figure A.2 depicts the production possibility of the two outputs.[*]

Let us assume, because of limited available inputs, that if no peas are produced, then X_1 bushels of tomatoes can be grown, or that if the production of tomatoes is zero, then Y_1 bushels of peas can be produced. Similarly, if the farmer chooses to produce X_2 bushels of tomatoes, his resources will allow him to produce no more than Y_2 bushels of peas (point P). The curve BB', therefore, shows the maximum amount of one product that can be produced for any level of production of the other product.

---

[*]The production-possibility frontier as shown in Figure A.2 is usually derived by means of the Edgeworth-Box diagram which relates inputs, outputs, and equilibrium allocations. For further discussion, see C. E. Ferguson, <u>Microeconomic Theory</u> (Homewood, Ill.: Richard D. Irwin, 1972), pp. 467-77.

FIGURE A.2

Production-Possibility Frontier

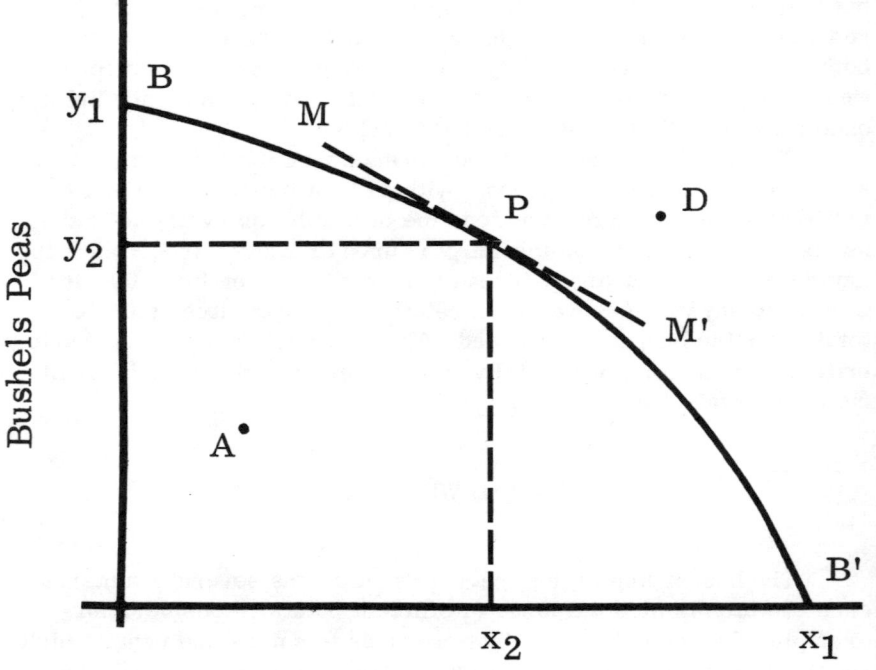

Bushels Tomatoes

Clearly, the farmer does not wish to operate at a point such as A since at such a point he would be forgoing profits needlessly. On the other hand, it is impossible for him to operate at a point such as D, since he does not possess sufficient inputs. The net, and possibly obvious, result of the analysis is that the farmer should operate somewhere on the production-possibility frontier (curve BB'). On this curve he can increase production of one item only at the expense of the other. This leads to a definition of the technological counterpart to Pareto-optimality, efficiency:

> A production arrangement is said to be efficient if, and only if, any alternative productive arrangement which increases the output of some commodity must also involve a decrease in the output of some other commodity.[2]

APPENDIX A

Now, let us assume that there exists a society of two individuals, S and T, each of whom has a known preference (indifference curve) for peas and tomatoes. If the marginal rate of substitution of tomatoes for peas is represented by the (slope of) the line MM' (which represents the price ratio that would be established for the two products), then production equilibrium is achieved at the tangency point P. Through use of the Edgeworth-Box diagram and the contract curve, it can be shown that for each efficient production equilibrium, there is an infinity of Pareto-optimal exchange (distribution) equilibria between the two consumers, S and T. The possible situations arising out of the production mix represented by P can be plotted in terms of the utility achieved by each of the two consumers. Since the total availability of the two goods is fixed, the total combined utility the two consumers can derive is also fixed. However, each consumer can derive varying utility, depending on the distribution of the two commodities.

In Figure A.3, the utility-possibility frontier for S and T is shown by the curve FF'. Note that the axes are labeled "preference index," reflecting the fact that the scale on which the utility of S is measured need not be the same as the scale on which T's utility is measured. All that is required is that preference increase as one moves from the origin. The graph is derived from the respective utilities derived by S and T from the consumption of different quantities of peas and tomatoes and from the production possibility of the two goods. There are several classical welfare criteria for determining how society should allocate its resources to optimize welfare and for testing whether a move from one point on the graph to another is an improvement.

The weakest, but perhaps the most useful, optimality condition is the Pareto criterion:

> Any change which harms no one and which makes some people better off (in their own estimates) must be considered an improvement.[3]

A societal organization is, therefore, Pareto-optimal, if any change that improves the situation of one or more people harms at least one other person. Conversely, an organization is Pareto-nonoptimal if changes can be made so that at least one person is better off without leaving anyone else worse off. In Figure A.4(a), a move from point A to points such as C and D are improvements, according to the Pareto principle. A move from point A to point E, however, cannot be judged by the Pareto principle, since it benefits T but harms S. The Pareto principle, thus, simply tells us that we should operate somewhere on the utility-possibility frontier. In so doing, it "sidesteps the crucial

FIGURE A.3

Utility-Possibility Frontier

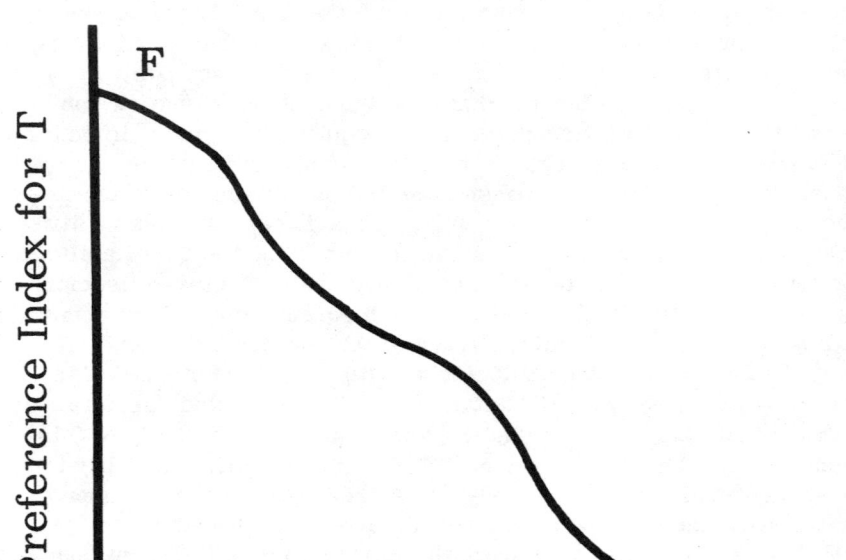

issue of interpersonal comparison by dealing only with situations where no one is harmed, so that the problem does not arise."[4]

Kaldor proposed a criterion to help in evaluating moves from points such as A to points such as E. The Kaldor principle requires that gainers be potentially able to compensate the losers out of their gain. Consider the point A in Figure A.4(b). A move to point E involves a gain for T, but a loss for S. Based on the Kaldor principle, such a move would be an improvement in social welfare if wealth (or utility) could be redistributed so that everyone is better off. Thus, the policy maker should ask S what he is willing to pay to avoid a move from A to E, and ask T what he is willing to pay in order not to forgo the move. If the gainer is willing to pay more than the loser, reasons Kaldor, then the move is beneficial because potentially the gainer could compensate the loser. The net result is that the loser

FIGURE A.4

Welfare Criteria

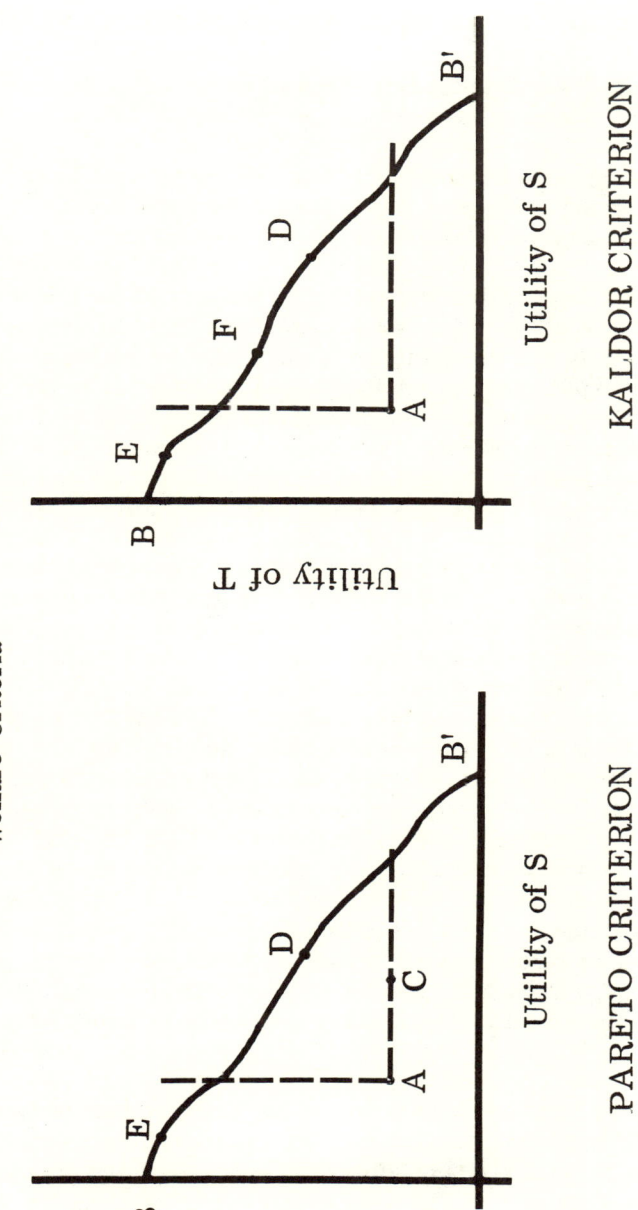

would be no worse off and the gainer still better off.* The Kaldor principle can, therefore, be defined as follows:

> A change is an improvement if those who gain evaluate their gains at a higher figure than the value which the losers set upon their losses.[5]

There is no question regarding the validity of the Pareto criterion, since the test applies only to situations where there are no losers. The Kaldor principle and its refinement, the Scitovsky double test, however, set up an interpersonal comparison based on potential money compensation.† This leads to the serious difficulties of comparing personal utilities. Suppose a hydroelectric project is proposed that will flood a family's entire estate. There is no balance sheet that could reasonably enable us to evaluate society's gain against the family's loss. Or suppose T evaluates his gain at $200, and his loss at $70. S may be poor or a miser and T a rich man. Thus, "unless S is actually compensated for his loss (in which case the Kaldor criterion is unnecessary and the Pareto criterion can do the job), the change (from A to E, Figure A.4(b)) may represent a major loss to S and a trivial gain to T even if it passes the Kaldor criterion with flying colors."[6]

A criterion that overcomes this difficulty, but that is of little use in practice, is the Bergson criterion. He suggested that the only way out of the problem of interpersonal monetary comparison is to establish a set of social indifference curves or welfare functions similar to the consumer indifference curves of Figure A.1. The point of tangency between the highest possible welfare curve and the utility-possibility frontier is the "constrained bliss"[7] at which society should operate. Needless to say, in addition to the moral and ethical question of proposing welfare functions, there are immense technical problems. Baumol notes, "Though it provides us with a highly useful frame of reference, unfortunately, it does not come equipped with a kit and a

---

*A more intuitive explanation of the Kaldor criterion is as follows: BB' in Figure A.4(b) is the utility-possibility frontier. From a point such as F, a simple redistribution of wealth (utility) can bring us to a point such as D. It is thus possible to slide along BB' by merely redistributing wealth. Therefore, if we move from point A to point E, and T can present some of his utility to S so that they will "slide" to a point such as D (at which they both are clearly better off than at A), then the move from A to E is an improvement.

†Scitovsky noticed the embarrassing paradox under which, using the Kaldor principle, a move from one point to another could be an improvement while the return move could also be an improvement!

set of instructions for collecting the welfare judgments which it requires."[8]

Thus, for practical purposes we are left with the weak, but generally useful, Pareto optimality principle. The Kaldor welfare criterion suffers from utility-comparison problems, and the Bergson framework is nearly impossible to implement. The Pareto criterion, however, is fundamentally unchallenged, has important and useful mathematical applications, and forms the basis for providing a set of efficient solutions to the policy-maker (Chapter 9).

SOCIAL CHOICE AND THE IMPOSSIBILITY THEOREM

In the analysis of consumer behavior, the assumption that bundles of goods can be ranked with respect to preference is essential in order to determine an equilibrium (optimum) solution. Thus, in Figure A.1, the consumer prefers any bundle of the goods X and Y represented by the indifference curve III to any combination represented by the curve II (III > II). By the principle of transitivity, if III > II, and II > I, then III > I. A second assumption is that the shape of the indifference curve is a function only of the consumer's marginal rate of substitution of the two goods, X and Y, and is in no way affected by the availability (or desirability) of a third product, Z. Finally, consider the utility-possibility frontier as represented by curves such as FF' in Figure A.3. It is assumed that the gains and losses accruing to an individual from a move along the frontier are evaluated by that individual only in terms of his own utility. Thus, there is no competition (in the common sense of the word) between the individuals, and one party will not oppose a reorganization simply because the other party will benefit as a result.

Kenneth Arrow has incorporated the above assumptions into a set of minimal conditions that all social choices must meet in order to properly reflect the preferences of individuals in a society.[9]

First, social choices must be transitive, in the sense that if the community prefers alternative A to B, and B to C, then, if faced with a choice between A and C, it cannot pick C over A.

Second, social preferences between two alternatives must depend only on the community's opinion of these two alternatives, and any other irrelevant alternatives should not affect the decision-making process. In the terms of the earlier discussion, this implies that $U(X, Y)$ is independent of $U(Z)$.

Third, social choices must not change in opposite directions from the choices of individual members of the society. That is, a preferred alternative must not be rejected simply because certain members of the group begin to support it. This criterion is similar to the assumption that a policy will be evaluated by an individual only in terms of his own utility.

Arrow's criteria for social choice seem appropriate and well-founded in microeconomic theory. However, as a central theorem of his book, he demonstrates that it is possible for democratic or social choices to violate the conditions outlined above. Consider the criterion of transitivity. Arrow demonstrates that while every member of the society may have a set of prioritized and transitive choices, the majority-rule decision could well lead to intransitive choices. Suppose that three individuals—Baker, Bailey, and Brown—are to vote their preference on three alternatives, A, B, and C by placing a 3 next to the alternative they consider most desirable, a 1 next to the alternative they consider least desirable, and a 2 for the alternative in between. The table below shows the outcome of the balloting.

	Alternative		
	A	B	C
Baker	3	2	1
Bailey	1	3	2
Brown	2	1	3

Both Baker and Brown prefer A to B, and Baker and Bailey prefer B to C. Hence, the majority clearly prefers A to B and B to C. Note, however, that Bailey and Brown prefer C to A. Thus, the majority also favors C over A!

Through the use of a table such as the one above, it can also be shown that irrelevant alternatives can have a definite impact on the outcome of a democratic decision-making process. One could construct a set of priorities to demonstrate that if a fourth alternative D is added to the table above (the rankings now range from 1 to 4), alternative A becomes tied with C rather than being preferred to it.

Several authors, in criticizing Arrow's theorem, have noted that his criteria, particularly the second part of the second condition, are more restrictive than appears at first glance.[10] William Baumol, for example, notes that the condition requires that only rankings, and not "intensity of desires," be considered in the decision-making process.[11] If half the community strongly wants a mass transit system because of environmental considerations, and the other half prefers a better highway system, the difference in the intensity of emotion must be disregarded. This would serve to argue that relative weighting in the solution of multiple-objective problems is not well-founded and that only preemptive ranking should be employed.

APPENDIX A

NOTES

1. For an introductory discussion of the analysis of consumer behavior, see Paul A. Samuelson, Economics: An Introductory Analysis (7th ed.; New York: McGraw-Hill, 1967), Ch. 22; or C. E. Ferguson, Microeconomic Theory (Homewood, Ill.: Richard D. Irwin, 1972), Ch. 2. A more mathematical approach is found in James Henderson and Richard Quandt, Microeconomic Theory (New York: McGraw-Hill, 1971), Secs. 2.1-2.4.
2. William J. Baumol, Economic Theory and Operations Analysis (3rd ed.; Englewood Cliffs, N.J.: Prentice-Hall, 1972), p. 527.
3. Ibid., p. 400.
4. Ibid.
5. Ibid., p. 402.
6. Ibid., p. 403.
7. Ferguson, op. cit., p. 490.
8. Baumol, op. cit., p. 404.
9. Kenneth J. Arrow, Social Choice and Individual Values (New York: John Wiley, 1963).
10. See Julian H. Blau, "The Existence of Social Welfare Functions," Econometrica 25 (April 1957): 302-13; Clifford Hildreth, "Alternative Conditions for Social Orderings," ibid. 21 (January 1953); Leo A. Goodman and Harry Markowitz, "Social Welfare Functions Based on Individual Rankings," American Journal of Sociology 58 (November 1952): 257-62.
11. Baumol, op. cit.

APPENDIX B: NOTES ON THE FUNCTIONAL IN THE QUADRATIC FORMULATION

FORM OF THE FUNCTIONAL

The quadratic function has the general form

$$\text{Min} \sum_{j=1}^{q} a_j [h_j(x_1 \cdots x_4) - G_j]^2$$

where a_j are the parameters weights and G_j are the desired goal levels. Let

$$f_j^2(X) = \{h_j(X_1 \cdots X_4) - G_j\}^2 \; ; \quad j = 1, q$$

We can now write the individual components of the objective function. The decision variables are x_1, x_2, x_3, and x_4.

Total Tax Rate

$$f_1(X) = \frac{K_0 \left(\sum_{i=1}^{4} K_i x_i \right)^2 - L_0 \left(\sum_{i=1}^{4} L_i x_i + M \right)}{T_0 + \sum_{i=1}^{4} T_i x_i} - G_1$$

Average Family Income

$$f_2(X) = \frac{Y_0 + \sum_{i=1}^{3} Y_i x_i}{N_0 + \sum_{i=1}^{3} x_i} - G_2$$

The authors wish to acknowledge the assistance of K. Brothers, Department of Mathematical Sciences, Rensselaer Polytechnic Institute, Troy, New York.

APPENDIX B

Percent Low-Income Families

$$f_3(X) = \frac{F_0 + \sum_{i=1}^{3} F_{ij} x_i}{N_0 + \sum_{i=1}^{3} x_i} - G_3 \qquad j = 1$$

Percent Elderly Households

$$f_4(X) = \frac{D_0 + \sum_{i=1}^{3} D_{ij} x_i}{N_0 + \sum_{i=1}^{3} x_i} - G_4 \qquad j = 5$$

Total Population

$$f_5(X) = P_0 + \sum_{i=1}^{3} P_i x_i - G_5$$

Total Retail Sales

$$f_6(X) = S_0 + \sum_{i=1}^{3} Y_i S_i x_i - G_6$$

Job Opportunity

$$f_7(X) = U x_4 - G_7$$

By using the theorems presented in Chapter 7 and 8, it is possible to find all efficient solutions if the functional is convex. For the discrete case, a function is convex if[1]

(1) $\quad g\{x+1\} - g\{x\} \geq g\{x\} - g\{x-1\}$

In the continuous case, a function is convex if[2]

(2) $\quad p \cdot g\{x_1\} + (1-p) \cdot g\{x_2\} \geq g\{p x_1 + (1-p) \cdot x_2\}$

for $x_1 < x_2$ and all p such that $0 \leq p \leq 1$.

(1) and (2) imply that a line connecting any two points on a convex curve will lie completely within that curve. Several other definitions of theorems regarding convexity are useful.

(3) A function that has a continuous second partial derivative is convex if and only if its Hessian matrix is positive, semidefinite (principal minors are nonnegative).[3]

(4) The square of a linear function is convex.

(5) The square of a positive convex function is convex.

Application

In the objective function f_5, f_6, and f_7 are of the form

$$[h(x_1 \cdots x_4) - G]$$

where $h(x_1 \cdots x_4)$ is a linear function of x. Therefore, by (4) above, f_5^2, f_6^2, and f_7^2 are everywhere convex.

Specifically, if $\partial^2 g = \partial(\partial g)$ is the Hessian matrix associated with the array $g(x_1 \cdots x_4)$, then

$$\partial^2 \{g^2\} = 2[g \cdot \partial^2 g + (\partial g) \cdot (\partial g)^t]$$

where superscript t indicates a matrix transpose. Now if $\partial^2\{g\} = 0$ (which is clearly the case when $g(x_1 \cdots x_4)$ is a linear function), then $\partial^2\{g^2\} = 2(\partial g) \cdot (\partial g)^t$, which is positive semidefinite.

The portions of the objective f_1, f_2, f_3, and f_4 have the form

$$\frac{h(x_2 \cdots x_4) + a}{g(x_1 \cdots x_4) + b}$$

It can be shown that these components have an associated Hessian matrix that is not positive, semidefinite, thus indicating that f_1^2, f_2^2, f_3^2, and f_4^2 are nowhere convex.

Discussion

The quadratic form of the functional consists of objectives that are everywhere convex, as well as of objectives that are nowhere convex. Thus, the shape of the functional depends on the value of the a_j parameters. For example, if $a_5 > 0$ with all other $a_j = 0$, then the functional is convex. In solving for efficient points, however, the

APPENDIX B

parameters must all be strictly positive (for instance, $a_i > 0$). Hence, in all cases the functional will not necessarily be convex. This has two important implications.

First, it may not be possible to find all efficient solutions, since there may be nonoptimal solutions that are efficient (as discussed in Chapter 7). The second question to be raised is whether any of the solutions obtained are in fact globally optimal.

In the analysis this problem was evaluated empirically. Nearly 50 runs of the model were made, with a different starting basis for each. In addition, several sets of weights were employed. With only one exception, the gradient search routine converged to the same solution for a given set of weights, suggesting that a global optimum has been obtained.

Refer to Figure 9.1. With starting bases outside the region of interest (say, around point 15), the computer code used had no difficulty in getting past the peak (point 12) to the desired minimum values. The population, sales, and employment objectives tend to drive the solution to a global minimum. In one run, the algorithm was started exactly at point 15 (a local minimum); and the weights associated with f_5, f_6, and f_7 were made very small ($a_5 = a_6 = a_7 = .001$; $\Sigma a_i = 10$). For this case the code converged on local minimum by remaining at point 15. The fact that a global minimum had not been achieved was revealed directly in the output; that is, the deviations from desired levels for the various objectives were large. This is an advantage of the quadratic form of the objective.

When all goals are completely satisfied, the objective

$$\text{Min: } Z = \sum_{i=1}^{q} a_i \{f_i(x) - G_i\}^2 = 0$$

After some experience with the formulation, there is no difficulty in determining when a proper minimum has not been achieved, because the value of some objective $a_k\{f_k(x) - G_k\}^2$ will be unreasonably large. Except for the one run described previously, no such difficulties were encountered.

When the parameter weights are all strictly positive, the solutions obtained all lie on the boundary (at least one of the constraints is binding). Note, however, that in runs such as Case 2, where $a_2 > 0$ and all other $a_i = 0$, the solution lies within the constraint set. The objective associated with a_2 (population) is strictly convex. However, even when convexity is exhibited, it is possible to choose a G such that the solution will lie on the boundary. In Case 2, for example, this will occur when $G_2 \leq 16,600$, in which case the optimal solution is $x_1 = x_2 = x_3 = 0$.

Empirical results therefore suggest that regardless of the convexity properties of the objective, the optimal solution can be made to lie on the boundary through the proper choice of goals. The following explanation may be offered for these empirical results: If G_j in the formulation $\{f_j(x) - G_j\}^2$ is outside the boundaries, and $f_j(x)$ is linear, then $\{f_j(x) - G_j\}^2$ decreases monotonically as we approach the bound. This apparently also holds for those $f_j(x)$ that are not linear.

As has been discussed in Chapter 9, when the solution falls inside the boundaries, the model merely serves to satisfice unless we take the narrow view that the policy-maker is simply not interested in any improvement beyond his chosen target levels. In order to develop solutions that are efficient, this narrow view notwithstanding, targets that are mutually unattainable should be specified. In the quadratic formulation presented this is assured. First, the choice for G_5 (percent low-income families) cannot be achieved within the bounds of the constraint set (see Case 5). Second, taxation is always minimized ($G_1 = 0$) and therefore also is not attainable. Finally, note that the remaining objectives can be met either inside the constraint set or on the boundary. Therefore, when all $a_i > 0$, the solutions will lie on the boundary. This feature enables us to describe the solution space analytically and directly.

AN ANALYTIC DESCRIPTION OF THE SOLUTION SPACE

Defining the Convex Hull

As described, if mutually unattainable goals are chosen, the solution will always lie on the boundary (at least one of the constraints is binding) of the constraint set, regardless of the shape of the functional.[4] Thus, finding the set of all optimal solutions reduces to describing all points on the bounds. Since the constraints are linear, these points can be written as convex combinations of the extreme points (the intersections of the bounding hyperplanes).[5]

The constraints used in the quadratic formulation are

$$x_1 \qquad\qquad\qquad - 1.045x_4 \geq 0 \qquad\qquad (1)$$

$$\qquad x_2 \qquad\qquad - .799x_4 \geq 0 \qquad\qquad (2)$$

$$\qquad\qquad x_3 - 2.468x_4 \geq 0 \qquad\qquad (3)$$

$$.4x_1 + .308x_2 + .02x_3 \qquad\qquad \leq 416 \qquad\qquad (4)$$

$$\qquad\qquad\qquad x_4 \leq 193 \qquad\qquad (5)$$

APPENDIX B 247

By solving this system as five different sets of four equalities, the intersections (extreme points) shown below are derived.

Set	Equations	Solutions			
		x_1	x_2	x_3	x_4
A	1, 2, 3, 4	609	466	1,410	583
B	1, 3, 4, 5	202	1,059	476	193
C	1, 2, 3, 5	202	154	476	193
D	1, 2, 4, 5	202	154	14,394	193
E	2, 3, 4, 5	898	154	476	193
F	—	0	0	0	0

Equations (1), (2), and (3) describe the housing demand generated by industrial acreage for each of the three housing types. Equations (4) and (5) define the total residential acreage and industrial acreage available.

We are now interested in describing the smallest convex set that contains all feasible points within the solution space. The first solution set (A) can therefore be discarded, since $x_4 = 583$ is infeasible by equation (5). Next, note that solutions B and C differ only with respect to the value of x_2. Since x_2 is greater than B, it can be taken as the bounding intersection, and solution C discarded. (The reader will recognize solution C as the one that minimizes taxation.) Solutions D and E remain, as well as the trivial solution F.

We are therefore left with the set

$$\begin{matrix} B & D & E & F \\ \begin{bmatrix} 202 \\ 1,059 \\ 476 \\ 193 \end{bmatrix} ; & \begin{bmatrix} 202 \\ 154 \\ 14,394 \\ 193 \end{bmatrix} ; & \begin{bmatrix} 898 \\ 154 \\ 476 \\ 193 \end{bmatrix} ; & \begin{bmatrix} 0 \\ 0 \\ 0 \\ 0 \end{bmatrix} \\ 1 & 2 & 3 & 4 \end{matrix}$$

This is the "convex hull," or smallest convex set containing all the feasible points.[6]

Now by the method of convex combinations (weighted averages), all points along the boundary can be written, using a weighting parameter, w, such that $0 \leq w \leq 1$. Thus a straightforward parameterization of the weighting factor, w, will yield only efficient points. Since it has already been argued that all optimal points lie on the boundary, this method therefore yields all efficient points, regardless of the shape of the functional, given that at least one "unattainable" goal is chosen, such that this goal cannot be met inside the bounds and that the remaining objectives can be met (for instance, $Z_j = 0$) either inside or on the bounds.

The following summarization is thus offered without rigorous proof:

1. If at least one objective is attainable only outside the bounds, with the remaining objectives attainable either inside or on the bounds, then the optimal solution (the vector minimum) will lie on the boundary, regardless of the shape of the objective.

2. Extreme points to the convex set can be found by solving the system of constraints as equalities.

3. It may be possible to discard some of the solutions in step 2, thereby reducing the problem.

4. Convex combinations of extreme points will yield all efficient points, since by step 1 above, these points lie on the boundary.

Discussion of the Analytic Approach

The analytic approach described is an alternative to nonlinear optimization, in the sense that efficient points can be generated so long as at least one goal is unattainable. As an aid to decision-making, however, this technique may not be as effective as the optimization method, since purposeful moves from one efficient point to another cannot be made.

In the optimization, the decision-maker's desire for improvement in a given objective is handled directly by increasing the associated weight. The analytic approach is potentially useful only in that it can quickly generate a large number of efficient points. To that extent, it is also useful in preparing two-dimensional attainment-possibility frontiers. However, it cannot deal explicitly with objectives, and this capability is the raison d'etre for using a normative approach.

The optimization process has been shown to be one of purposeful incrementalism—that is, the decision-maker is guaranteed that an end is in sight. The analytic technique does not have this property. While there may be applicable algorithms that evaluate the objective at each point and provide guidance as to the direction in which to proceed,[7] this brings us right back to a nonlinear optimization, albeit with the search constrained to the boundary. The gradient search code described in Chapter 9 was found to be highly efficient and straightforward in its application. Thus, it is felt that a constrained search would not lead to significant improvement for the nonlinear problem presented.

APPENDIX B

CONCLUSION

The quadratic form of the objective has a definite, known minimum ($Z = 0$). This minimum may lie inside or outside the constraints, depending on the values chosen for G. If these values are chosen so that $Z = 0$ is a feasible solution, then the model is only satisficing. If the G are chosen so that $Z = 0$ cannot be reached, the solution will lie on the constraint-set boundary. (See Chapter 7.)

The computer code used does not have difficulty dealing with the nonconvexity of the functional. The quadratic form of the objectives is useful in that it shows large variations from desired values, should an "improper" optimum be obtained. When the G are chosen so that the optimal solution lies outside the bounds, two advantages result. First, it guarantees proper efficiency of the optimal solution. Second, since these solutions will lie on the boundary, the entire set of efficient solutions can be written directly as the weighted average or convex combination of the extreme points.

NOTES

1. Harvey M. Wagner, Principles of Operations Research (Englewood Cliffs, N.J.: Prentice-Hall, 1969), p. 292.

2. Ibid., p. 523.

3. For further discussion on the Hessian matrix, see James Henderson and Richard Quandt, Microeconomic Theory (New York: McGraw-Hill, 1971), p. 401.

4. A. Charnes and W. W. Cooper, Management Models and Industrial Applications of Linear Programming (New York: John Wiley, 1964), have already shown this to be a necessary, but not sufficient, condition for the linear case; see Ch. 7, "Efficiency: A Mathematical Approach."

5. Wagner, op. cit., pp. 460, 580.

6. Ibid., p. 460. Also see W. A. Spivey and R. M. Thrall, Linear Optimization (New York: Holt, Rinehart, and Winston, 1970), Appendix B.16.

7. Wagner, op. cit., pp. 582-92.

APPENDIX C: A SAMPLE OF EFFICIENT SOLUTIONS FOR THE COMMUNITY DEVELOPMENT PROBLEM

This appendix contains sample results obtained by using the quadratic form of the objective discussed in Chapter 9. These results represent the more interesting cases studied during the course of this work.

The solutions presented are all efficient except for Cases 1-7, 201-07, 501-07, and 701-07. In these cases only one parameter weight, a_i, is greater than zero, with all other a_j equal to zero.

The appendix is separated into four tables, each containing selected runs from Cases 1-138, 201-338, 501-638, and 701-838. As discussed in Chapter 9, Table C.1 gives results with the original set of objectives. In Table C.2, the population goal is reduced from 20,000 to 18,000 and the employment goal is reduced from 1000 to 50. The last tables test sensitivity of the results to uncontrollable factors, such as state aid, and the objectives are the same as in the first section. In Table C.3, the external aid was reduced by 25 percent, while in Table C.4 it was increased by 25 percent.

The tables in this appendix are arranged as follows: the first line for each case gives the deviation from each of the seven objectives, with the parentheses indicating a negative deviation; the second line gives the associated parameter weights; the solution itself is given at the right-hand side. X_1, X_2, X_3, and X_4 are the decision variables: four-bedroom, single-family units; three-bedroom, single-family units; apartment units; and acres of industrial land.

TABLE C.1

Sample Results from Cases 1-138, Using Original Objectives

Objective	Taxation (minimized)	Population 20,000	Retail Sales $34 Million	Average Income $9,633	Percent Low Income Families 15	Percent Elderly Families 22.7	Added Employment 1000	x_1	x_2	x_3	x_4
Case											
1	120.64	(1252)	(2.0)	(608)	12.7	3.2	2860	202	154	476	193
	10.0	0	0	0	0	0	0				
2	141.42	0	(0.9)	(336)	11.5	2.2	0	331	307	610	50
	0	10.0	0	0	0	0	0				
3	140.71	945	0	(131)	10.7	1.5	0	460	369	744	50
	0	0	10.0	0	0	0	0				
4	140.04	1392	0.4	0	10.3	1.2	0	615	347	709	50
	0	0	0	10.0	0	0	0				
5	149.46	6723	6.6	391	6.6	1.5	(1000)	0	1125	3500	0
	0	0	0	0	10.0	0	0				
6	140.36	3103	2.1	48	8.8	0	0	195	915	1472	50
	0	0	0	0	0	10	0				
7	143.22	(1780)	(2.4)	(749)	13.2	3.7	0	100	100	500	50
	0	0	0	0	0	0	10				
15	124.51	123	0.2	(336)	11.2	2.2	2430	179	137	1320	172
	1.43	1.43	1.43	1.43	1.43	1.43	1.43				
100	134.37	225	0.1	(332)	11.0	2.2	1078	109	83	1628	104
	1.0	1.0	0.5	1.0	2.0	1.0	3.0				
102	122.32	444	0.1	(275)	10.9	2.0	2860	201	154	1419	193
	2.0	0.5	0.5	2.0	2.0	2.0	1.0				
103	134.85	1014	0.02	(292)	10.4	1.3	738	91	728	884	87
	1.0	0.1	0.9	1.0	1.0	1.0	5.0				

105	129.33	121	(0.1)		11.1	2.2	1704	141	108	1454	135
	1	1.6	1	(344)	1.6	1.6	1.6				
110	124.46	190	(0.1)	(324)	11.1	2.2	2449	180	138	1354	172
	1.6	0.1	0.1	1.6	1.6	1.6	1.6				
111	121.96	41	(0.4)	(347)	11.3	2.3	2860	202	154	1195	193
	2.0	3.0	1.0	1.0	1.0	1.0	1.0				
112	122.03	126	(0.3)	(331)	11.2	2.2	2860	202	154	1242	193
	2.0	1.0	3.0	1.0	1.0	1.0	1.0				
113	122.03	120	(0.3)	(332)	11.2	2.2	2860	202	154	1238	193
	2.0	1.0	1.0	3.0	1.0	1.0	1.0				
114	122.21	322	(0.02)	(296)	11.0	2.1	2860	202	154	1351	193
	2.0	1.0	1.0	1.0	3.0	1.0	1.0				
115	121.06	160	(1.0)	(389)	11.3	1.9	2860	202	562	491	193
	2.0	1.0	1.0	1.0	1.0	3.0	1.0				
118	121.04	152	(1.0)	(391)	11.3	1.9	2860	202	567	476	193
	2.0	0.9	0.1	3.0	1.0	2.0	1.0				
119	121.15	818	(0.5)	(296)	10.7	1.3	2860	202	763	476	193
	3.0	0.1	0.1	0.1	0.1	6.5	0.1				
120	122.58	3675	2.7	122	8.4	0.3	2860	202	983	1649	193
	3.0	0.1	0.1	0.1	6.5	0.1	0.1				
122	121.02	98	(1.0)	(399)	11.4	2.0	2860	202	551	476	193
	3.0	0.1	0:1	6.5	0.1	0.1	0.1				
124	123.36	336	(0.3)	(321)	11.0	2.0	2579	187	307	1101	179
	3.0	0.5	0.1	0.4	1.5	1.5	3.0				
125	137.84	152	(1.4)	(491)	11.3	1.7	240	65	891	153	62
	0.5	0.1	0.1	0.1	0.1	0.1	9.0				
129	129.20	3693	2.7	94	8.4	0.4	1572	134	1071	1634	129
	0.5	0.1	1.0	1.0	7.0	0.1	0.3				
133	148.17	628	0.8	(277)	10.6	2.0	(216)	41	31	2092	39
	0.1	0.5	0.2	0.2	3.0	3.0	3.0				
135	144.33	118	0.1	(362)	11.0	2.3	81	56	43	1754	54
	0.1	1.0	1.0	5.0	1.0	1.0	0.9				
138	131.79	150	(1.3)	(461)	11.3	1.8	1016	105	795	249	101
	2.0	0.2	0.2	0.2	0.2	0.2	7.0				

TABLE C.2

Sample Results from Cases 201-338, Using Modified Objectives

Objective Case	Taxation (minimized)	Population 18,000	Retail Sales $34 Million	Average Income $9,633	Percent Low Income Families 15	Percent Elderly Families 22.7	Added Employment 50	x_1	x_2	x_3	x_4
201	120.64	748	(2.0)	(974)	12.7	3.2	3810	202	154	476	193
	10.0	0	0	0	0	0	0				
202	137.64	0	(2.6)	(1164)	13.4	3.9	1481	80	61	493	77
	0	10.0	0	0	0	0	0				
203	140.71	2945	0	(497)	10.7	1.5	950	460	369	745	50
	0	0	10.0	0	0	0	0				
204	149.92	4850	2.3	0	9.2	0.6	(50)	969	0	1428	0
	0	0	0	10.0	0	0	0				
205	149.46	8723	6.6	25	6.6	1.5	(50)	0	1125	3500	0
	0	0	0	0	10.0	0	0				
206	140.36	5103	2.1	(318)	8.8	0	950	195	915	1472	50
	0	0	0	0	0	10.0	0				
207	156.40	220	(2.4)	(1115)	13.2	3.7	0	100	100	500	2.5
	0	0	0	0	0	0	10.0				
215	129.13	226	(2.5)	(1104)	13.2	3.7	2435	130	99	442	124
	1.43	1.43	1.43	1.43	1.43	1.43	1.43				
300	141.27	368	(2.1)	(1080)	12.9	3.6	1188	65	49	752	62
	1.0	1.0	0.05	1.0	2.0	1.5	3.0				
302	121.61	722	(2.0)	(981)	12.7	3.3	3632	192	147	495	184
	2.0	0.5	0.5	2.0	2.0	2.0	1.0				
303	143.87	1457	(0.7)	(851)	11.7	2.7	1038	57	43	1385	54
	1.0	0.1	0.9	1.0	1.0	1.0	5.0				

305	135.45	213	(2.4)	(1112)	13.2	3.7	1717	92	71	568	88
	1.0	1.6	1.0	1.6	1.6	1.6	1.6				
310	128.56	332	(2.3)	(1078)	13.1	3.6	2524	134	103	484	129
	1.6	1.0	1.0	1.6	1.6	1.6	1.6				
311	127.42	96	(2.7)	(1134)	13.4	3.8	2638	140	107	332	134
	2.0	3.0	1.0	1.0	1.0	1.0	1.0				
312	124.98	306	(2.4)	(1081)	13.2	3.6	3017	160	123	378	153
	2.0	1.0	3.0	1.0	1.0	1.0	1.0				
313	125.45	264	(2.5)	(1092)	13.2	3.7	2940	156	119	369	149
	2.0	1.0	1.0	3.0	1.0	1.0	1.0				
314	124.86	520	(2.2)	(1031)	12.9	3.4	3070	163	125	487	156
	2.0	1.0	1.0	1.0	3.0	1.0	1.0				
315	124.83	320	(2.4)	(1078)	13.1	3.6	3041	161	123	381	154
	2.0	1.0	1.0	1.0	1.0	3.0	1.0				
318	124.06	299	(2.5)	(1083)	13.2	3.6	3003	159	122	377	153
	2.0	0.9	0.1	3.0	1.0	2.0	1.0				
319	120.90	1567	(1.4)	(845)	11.9	2.5	3810	202	395	476	193
	3.0	0.1	0.1	0.1	0.1	6.5	0.1				
320	123.79	4357	2.6	345	9.3	0.9	3810	202	154	2481	193
	3.0	0.1	0.1	0.1	6.5	0.1	0.1				
322	120.64	748	(2.0)	(974)	12.7	3.2	3810	202	154	476	193
	3.0	0.1	0.1	6.5	0.1	0.1	0.1				
324	125.89	531	(2.2)	(1030)	12.9	3.4	2920	155	119	521	149
	3.0	0.5	0.1	0.4	1.5	1.5	3.0				
325	148.80	247	(2.9)	(1207)	13.3	3.4	365	22	433	51	21
	0.5	0.1	0.1	0.1	0.1	0.1	9.0				
329	135.80	4345	2.8	(369)	9.2	1.0	2009	107	82	2809	103
	0.5	0.1	1.0	1.0	7.0	0.1	0.3				
333	152.12	8.0	(3.1)	(1260)	13.6	3.7	155	11	389	25	10
	0.1	5.0	0.1	0.1	0.1	0.6	4.0				
335	159.64	216	(2.1)	(1123)	13.0	3.7	(50)	0	0	898	0
	0.1	1.0	1.0	5.0	1.0	1.0	0.9				
338	137.63	235	(2.7)	(1164)	13.3	3.6	1371	74	305	175	71
	2.0	0.2	0.2	0.2	0.2	0.2	7.0				

TABLE C.3

Sample Results from Cases 501-638, Assuming a Decrease in External Funding

Case	Objective Taxation (minimized)	Population 20,000	Retail Sales $34 Million	Average Income $9,633	Percent Low Income Families 15	Percent Elderly Families 22.7	Added Employment 1000	x_1	x_2	x_3	x_4
501	145.63	(1252)	(2.0)	(608)	12.7	3.2	2860	202	154	476	193
	10.0	0	0	0	0	0	0				
502	170.89	0	(0.9)	(335)	11.5	2.2	0	331	307	610	50
	0	10.0	0	0	0	0	0				
503	170.36	945	0	(131)	10.7	1.5	0	460	369	745	50
	0	0	10.0	0	0	0	0				
504	169.72	1392	0.4	0	10.3	1.2	0	615	347	709	50
	0	0	0	10.0	0	0	0				
505	182.61	6723	6.6	391	6.6	1.5	0	0	1125	3500	0
	0	0	0	0	0	0	(1000)				
506	170.53	3103	2.1	48	8.8	0	0	195	915	1472	50
	0	0	0	0	10.0	0	0				
507	172.38	(1780)	(2.4)	(749)	13.2	3.7	0	100	100	500	50
	0	0	0	0	0	10.0	0				
515	148.30	122	(0.3)	(333)	11.2	2.2	2746	196	150	1261	187
	1.43	1.43	1.43	1.43	1.43	1.43	1.43				
600	160.42	224	0.1	(330)	11.0	2.2	1266	118	91	1593	113
	1.0	1.0	0.5	1.0	2.0	1.5	3.0				
602	147.95	437	0.1	(276)	10.9	2.0	2860	202	154	1415	193
	2.0	0.5	0.5	2.0	2.0	2.0	1.0				
603	161.92	1009	0.1	(295)	10.5	1.2	865	97	760	809	93
	1.0	0.9	0.9	1.0	1.0	1.0	5.0				

	1.0			1.6	1.6	1.6				148
610	148.25	189	1.0 (0.2)	1.6 (321)	11.1	2.2	2766	197	151	1294	188
611	147.44	40	1.0 (0.4)	1.6 (347)	11.6	1.6	1.6	202	154	1194	193
612	147.55	123	1.0 (0.3)	1.0 (332)	11.3	2.3	2860 1.0	202	154	1240	193
613	147.54	116	3.0 (0.3)	1.0 (333)	11.2 1.0	1.0 2.2	2860 1.0	202	154	1236	193
614	147.80	319	1.0 (0.02)	3.0 (297)	11.2 1.0	1.0 2.2	2860 1.0	202	154	1349	193
615	146.48	157	1.0 (1.0)	1.0 (390)	11.0 3.0	2.1 1.0	2860 1.0	202	569	476	193
618	146.48	149	1.0 (1.0)	1.0 (392)	11.3 1.0	1.9 3.0	2860 1.0	202	566	476	193
619	146.78	790	0.1 (0.5)	3.0 (300)	11.3 1.0	1.9 2.0	2860 1.0	202	755	476	193
620	149.05	3649	0.1 2.7	0.1 118	10.7 0.1	1.4 6.5	2860 0.1	202	984	1632	193
622	146.43	54	0.1 (1.1)	0.1 (406)	8.4 6.5	0.3 0.1	2860 0.1	202	538	476	193
624	147.44	326	0.1 (0.3)	11.4 0.1	11.0	2.0 0.1	2860 0.1	202	289	1099	193
625	166.27	147	0.5 0.1	0.4 (315)	1.5	2.0 1.5	2860 3.0	202	884	159	64
	0.5		(1.4)	(490)	11.3	1.7	285 9.0	67	1037	1642	153
629	153.81	3691	0.1 2.7	0.1 105	0.1 8.4	0.1 0.3	2065 0.3	160	33	2085	41
633	178.33	628	0.1 0.8	1.0 (276)	7.0 10.6	0.1 2.0	(178) 3.0	43			
635	172.82	118	0.5 0.2	0.2 (361)	3.0 11.0	3.0 2.3	178 0.9	62	47	1736	59
638	158.07	134	0.1 1.0	0.2 (457)	1.0 11.3	1.0 1.8	1179 7.0	114	770	269	109
	2.0	0.2	(1.2)	0.2	0.2	0.2					

257

TABLE C.4

Sample Results from Cases 701-838, Assuming an Increase in External Funding

Objective	Taxation (minimized)	Population 20,000	Retail Sales $34 Million	Average Income $9,633	Percent Low Income Families 15	Percent Elderly Families 22.7	Added Employment 1000	x_1	x_2	x_3	x_4
Case											
701	95.30	1393	0.3	127	10.5	1.3	2860	898	154	476	193
	10.0	0	0	0	0	0	0				
702	101.94	0	(0.9)	(336)	11.5	2.2	0	331	307	610	50
	0	10.0	0	0	0	0	0				
703	101.06	945	0	(131)	10.7	1.5	0	460	369	745	50
	0	0	10.0	0	0	0	0				
704	110.37	1392	0.4	0	10.3	1.2	0	615	347	709	50
	0	0	0	10.0	0	0	0				
705	116.31	6723	6.6	392	6.6	1.5	1000	0	1125	3500	0
	0	0	0	0	10.0	0	0				
706	110.19	3103	2.1	49	8.8	0	0	195	915	1472	50
	0	0	0	0	0	10.0	0				
707	114.06	(1780)	(2.4)	(749)	13.2	3.7	0	100	100	500	50
	0	0	0	0	0	0	10.0				
715	100.31	123	(0.2)	(340)	11.1	2.2	2077	161	123	1385	154
	1.43	1.43	1.43	1.43	1.43	1.43	1.43				
800	107.91	226	0.2	(334)	11.0	2.2	873	98	75	1667	94
	1.0	1.0	0.5	1.0	2.0	1.5	3.0				
802	96.69	450	0.1	(273)	10.9	2.0	2860	202	154	1422	193
	2.0	0.5	0.5	2.0	2.0	2.0	1.0				
803	107.45	1017	0.1	(288)	10.4	1.3	604	84	691	971	80
	1.0	0.1	0.9	1.0	1.0	1.0	5.0				

258

810	1.0 100.26 1.6	192	1.0 (0.1) 1.0	1.6 (328) 1.6	1.6 11.1 1.6	1.6 2.2 1.6	1.6 2094 1.6	162	124	1420	155
811	96.47 2.0	42 3.0	(0.4) 1.0	(346) 1.0	11.3 1.0	2.3 1.0	2860 1.0	202	154	1195	193
812	96.52 2.0	130 1.0	(0.3) 3.0	(331) 3.0	11.2 1.0	2.2 1.0	2860 1.0	202	154	1244	193
813	96.51 2.0	123 1.0	(0.3) 1.0	(332) 3.0	11.2 1.0	2.2 1.0	2860 1.0	202	154	1240	193
814	96.98 2.0	325 1.0	0 1.0	(296) 1.0	11.0 3.0	2.1 1.0	2781 1.0	197	151	1367	189
815	95.69 2.0	162 1.0	(0.9) 1.0	(382) 1.0	11.3 1.0	2.0 3.0	2860 1.0	202	524	563	193
818	95.59 2.0	155 0.9	(1.0) 0.1	(391) 3.0	11.3 1.0	1.9 2.0	2860 1.0	202	568	476	193
819	95.52 3.0	845 0.1	(0.5) 0.1	(292) 0.1	10.7 0.1	1.3 6.5	2860 0.1	202	771	476	193
820	96.21 3.0	3687 0.1	2.8 0.1	129 0.1	8.4 6.5	0.3 0.1	2860 0.1	202	925	1764	193
822	95.60 3.0	142 0.1	(1.0) 0.1	(393) 6.5	11.3 0.1	1.9 0.1	2860 0.1	202	564	476	193
824	99.14 3.0	346 0.5	(0.3) 0.1	(330) 0.4	11.0 1.5	2.0 1.5	2211 3.0	168	339	1087	161
825	109.27 0.5	157 0.1	(1.4) 0.1	(492) 0.1	11.3 0.1	1.7 0.1	193 9.0	62	899	147	60
829	104.00 0.5	3697 0.1	(2.7) 1.0	(81) 1.0	8.4 7.0	0.4 0.1	1008 0.3	105	1110	1625	100
833	117.84 0.1	628 0.5	1.0 0.8	(277) 0.2	10.6 3.0	2.0 3.0	(255) 3.0	39	30	2099	37
835	115.49 0.1	118 1.0	0.2 0.2	(363) 5.0	11.0 1.0	2.3 1.0	(23) 0.9	51	39	1773	49
838	105.14 2.0	166 0.2	1.0 (1.3) 0.2	(466) 0.2	11.3 0.2	1.8 0.2	841 7.0	96	831	227	92

BIBLIOGRAPHY

Ackoff, Russell L. The Scientific Method. New York: John Wiley, 1962.

_____. A Concept of Corporate Planning. New York: John Wiley, 1970.

Alonso, William. "Cities and City Planners," Daedalus 92 (Fall 1963): 825-26.

Altshuler, Alan. The City Planning Process. Ithaca: Cornell University Press, 1965.

_____. The Goals of Comprehensive Planning. Reprint 12. AIP Journal 31, no. 3 (August 1965): 186-95.

American Society of Planning Officials. School Enrollment by Housing Type. Planning Advisory Report no. 210. Chicago: The Society.

Anderson, Robert M. Zoning Law and Practice in New York State. New York: Lawyer's Cooperative, 1963.

Andrews, Richard B. "Comment re Criticisms of the Economic Base Theory." Journal of the American Institute of Planners no. 1 (1958).

"Apartments? Here? Never.'" Changing Times, March 1965.

Arrow, Kenneth J. Social Choice and Individual Values. New York: John Wiley, 1963.

Balinsky, M. L., and Baumol, W. J. "The Dual in Non-Linear Programming and Its Economic Interpretation." Review of Economic Studies 30 (July 1968): 237-56.

Barton, Richard T. A Primer on Simulation and Gaming. Englewood Cliffs, N.J.: Prentice-Hall, 1970.

Bassett, Edward M. Zoning. New York: Russell Sage Foundation, 1946.

Bassett, Edward M.; Williams, F.; Bettman, A.; and Whitten, R. *Model Planning Laws*. Cambridge, Mass.: Harvard University Press, 1935.

Bauer, Raymond, ed. *Social Indicators*. Cambridge, Mass.: MIT Press, 1966.

Baumol, William J. *Economic Theory and Operations Analysis*. 3rd ed. Englewood Cliffs, N.J.: Prentice-Hall, 1972.

Benayoun, R., et al. "Linear Programming with Multiple Objective Functions: Step Method." *Mathematical Programming* 1 (1971): 366-75.

Beshers, James M., ed. *Computer Methods in the Analysis of Large-Scale Social Systems*. Cambridge, Mass.: MIT Press, 1965.

Beuscher, Jacob, and Wright, R. *Land Use, Cases and Materials*. St. Paul, Minn.: West Publishing Co., 1969.

Birstein, Samuel J.; Hossaire, A.; and Sheldon, R. "Urban Residential Renewal Investments: A Policy Analysis Employing Linear Programming." *Socio-Economic Planning Sciences* 6 (1972), pp. 251-62.

Blau, Julian H. "The Existence of Social Welfare Functions." *Econometrica* 25 (April 1957): 302-13.

Bourne, Larry S., ed. *Internal Structure of the City, Readings on Space and Environment*. New York: Oxford University Press, 1971.

Branch, Melville C., Jr. "Comprehensive Planning: A New Field of Study." *Journal of the American Institute of Planners* 28 (1959): 115-20.

_____. *The Corporate Planning Process*. New York: American Management Association, 1962.

_____. "Delusions and Diffusions in City Planning." *Management Science*; Applications ser. 16, no. 12 (August 1970): B-714-31.

Brewer, Garry. *Politician, Bureaucrats and the Consultant*. New York: Basic Books, 1973.

Brewer, Garry. What's the Purpose? What's the Use? Santa Monica, Calif.: RAND Corp., 1973.

Bryce, Lord James. Housing Problems in America, 1909. Proceedings, Second National Conference on Housing (Cambridge: 1912).

Burnham, Daniel H., and Bennett, Edward. Plan of Chicago, 1909. Chicago: Commercial Club, 1909. Reprinted New York: Da Capo Press, 1970.

Capital District Regional Planning Commission. Housing. Albany: The Commission, 1970.

Center for Real Estate and Urban Economics, Institute of Urban Regional Development. Jobs, People and Land: Bay Area Simulation Study. Berkeley: University of California, 1968.

Chapin, F. Stuart, Jr. Urban Land Use Planning. Urbana: University of Illinois Press, 1957. Reprint 1965.

_____. "Foundations of Urban Planning." In Urban Life and Form, edited by Werner Hirsch. New York: Holt, Rinehart, and Winston, 1963.

Charnes, A., and Cooper, W. W. "Programming with Linear Fractional Functionals." Naval Research Log Quarterly 9 (1962): 181-86.

_____. Management Models and Industrial Applications of Linear Programming. New York: John Wiley, 1964.

Charnes, A., and Stedry, A. C. "Investigations into the Theory of Multiple-Budgeted Goals." In Management Controls: New Directions in Basic Research, edited by C. Bonini, R. Jaedicke, and H. Wagner. New York: McGraw-Hill, 1964.

Chase, Samuel B., ed. Problems in Public Expenditure Analysis. Washington, D.C.: The Brookings Institution, 1968.

Chase Manhattan Bank, N.A., Economic Resource Division. Improving Quality of Life, a Study of the Economics of Pollution Control. New York: The Bank, n.d.

Chermayeff, Serge, and Tzonis, A. Shape of Community Realization of Human Potential. Baltimore: Penguin Books, 1971.

Chimura, Thomas J., and Wallace, William A. "A Test of a Municipal Budgeting Simulation in a Small City." Socio-Economic Planning Sciences 9 (June 1975): 131-36.

Cincinnati City Planning Commission. Industrial Areas. Cincinnati: The Commission, 1946.

Clavel, Pierre. "Planners and Citizen Boards: Some Applications of Social Theory to the Problem of Plan Implementation." Journal of the American Institute of Planners 34 (May 1968): 130-39.

Clawson, Marion. Suburban Land Conversion in the U.S.: An Economic and Governmental Process. Baltimore: Johns Hopkins Press, 1971.

Coger, Lewis A., ed. Political Sociology—Selected Essays. New York: Harper and Row, 1966.

Cohoes Planning and Development Agency. Cohoes Housing Study. Cohoes: The Agency, 1971.

_____. Economic and Marketing Study. Cohoes: The Agency, 1972.

_____. Fiscal Impact of Equinox Estates, National Homes and Columbia Gardens on the City of Cohoes. Cohoes: The Agency, 1972.

_____. Impact Analysis of Equinox Estates, National Homes and Columbia Gardens on the Cohoes Public School District. Cohoes: The Agency, 1972.

Coke, James G. "Antecedents of Local Planning." In Principles and Practice of Urban Planning, edited by William Goodman. Washington, D.C.: International City Managers' Association, 1971.

Committee for Economic Development. Budgeting for National Objectives, A Statement by the Research and Policy Committee. New York: The Committee, 1966.

Cooper, W. W.; Eastman, C.; Johnson, N.; and Kortanek, K. O. Systems Approaches to Urban Planning: Mixed, Conditional, Adaptive and Other Alternatives. Pittsburgh: Carnegie-Mellon University, 1971.

Coplin, William D. Simulation in the Study of Politics. Chicago: Markham Publishing Co., 1968.

Coughlin, Robert E., and Isard, Walter. Municipal Costs and Revenues Resulting from Community Growth. Wellesley, Mass.: Chandler-Davis, 1957.

Council of Environmental Quality. The Cost of Sprawl. 411-00022. Washington, D.C.: U.S. Government Printing Office, 1974.

County and Municipal Government Study Commission. Housing and Suburbs: Fiscal and Social Impact of Multi-family Development. Trenton, N.J.: The Commission, 1974.

Courtney, James, et al. "A Goal-Programming Approach to Urban-Suburban Location Preferences." Management Science 18, no. 6 (February 1972): B258-68.

Crecine, John P. Governmental Problem Solving. Chicago: Rand McNally, 1969.

_____. Financing the Metropolis Pubic Policy in Urban Economics. Beverly Hills, Calif.: Sage Publishers, 1970.

Cross, Kenneth E. A Gradient Projection Method for Constrained Optimization. Oak Ridge, Tenn.: Union Carbide Corp., Nuclear Division, Computing Technology Center, 1968.

Curtiss, David W. "Tax Exemption of Educational Property in New York." Cornell Law Quarterly 52, no. 4 (1967): 1-16.

Czamanski, Stanislaw. "A Method of Forecasting Metropolitan Growth by Means of Distributed Logs Analysis." Journal of Regional Science 6, no. 1 (1965): 1-15.

_____. "Effects of Public Investments on Urban Land Values." Journal of the American Institute of Planners (July 1966): 204-17.

Dalkey, Norman C. Delphi. P-3704. Santa Monica, Calif.: RAND Corp., 1967.

_____. Quality of Life. P-3805. Santa Monica, Calif.: RAND Corp., 1968.

Davidoff, Paul, and Reiner, T.A. "A Choice Theory of Planning." Journal of the American Institute of Planners 28 (May 1962): 103-15.

Department of Audit and Control, Division of Municipal Affairs, New York State. <u>Overall Real Property Tax Rates Local Government in New York State</u>. Albany: The Department, 1971 and 1972.

Department of City Planning. <u>A Land Use Plan for the Roanoke Valley Region</u>. Roanoke, Va.: The Department, 1963.

Dorfman, Robert, ed. <u>Measuring Benefits of Government Investments</u>. Washington, D.C.: The Brookings Institution, 1965.

Dorsett, L. W., ed. <u>The Challenge of the City</u>. Lexington, Mass.: D.C. Heath, 1968.

Dror, Yehezekel. <u>Analytical Approaches and Applied Social Science</u>. P-4248. Santa Monica, Calif.: RAND Corp., 1969.

_____. <u>Law as a Tool of Directed Social Change: A Framework for Policy-makers</u>. P-4285. Santa Monica, Calif.: RAND Corp., 1970.

_____. <u>Urban Metapolicy and Urban Education</u>. P-4314. Santa Monica, Calif.: RAND Corp., 1970.

Duncan, Beverly. "Factors in Work-Residence Separation." <u>American Sociological Review</u> 21 (February 1956).

Dyckman, John W. "Planning and Decision Theory." <u>Journal of the American Institute of Planners</u> 27 (November 1961): 335-43.

Dyer, James R. "Interactive Goal Programming." <u>Management Science</u> 19, no. 1 (September 1972): 62-70.

Eastman, Charles M., and Kortanek, L. O. "Modeling School Facility Requirements in New Communities." <u>Management Science</u> 10, no. 12 (August 1970): B784-98.

Economic Developmental Administration. <u>Feasibility Study for an Industrial Park Development in Bisbee, Arizona</u>. Washington, D.C.: U.S. Department of Commerce, 1972.

_____. <u>Feasibility Study of Industrial Park Locations in Fulton and Schoharie Counties, New York</u>. Washington, D.C.: U.S. Department of Commerce, 1974.

Eddy, Elizabeth M., ed. <u>Urban Anthropology: Research Perspectives and Strategies</u>. Athens: University of Georgia Press, 1968.

Edel, Matthew, and Rothenberg, J. <u>Readings in Urban Economics</u>. New York: Macmillan, 1972.

Eldredge, Wenthworth, ed. <u>Taming Megalopolis</u>. Garden City, N.Y.: Doubleday, 1967.

Evans, J. P., and Steuer, R. E. "A Revised Simplex Method for Linear Multiple-Objective Programs." <u>Journal of Mathematical Programming</u> 5 (1973): 54-72.

Fairfax County Planning Division. <u>Student Contribution from Apartments and Mobile Homes</u>. Fairfax, Va.: The Division, 1966.

Feldt, Allan G. "The Metropolitan Area Concept: An Evaluation of the 1950 SMA's." <u>Journal of the American Statistical Association</u> 60, no. 310 (June 1965).

_____. "Operational Gaming in Planning Education." <u>Journal of the American Institute of Planners</u> 22, no. 1 (January, 1966): 17-23.

_____, and Wheeler, R. H. <u>The Balance of Social Economic and Demographic Language in Puerto Rico—1956-60</u>. Ithaca, N.Y.: Center for Housing and Environmental Studies, Cornell University.

Ferguson, C. E. <u>Microeconomic Theory</u>. Homewood, Ill.: Richard D. Irwin, 1972.

First National Bank of Boston, Municipal Securities Department. <u>Debt Service Schedule</u>. Boston: The Bank, 1970.

Fisch, Oscar. "Impact Analysis and Optimal Urban Densities and Optimal City Size." <u>Journal of Regional Science</u> 14, no. 2 (1974): 233-47.

Fishburn, Peter C. "Methods of Estimating Additive Utilities." <u>Management Science</u> 13, no. 7 (March 1967): 435-53.

_____. "Preferences, Summation and Social Welfare Functions." <u>Management Science</u> 16, no. 3 (November 1969): 179-86.

_____. <u>Utility Theory for Decision Making</u>. New York: John Wiley, 1970.

Fisher, Gene H. *Cost Considerations in Systems Analysis*. New York: American Elsevier, 1971.

Fite, Harry H. *The Computer Challenge to Urban Planners and State Administrators*. The American University Technology of Management Series, vol. 2. London: Macmillan, 1965.

Forrester, Jay W. *Urban Dynamics*. Cambridge, Mass.: MIT Press, 1968.

Forsyth, J. "Utilization of Goal Programming in Production and Capital Expenditure Planning." *CORS Journal* 7, no. 2 (July 1969): 136-40.

Friedman, John. "Comprehensive Planning as a Process." *Journal of the American Institute of Planners* 31 (August 1965): 195-97.

Gaffney, Mason M. "The Property Tax Is a Progressive Tax." Washington, D.C.: Resources for the Future, 1971. (Mimeo.).

Gallion, Arthur, and Eisner, Simon. *The Urban Pattern*. Princeton, N.J.: D. Van Nostrand, 1963.

Garn, Harvey, and Wilson, Robert. *A Critical Look at Urban Dynamics, The Forrester Model and Public Policy*. Washington, D.C.: The Urban Institute, 1970.

Genesky, S. M. *Some Comments on Urban Research*. P-3827. Santa Monica, Calif.: RAND, 1968.

Geoffrion, Arthur M. "Strictly Concave Parametric Programming, Part I: Basic Theory." *Management Science* 13, no. 3 (November 1966): 244-53.

_____. "Strictly Concave Parametric Programming, Part II: Additional Theory and Computational Consideration." *Management Science* 13, no. 5 (January 1967): 359-70.

_____. "Proper Efficiency and the Theory of Vector Maximization." *Journal of Mathematical Analysis and Applications* 22 (1968): 618-30.

George, Henry. *City and Country*. Vol. 3. New York: Doubleday and McClure, 1898.

Gerra, M. J., and Ross, M. S. "An Interactive City Planning Model." *Omega* 1, no. 6 (1973).

Gist, Noel, and Fava, Sylvia. *Urban Society*. New York: Thomas Crowell, 1964.

Glaab, Charles, and Brown, T., eds. *A History of Urban America*. New York: Macmillan, 1967.

Goals for Dallas. Submitted for consideration by Dallas citizens. Dallas: Goals for Dallas, 1966.

Goodman, David A. "A Goal Programming Approach to Aggregate Planning of Production and Work Force." *Management Science* 20, no. 12 (August 1974).

Goodman, Leo, and Markowitz, Harry. "Social Welfare Functions Based on Individual Rankings." *American Journal of Sociology* 58 (November 1952).

Gordon, Peter, and MacReinold, W. K. "Optimal Urban Forms." *Journal of Regional Science* 14, no. 2 (1974): 217-33.

Granger, Charles H. "The Hierarchy of Objectives." *Harvard Business Review* 42 (May-June 1964): 63-74.

Greene, Kenneth; Neenan, Lillian; and Scott, Claudia. *Fiscal Interactions in a Metropolitan Area*. Washington, D.C.: The Urban Institute, 1974.

Groves, Harold M., and Riew, John. "The Impact of Industry on Local Taxes." *National Tax Journal* 16, no. 2 (June 1963): 137-46.

Gruen, Victor. *The Heart of Our Cities*. New York: Simon and Schuster, 1964.

Guetzkow, Harold; Kotler, P.; and Schultz, R. L. *Simulation in Social and Administrative Science, Overview and Case-Example*. Englewood Cliffs, N.J.: Prentice-Hall, 1972.

Hadley, G. *Non-Linear and Dynamic Programming*. Reading, Mass.: Addison-Wesley, 1964.

Haggard, Sue A., et al. *Program Budgeting for School District Planning: Concepts and Applications*. RM-6116-RC. Santa Monica, Calif.: RAND, 1969.

Haines, Yacov Y., and Hall, W. A. "Multi-objectives in Water Resource Systems Analysis: The Surrogate World Trade Off Method." Water Resources Research 10, no. 4 (August 1974): 615-24.

Harland Bartholomew and Associates. A Major Street Plan for Rochester. St. Louis, 1929.

Harris, Britton. "The Uses of Theory in the Simulation of Urban Phenomena." Journal of the American Institute of Planners (September 1967).

Hatry, Harry P.; Winme, R. E.; and Fish, D. M. Practical Program Evaluation for State and Local Government Officials. Washington, D.C.: The Urban Institute, 1973.

Henderson, James M., and Quandt, Richard. Microeconomic Theory: A Mathematical Approach. New York: McGraw-Hill, 1971.

Hildreth, Clifford. "Alternative Conditions for Social Orderings." Econometrica 21 (January 1953): 81-95.

Hill, Morris. "A Goals-Achievement Matrix for Evaluating Alternative Plans." Journal of the American Institute of Planners (May 1968): 19-29.

Hirsch, Werner Z. "Fiscal Impact of Industrialization on Local Schools." Review of Economics and Statistics 46, no. 2 (May 1964): 191-99.

_____. The Economics of State and Local Government. New York: McGraw-Hill, 1970.

_____. Urban Economic Analysis. New York: McGraw-Hill, 1973.

Hodge, Gerald. "Use and Mis-Use of Measurement Scales in City Planning." Journal of the American Institute of Planners (May 1963): 112-21.

Hudson, Barclay M.; Wachs, M.; and Schofer, J. "Local Impact Evaluation in the Design of Large-Scale Urban Systems." Journal of the American Institute of Planners 40, no. 4 (July 1974): 255-65.

Ijiri, Yuri. Management Goals and Accounting for Control. Chicago: Rand-McNally, 1965.

International City Managers' Association. <u>Municipal Finance Administration</u>. Washington, D.C.: The Association, 1962.

Isard, Walter, et al. <u>General Theory: Social, Political, Economical and Regional</u>. Cambridge, Mass.: MIT Press, 1969.

_____, and Czamanski, S. <u>Techniques for Estimating Local and Regional Multiplier Effects of Changes in the Level of Major Governmental Programs</u>. N.Y.: Reprinted from Peace Research Society: Papers, 3, Chicago Conference, 1965.

Jacobs, Jane. <u>The Death and Life of Great American Cities</u>. New York: Random House, 1961.

Johnson, N., and Ward, E. "Citizen Information Systems: Using Technology to Extend the Dialogue Between Citizens and Their Government." <u>Management Science</u> 19, no. 4 (December 1972): 21-34.

Joine, Charles A. <u>Organizational Analysis, Political Sociological Administrative Process of Local Government</u>. East Lansing: Institute for Community Development and Services, Continuing Education Services, Michigan State University, 1964.

Jones, Martin, and Flax, Michael. <u>The Quality of Life in Metropolitan Washington, D.C</u>. Washington, D.C.: The Urban Institute, 1970.

Kalbach, Warren E.; Meyer, George C.; and Walker, John R. <u>Metropolitan Area Mobility, A Comparative Analysis of Family Spatial Mobility in a Central City and Selected Suburbs</u>. Reprint 6. Ithaca, N.Y.: Center for Housing and Environmental Studies, Cornell University.

Kee, Woo Sik. "Industrial Development and Its Impact on Local Finance." <u>Quarterly Review of Economics and Business</u> 8 (1968): 19-24.

Kephart, W. L., and Copper, J. R. <u>Some Improvements in the Gradient Search Method of Optimization</u>. Oak Ridge, Tenn.: Union Carbide Corp., Nuclear Division, Computing Technology Center, 1965.

Kilbridge, Maurice D., et al. <u>Urban Analysis</u>. Cambridge, Mass.: Harvard University Press, 1970.

Kinnard, William N. Industrial Real Estate. Washington, D.C.: Society of Industrial Realtors, 1967.

Koopmans, Tjaling C. Activity Analysis of Production and Allocation. Cowles Commission Monograph no. 13. New York: John Wiley, 1951.

Kornbluth, J. S. H. "A Survey of Goal Programming." Omega 1, no. 2 (1973): 193-205.

Kouwenhoven, John. Adventures of America: A Pictorial Record from Harper's Weekly. New York: Harper Brothers, 1938.

Kristof, Frank S. "Housing Policy Goals and the Turnover of Housing." Journal of the American Institute of Planners 31 (August 1965): 232-45.

Kuhn, H. W., and Tucker, A. W. Proceedings, Second Berkeley Symposium on Mathematical Statistics and Probability. Berkeley, Calif.: 1950.

Laidlaw, Charles D. Linear Programming for Urban Development Plan Evaluation. New York: Praeger, 1972.

Lee, Sang M. Goal Programming for Decision Analysis. Philadelphia: Auerbach, 1972.

_____, and Clayton, Edward. "Goal Programming Model for Academic Resource Allocation." Management Science 18, no. 8 (April 1972): B395-408.

_____, and Nicely, R. E. "Goal Programming for Marketing Decisions: A Cash Study." Journal of Marketing 38 (January 1974).

Leven, Charles L. "Establishing Goals for Regional Economic Development." Journal of the American Institute of Planners 30 (May 1964): 100-10.

Lieftinck, P.; Sadove, A. R.; and Creyke, T. Water and Power Resources of West Pakistan. vol. 3. Baltimore: Johns Hopkins Press, 1969.

Lindblom, Charles E. "The Policy Making Process." In Foundations of Modern Political Science Service, edited by R. A. Dahl. Englewood Cliffs, N.J.: Prentice-Hall, 1968.

Lindblom, Charles E. "The Science of Muddling Through." Public Administration Review 19 (Spring 1959): 78-89.

Litchfield, Nathaniel. "Cost-Benefit Analysis in City Planning." Journal of the American Institute of Planners 26 (November 1960).

_____, and Margolis, Julius. "Benefit-Cost Analysis as a Tool in Urban Government Decision-Making." In Public Expenditure Decisions in the Urban Community, edited by Howard C. Schaller, pp. 118-46. Baltimore: Johns Hopkins Press, 1963.

Loewenstein, Louis K. "The Impact of New Industry on the Fiscal Revenues and Expenditures of Suburban Communities," National Tax Journal 16, no. 2 (June 1963): 113-36.

Lowry, Ira S. A Model of Metropolis. RM-4035. Santa Monica, Calif.: RAND Corp., 1964.

Mace, Ruth, and Wicker, Warren. Do Single Family Homes Pay Their Way? Research Monograph no. 15. Washington, D.C.: The Urban Institute, 1968.

MacRae, Duncan C. An Economic Evaluation of Urban Development. URI 10011. Washington, D.C.: The Urban Institute.

Margolis, Julius. "Municipal Fiscal Structure in a Metropolitan Region." Journal of Political Economy 65, no. 3 (1957): 232.

_____, ed. The Public Economy of Urban Community. Baltimore: Johns Hopkins Press, 1965.

Maryland National Park and Planning Commission. Population and Household Growth Forecast. Silver Spring: The Commission, 1972.

Masser, Ian. Analytical Models for Urban and Regional Planning. New York: John Wiley, 1972

McKeener, J. Ross. Business Parks. Washington, D.C.: The Urban Land Institute, 1970.

McLoone, Eugene P., et al. Long-Range Revenue Estimation. Washington, D.C.: George Washington University Press, 1967.

Metropolitan Planning Commission. How Should Our Community Grow? Portland, Ore.: The Commission, 1966.

Metropolitan Washington Council of Governments. "EMPIRIC" Activity Allocation Model: Application to Washington Metropolitan Region. Washington, D.C.: Peat, Marwick, Mitchell and Co., The Council, 1972.

Meyerson, Martin. "Building the Middle-Range Bridge for Comprehensive Planning." Journal of the American Institute of Planners 22 (Spring 1956): 58-64.

―――. "Some Changing Patterns of American Urbanism." In Education for Urban Administration, American Academy of Political and Social Science, Monograph no. 16, edited by F. Cleavland. 1973.

―――, and Banfield, Edward. Politics, Planning and the Public Interest—The Case of Public Housing in Chicago. New York: Free Press of Glencoe, 1955.

Michael, Donald N. "Urban Policy in the Rationalized Society." Journal of the American Institute of Planners 31 (November 1965): 283-88.

Miller, Irwin, and Freund, John. Probability and Statistics for Engineers. Englewood Cliffs, N.J.: Prentice-Hall, 1965.

Mocine, Corwin R. "Urban Physical Planning and the 'New Planning.'" Journal of the American Institute of Planners 32 (May 1966): 234-37.

Montgomery County Planning Board. Fiscal Impact Analysis, Germantown Master Plan. Silver Spring, Md.: The Board, 1974.

Morris, William T. "On the Art of Modeling." Management Science 13, no. 12 (August 1967): B707-17.

Morse, Philip M., and Bacon, L. W. Operations Research for Public Systems. Cambridge, Mass.: MIT Press, 1967.

Mortimore, Roger. "Corporate Planning in Local Government: Some Measurement Problems." Omega 1, no. 6 (1973): 711-19.

Muller, Thomas, and Dawson, Grace. The Fiscal Impact of Residential and Commercial Development: A Case Study. Washington, D.C.: The Urban Institute, 1972.

Mumford, Lewis. The City in History. New York: Harcourt, Brace, 1961.

Muncy, Dorothy A. Space for Industry, an Analysis of Site and Location Requirements. Technical Bulletin no. 23. Washington, D.C.: The Urban Land Institute, 1954.

Mushkin, Selma, ed. Public Prices for Public Products. Washington, D.C.: The Urban Institute, 1972.

National Academy of Sciences. Long-Range Planning for Urban Research and Development of Technological Considerations. Washington, D.C.: The Academy, 1969.

_____. National Academy of Engineering. Urban Growth and Land Development, the Land Conversion Process. Washington, D.C.: The Academy, 1972.

_____. National Academy of Engineering. Revenue Sharing and the Planning Process, Shifting the Focus of Responsibility for Domestic Problem Solving. Washington, D.C.: The Academy, 1974.

National Association of Home Builders. Garden Apartments and School Age Children. Washington, D.C.: The Association, 1962.

_____. "Schools and Urban Growth." Washington, D.C.: The Association, n.d. (mimeo.).

National Association of Industrial Parks. Reconnaissance Study, The Community Impact of Industrial Parks. Washington, D.C.: The Association, 1974.

National Commission on Urban Problems. Building the American City, Report of the National Commission on Urban Problems. New York: Praeger, 1971.

National Resource Committee. Our Cities, Their Role in the National Economy. Washington, D.C.: U.S. Government Printing Office, 1937.

National Science Foundation. An Evaluation of Policy-Related Research in the Field of Municipal Economic Development. Washington, D.C.: The Foundation, 1974.

Netzer, Dick. Economics of the Property Tax. Washington, D.C.: The Brookings Institution, 1966.

Niedercorn, John H., and Kain, J. F. Suburbanization of Employment and Population 1948-75. Santa Monica, Calif.: RAND Corp., 1963.

Nolen, John, ed. City Planning. New York: D. Appleton and Co., 1916 and 1929.

Office of Planning Coordination. Control of Land Subdivisions. Albany, N.Y.: The Office, 1967.

Pascal, Anthony A., ed. Contributions to the Analysis of Urban Problems. P-3868. Santa Monica, Calif.: RAND, 1968.

Pasma, Theodore. "Characteristics of 63 Modern Industrial Plans." Industrial Development (March/April 1970).

Peattie, Lisa R. "Reflections on Advocacy Planning." Journal of the American Institute of Planners 34 (March 1968).

Perkins, Homer. "Urban Design and City Planning." In Planning and the Urban Community, edited by Harvey Perloff. Pittsburgh: University of Pittsburgh Press, 1961.

Perloff, Harvey. Education for Planning: City, State, and Regional. Washington, D.C.: Resources for the Future, 1957.

Phillip, J. "Algorithms for the Vector Maximum Problem." Mathematical Programming 2 (1972): 207-29.

Port of New York Authority. The New York-New Jersey Metropolitan Area Industrial Development Guide. New York: The Authority, 1971.

Rathkopf, Charles. The Law of Zoning and Planning. New York: Crosby Press, 1949.

Reps, John W. The Making of Urban America, A History of City Planning in the United States. Princeton, N.J.: Princeton University Press, 1965.

———. *Town Planning in Frontier America*. Princeton, N.J.: Princeton University Press, 1969.

———, and Smith, J. L. "Control of Urban Land Subdivision." *Syracuse Law Review* 14, no. 3 (1963).

Riis, Jacob. *How the Other Half Lives: Studies Among the Tenements of New York*. New York: Charles Scribner's Sons, 1890.

Robinson, Charles Mulford. *City Planning*. New York: G.P. Putnam's Sons, Knickerbocker Press, 1916.

Robinson, Ira M. "Beyond the Middle-Range Planning." *Journal of the American Institute of Planners* 31 (November 1965): 304-12.

———, et al. "A Simulation Model for Renewal Programming." *Journal of the American Institute of Planners* 31 (May 1965): 126-34.

Ross, P. S., and Partners. *Promus, A Simulation System for Urban Analysis and Management*. Toronto: n.d.

Roy, B. "Problems and Methods with Multiple Objective Functions." *Mathematical Programming* 1 (1972): 239-66.

Rutherford, Scott G., Schofer, J. L., et al. "Goal Formulation for Socio-Technical Systems." *Journal of the Urban Planning and Development Division ASCE* (September 1973): 157-69.

Said, Kamal. "A Policy Selection/Goal-Formulation Model for Public Systems." *Policy Sciences* 55 (1974): 89-100.

Samuelson, Paul A. *Economics: An Introductory Analysis*. 7th ed. New York: McGraw-Hill, 1967.

Savage, E. J. *The Advisory Community on Intergovernmental Relations—A Data Base for Urban Planners*. P-4346. Santa Monica, Calif.: RAND Corp., 1970.

———. *A Case Study in Urban Development: From "Factory Town" to Balanced Community*. P-4345. Santa Monica, Calif.: RAND Corp., 1970.

Schaenman, Phillip S., and Muller, Thomas. *Measuring Impacts of Land Development: An Initial Approach*. Washington, D.C.: The Urban Institute, 1974.

Schlager, Kenneth J. "A Land Use Plan Design Model. In <u>Models of Urban Structure</u>, edited by David C. Sweet. Washington, D.C.: Heath, 1972.

Schmid, Alan A. <u>Converting Land from Rural to Urban Uses</u>. Washington, D.C.: Resources for the Future, 1968.

Schneider, Jerry B., and Jehner, C. D. <u>The Interactive Graphic Transit Design System: A Brief Non-Technical Overview of Its Structure and Operation</u>. Seattle: Urban Systems Research Center, Department of Urban Planning and Civil Engineering, University of Washington, 1972.

Schroeder, R. "Resource Planning in University Management by Goal-Programming." <u>Operations Research</u> 22, no. 4 (July/August 1974): 700-09.

Simon, Herbert. <u>Administrative Behavior</u>. New York: Macmillan, 1947.

Skutsch, Margaret, and Schofer, J. L. "Goals-Delphis for Urban Planning: Concepts in Their Design." <u>Socio-Economic Planning Science</u> 7 (1973): 305-13.

Smith, N. J., and Sage, A. P. "Hierarchical Systems Identification of Models for Urban Dynamics." <u>Socio-Economic Science</u> 7 (1973): 545-70.

Sonenblum, Sidney, and Stern, L. H. "The Use of Economic Projections in Planning." <u>Journal of the American Institute of Planning</u> 3 (May 1964): 110-23.

Spangler, Richard. "The Effect of Population Growth upon State and Local Government Expenditures." <u>National Tax Journal</u> 16, no. 2 (June 1963): 193-96.

Spivey, W. Allen, and Thrall, R. N. <u>Linear Optimization</u>. New York: Holt, Rinehart, and Winston, 1970

State of New York, Office of the Comptroller. <u>Special Report on Municipal Affairs</u>. Albany, annual.

Steger, Wilbur A. "The Pittsburgh Urban Renewal Simulation Mode." <u>Journal of the American Institute of Planners</u> 31 (May 1965): 144-50.

Steger, Wilbur A. "Review of Analytic Techniques for the CRP." Ibid., 166-72.

Sternlieb, George. Housing Development and Municipal Costs. New Brunswick, N.J.: Center for Urban Policy Research, Rutgers University, 1973.

Steward, Thomas R., and Carter, J. E. POLICY: An Interactive Computer Program for Externalizing, Executing and Refining Judgmental Policy. Boulder: Institute of Behavioral Science, University of Colorado, 1973.

Stuart, Darwin G. "Urban Improvement Programming Models." Socio-Economic Planning Science 4 (1970): 217-38.

Sweet, David C. Models of Urban Structure. Lexington, Mass.: D.C. Heath Co., 1972.

Syracuse University Research Corp. and Maxwell School of Citizenship and Public Affairs. A Framework for Fiscal Planning: Binghamton, New York. Syracuse: Syracuse University Press, 1972.

Szanton, Peter L. Working with a City Government, Rand's Experience in New York. RM 6236. New York City Rand Institute, 1970.

Tempkin, Sanford. "A Comprehensive Planning Mode." Socio-Economic Planning Science 6 (1972): 241-56.

Thompson, Wilbur R. "Internal and External Factors in the Development of Urban Economics." In Issues in Urban Economics, edited by H. Perloff and L. Wingo, Jr. Baltimore: Johns Hopkins Press, 1968.

──────. A Preface to Urban Economics. Baltimore: Johns Hopkins Press, 1965.

Tiebout, Charles M. The Community Economic Base Study. Supplementary Paper no. 16. New York: Committee for Economic Development, 1962.

Tufte, Edward R., ed. The Quantitative Analysis of Local Problems. Reading, Mass.: Addison-Wesley, 1970.

Tunnard, Christopher, and Reed, Henry Hope. American Skyline. New York: New American Library, 1956.

United States Congress, House Committee on Banking and Currency. Industrial Location Policy. Washington, D.C.: U.S. Government Printing Office, 1971.

United States Department of Housing and Urban Development. Federal Housing Administration Techniques of Housing Marketing Analysis. Washington, D.C.: FHA, 1970.

_____. The Changing Demand for Local Capacity—An Analysis of Functional Programming and Policy Planning. Community Development Evaluation Series no. 12. Washington, D.C.: 1972.

_____. Local Government Approaches to Capacity Building. Community Development Evaluation Series no. 15. Washington, D.C.: 1973.

_____. The Model Cities Program: A Comparative Analysis of the Planning Process in Eleven Cities. Washington, D.C.: n.d.

_____ and National League of Cities. Alternative Study: Model Cities Phase-out, Community Development Phase-in. NTIS PB-234-754. Alexandria, Va.: 1973.

_____, Office of Community Development Evaluation. The Model Cities Program, a Comparative Analysis of City Response Patterns and Their Relation to Future Urban Development. Washington, D.C.: n.d.

United States Department of Transportation, Federal Highway Administration, Bureau of Public Roads. Metropolitan Plan Evaluation Methodology. Washington, D.C.: 1969.

Urban Institute. The Struggle to Bring Technology to Cities. Washington, D.C.: The Institute, 1971.

Urban Land Institute. Industrial Districts—Principles in Practice. Technical Bulletin no. 44. Washington, D.C.: The Institute, 1962.

_____. The Community Builder's Handbook. Washington, D.C.: The Institute, 1968.

Vernon, Raymond. Metropolis 1985. Cambridge, Mass.: Harvard University Press, 1960.

Vernon, Raymond. The Changing Economic Function of the Central City. New York: Committee for Economic Development, 1963.

Wade, Richard C. The Urban Frontier. Chicago: University of Chicago Press, 1964.

Wagner, Harvey M. Principles of Operations Research. Englewood Cliffs, N.J.: Prentice-Hall, 1969.

Walker, Mabel. Business Enterprises and the City. Princeton, N.J.: Tax Institute Inc., 1957.

Walker, Robert. The Planning Function in Urban Government. Chicago: University of Chicago Press, 1941.

Wallace, W. A., and Orne, D. "Alternative Mathematical Programming Approaches to New Town Planning." In Urban Simulation: Models for Policy Analysis, edited by M. Whithed and R. M. Sarly. Leiden: A. W. Sijthoff, 1974.

Warren, Ronald L. "Model Cities First Round: Politics, Planning and Participation." Journal of the American Institute of Planners 35 (July 1969): 245-52.

Webber, Melvin M. "The Roles of Intelligence Systems in Urban-Systems Planning." Journal of the American Institute of Planners 31 (November 1965): 289-96.

Weisbrod, Burton A. "Preventing High School Dropouts." In Measuring Benefits of Government Investments, edited by R. Dorfman. Washington, D.C.: The Brookings Institution, 1965.

Wheaton, William C. "Application of Cost Revenue Studies to Fringe Areas." Journal of the American Institute of Planners 25, no. 4 (1959): 170-73.

Wholey, Joseph S., et al. Federal Evaluation Policy—Analyzing the Effect of Public Programs. Washington, D.C.: The Urban Institute, 1970.

Williams, A. C. "Marginal Values in Linear Programming." Journal of the Society for Industrial and Applied Mathematics 11 (1963): 82-94.

Williams, Norman, Jr. The Structure of Urban Zoning. New York: Buttenheim, 1966.

Wingo, Lowdon, Jr., ed. Cities and Space, The Future Use of Urban Land. Baltimore: Johns Hopkins Press, 1963.

Wolfe, Phillip. "A Duality Theorem for Non-Linear Programming." Quarterly of Applied Mathematics 19 (1961): 239-44.

WPA. St. Louis—Income and Cost of Municipal Services. Entry no. 3436. Washington, D.C.: 1937.

_____. Index of Research Projects. 1938 and 1939.

Young, Robert C. "Goals and Goal-Setting." Journal of the American Institute of Planners 32 (March 1966): 76-85.

INDEX

Ackoff, R., 41
Alonso, W., 31, 46, 51
assessment ratio, 101

Balinsky, M. L., 182
Banfield, E., 40
Baumol, W. J., 59, 182
Branch, M., 32, 42-43 (see also, municipal planning)
Brewer, G. D., 7, 8, 29
Burnham, D. H., 7, 8, 29 (see also, "city beautiful" planning)

Chapin, S., 37, 44
Charnes, A., 166, 185
citizen participation in planning: application of cost-revenue techniques as an aid, 222-24; advocacy in planning, 39-40; Davidoff, P., 31, 37, 39-40; Dunbar, Pennsylvania, 221-22; evaluation of land development proposals, 224-25; Jacobs, J., 26, 37, 39; Johnson, N., 222; pluralism, 38
"city beautiful" planning: Burnham, D., 7, 8, 29; Chicago, plan of, 7, 29; "city beautiful," as a compromise solution, 25; "city beautiful," methods of practice, 28-29; "city beautiful" movement, 7-8, 24; Columbian Exposition, 7, 22; Olmstead, Frederick Law, 8, 15, 23; planning axioms, basis for, 25-26; Trasney

Act of 1893, 27
"city pestilential": contemporary commentaries: Bryce, Lord James, 22-23, 25-26; Flower, Benjamin, 22, 24; George, Henry, 23; Riis, Jacob, 22, 24; dumbbell plan, 24; evils of, 22-25; health and sanitary problems, 23; New York City Tenement House Act of 1901, 24; "railroad flats", 24
cohort survival analysis, 83-84
colonial planning: colonial zoning, 8-9; New York City, 10; Nicholson, F., 8; Penn, W., 9; Philadelphia, 9-10, 15-16; Williamsburg, Virginia, 8-9
community renewal program, 47 (see also, municipal planning)
"commuter tax", 168
computer models in planning: applicability to small cities, 50-51; Chicago Area Transportation Study, 33; computer models, 47; Forrester, J., 51; Kilbridge, M., 48; land-use plan design model, 37; linear program formulation, 50; Lowry, I. S., 37, 47; Schlager, K. J., 50; Steger, W. A., 48; TOMM, 47-48; urban renewal models: Pittsburgh, 37; San Francisco, 37
consumer behavior, 154 (see also, utility theory)
Cooper, W. W., 166, 185
cost-benefit analysis in municipal planning (see, municipal cost-revenue studies)

282

INDEX

Davidoff, P. (see, citizen participation in planning)
demonstration cities and Metropolitan Development Act of 1966 (see, Model Cities)
dumbbell plan (see, "city pestilential")
Duncan, B., 70, 73

Edgeworth, F., 154
education expenditures (see, municipal finances)
efficiency: attainment possibility frontier concept, 182, 184, 205; solutions, 211-12; taxation vs. industrial land, 209; taxation vs. population, 205-07; computational techniques, 160-61; definition of, 157-58; geometric representation, 159-60; Koopmans, T., 157-58; local efficiency, 159; nonlinear goal-programming formulation, 191-93; parameter weights, 161; production, 157-58; production possibility frontier, 155-56, 171, 231-41; proper efficiency, 162-63; "satisficing" constraints, 167-69, 171
eminent domain, 159 (see also, legal foundations in planning)
"equalization rate", 101-02

Fisher, I., 154

Geoffrion, A. M., 162 (see also, multiple-objective optimization)
goal programming: efficient goals, 172; goal variables, 182-84; linear formulation: objective function, 177; policy constraints, 177; results, 180; structural constraints, 176-77; nonlinear formulation: disadvantages, 193; objective function, 190-91, 242-49; policy constraints, 190; preemptive ordering, 163-64, 170, 171; results, 191-93; structural constraints, 190
goal setting: goal decomposition, 45; goals, as measurable end states, 152-53; goals, hierarchy of, 45-46; in planning, 44-45; "muddling through", as a method of goal setting, 152-53; operational objectives in planning, 44; planning, as a problem-solving process, 44; "purposeful incrementalism", 153; "satisficing", 45
gridiron plan, 8 (see also, municipal planning)

Hadley, G., 184
Harris, B., 37
Howard, Ebenezer, 36 (see also, "city beautiful" planning)

Ijiri, Y., 166
industrial development: capture rate, 70-74; determination of labor force, 70; housing demand, 74-75; Margolis effect, 65
Isard, W., 65

Jacobs, Jane, 26, 37 (see also, citizen participation in planning)
Jefferson, Thomas, 17

Laidlaw, C. D., 166, 167, 184
land development processes: Connecticut Land Company, 19; District of Columbia, 13; economic pressures, influence on land development, 17-18; Greenleaf, James, 17; Jeffer-

sonville, Indiana, 17; land speculation, 14, 18-19; new towns, 18; New York City commissioners' plan, 15-16; North American Land Company, 18; Ohio Company of Associates, 18-19; Washington, D.C., 16-17, 29

legal foundations in planning: antinuisance ordinance, 10, 11; Brown v. Maryland, 12; common law of nuisances, 10-11, 13; comprehensive zoning ordinances, 12, 13, 22, 27-28; eminent domain, 13; Euclid v. Ambler Realty, 11, 28; Land Ordinance of 1785, 14, 16, 18-19; legal vacuum, weakness of government, 11, 14; Mansfield and Swett v. Town of West Orange, 28; Marshall, Chief Justice J., 12; New Jersey Supreme Court, 28; New York City, commissioners' plan 1807, 15-16; New York City, Comprehensive Zoning Ordinance of 1916, 22, 26-27; police powers, 10-11, 12-13; zoning law, 10

L'Enfant, Pierre, 16-17
Lindblom, C., 153
Loewenstein, L. K., 73
Lorenz curves, 94-95

Margolis, J., 65 (see also, industrial development)
market ratio, 100, 101
mathematical programming: applied in public sector, 166; single v. multiple criteria, 166-67
Meyerson, M., 40, 44
Model Cities; evaluation, 38
Muller, T., 224 (see also, municipal cost-revenue studies)

multiple-objective optimization: as a vector-maximization problem, 158; computational anomalies in, 162-63; Geoffrion, A. M., 162, 163, 259; multiple-objective programming, 158; nonlinear multiple-objective formulation: advantages, 199-200; constraints, 195; evaluation of competing objectives, 205; general, 194-95; improvement of initial solutions, 200-05; level of the goals, 198; objective, 195-97, 199, 200; policy evaluation, 216; results, 212; single v. multiple criteria, 166-67

Mumford, Lewis, 16
municipal cost-revenue studies: basis for planning, 58-60; Boston, 32; cost-benefit analysis, 168; examples of, 60; external economies and costs, 168-69; industrial development, 65-66;Litchfield, N., 62; Muller, T., 224; political considerations, 169; St. Louis, 32; Sternlieb, G., 91

municipal finances: computation of expenditures, 106-14; education expenditures and revenues, 114-17; general, 62; nonproperty tax revenues, 103, 106; scenario analysis, use in computing municipal costs, 109-14; tax base, 101-03; types of expenditures, 106-08

municipal planning: automobile, impact on planning, 29-30; Branch, M., 32, 37, 42-43; comprehensive master plans, difficulty with, 42-43; comprehensive planning, 42; "continuous master planning," 32;

INDEX

[municipal planning] functional planning, 42; gridiron plan, 8, 9, 15-16; Housing Act of 1949, 38, 47; Housing and Urban Development Act of 1974, 1; new approaches to planning, 36-37; physical planning, 42; planning commissions, 27, 30, 31-32; planning foundations in 1930s, 31; planning process: characteristics of, 37, 41, 43-44; deficiencies of, 41-42

new towns: Garden City, N.Y., 36; Radburn, N.J., 31, 36; Resettlement Administration projects, 36; Sunnyside, N.Y., 36
New York City (see, colonial planning, legal foundations in planning)
nonlinear programming, 187-88 (see also, multiple-objective optimization)

Olmstead, Frederick Law, 8, 15, 23 (see also, "city beautiful" planning)

Pareto, Vilfredo, 154
Philadelphia (see, colonial planning)
police powers, origin of concept, 12 (see also, legal foundations in planning)
production-possibility frontier, 155-56 (see also, efficiency)
property taxes (see, municipal finances)

Radburn, N.J., 31, 36 (see also, new towns)
Reps, J., 8
residential development: cohort survival analysis, 82; demographic considerations, 82; demographic predictions based on housing availability, 83-84; general, 70, 71, 73; impact of physical characteristics, 70, 72-75
Robinson, Charles Mulford, 28-29

Samuelson, P. A., 100
Satisficing (see, goal setting; efficiency)
scenario analysis, 41: applied to development, 60-62; computing municipal costs, 109-14 (see also, municipal cost-revenue studies)
speculation in land (see, land development processes)
Sternlieb, G., 91, 228 (see also, municipal cost-revenue studies)

TOMM, 47-48 (see also, computer models in planning)

utility theory: attainment-possibility frontier, 155-57; consumer behavior, 154; general, App. A; Marshallian, 154; utility, cardinal measure of, 154-55; welfare function, 158; welfare maximization, 168

vector-maximization problem, 158 (see also, multiple-objective optimization)

Wagner, H. M., 185
Webber, M., 42
welfare theory, App. A (see also, utility theory)
Wheaton, W. C., 66
"white city" forms, 7 (see also, "city beautiful" planning)

Williamsburg, Va., 8-9 (see also, colonial planning)

zoning law, 10 (see also, legal foundations in planning)

ABOUT THE AUTHORS

SHIMON AWERBUCH is the Director, Policy Analysis and Planning Project, New York State Department of Education. He holds an M.S. and a Ph.D. in Urban-Environmental Studies from Rensselaer Polytechnic Institute.

Previous to his present assignment, Dr. Awerbuch held positions with the firm of Ernst & Ernst, the New York State Legislature, and the Cohoes Planning and Development Agency. Dr. Awerbuch has published in areas of community development and multi-criteria optimization. He is a member of The Institute for Management Science and the American Society for Public Administration, and has consulted for several local, state, and federal agencies.

WILLIAM A. WALLACE is Professor of Public Management, Rensselaer Polytechnic Institute, and holds an M.S. and Ph.D. in Management from Rensselaer Polytechnic Institute.

Professor Wallace has published in areas of environmental management, planning for higher education, and community development in such journals as Management Science, Economic Geography, Socio-Economic Planning Sciences, and American Society of Mining Engineers: Transactions. He has co-authored another book in this series, Financial Analysis and the New Community Development Process. He is a member of the Operations Research Society of America, The Institute of Management Sciences, and Sigma Xi.

RELATED TITLES
Published by
Praeger Special Studies

THE EFFECTS OF URBAN GROWTH: A Population
Impact Analysis
        Richard P. Appelbaum
        Jennifer A. Bigelow
        Henry P. Kramer
        Harvey L. Molotch
        Paul Relis

URBAN PROBLEMS AND PUBLIC POLICY CHOICES
      edited by Joel Bergsman
        Howard L. Weiner

PRIVACY, SECURITY, AND COMPUTERS: Guidelines
for Municipal and Other Public Information Systems
        O. E. Dial
        Edward M. Goldberg

URBAN NONGROWTH: Planning for People
        Earl Finkler
        William J. Toner
        Frank J. Popper

BUDGETING MUNICIPAL EXPENDITURES: A Study
in Comparative Policy Making
        Lewis B. Friedman

CULTURAL RESOURCE DEVELOPMENT: Planning
Survey and Analysis
        Janet I. Harris

SYSTEMATIC URBAN PLANNING
        Darwin G. Stuart